# QUEEN, EMPRESS, CONCUBINE

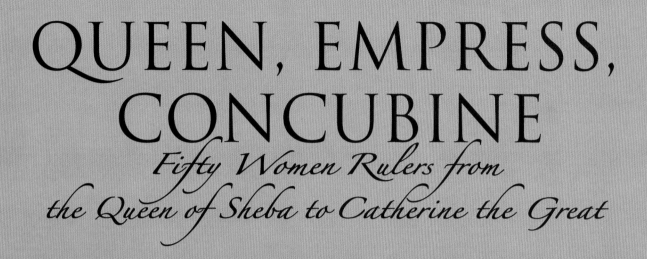

# QUEEN, EMPRESS, CONCUBINE

## Fifty Women Rulers from the Queen of Sheba to Catherine the Great

## CLAUDIA GOLD

Quercus

# CONTENTS

*Blanche of Castile*

*Cleopatra*

*Queen Victoria*

*Queen Anne of England*

# INTRODUCTION

In 1488, Caterina Sforza faced near certain defeat at the hands of her bitter rivals. She and her modest forces had been overwhelmed by a much larger army, and her enemies were now gleefully surveying their prize, the Italian city state of Forlì.

Feigning surrender, Caterina asked to enter the Forlì gates to convince the population to capitulate. She was allowed through, but threatened with the murder of her children if she did not succeed. Once inside, Caterina mounted the battlements, lifted her skirts for all to see – and screamed that her rivals had no power over her because she could still bear more children; Forlì, she declared, would never surrender. Stunning the enemy by her act, the fearless Caterina seized the moment to destroy its forces and rescue her children.

Caterina Sforza belongs to an exclusive club of extraordinary women rulers, 50 of whose lives, struggles and achievements are recounted in this book. Starting with Hatshepsut, queen of Egypt in the 15th century BC and ending with Pakistan's Benazir Bhutto, assassinated in 2007, their stories are told in chronological order. Together these women have had a hugely disproportionate impact on history. The achievements of Elizabeth I, who fashioned England into a major European power, and Catherine the Great, the obscure German princess who dragged the lumbering Russian bear into the modern world, are among the more familiar to a modern audience. But no less remarkable were the likes of Zenobia, the Palmyran princess who took on Rome; Queen Tomyris of the Massagetae, nemesis of the seemingly unstoppable Persian conqueror, Cyrus the Great; and Empress Wu Hou, whose brilliance laid the foundations of China's golden age.

Perhaps it was a keen awareness of the ever-present danger in which they found themselves – in some cases, the threat of an assassin's rope or a poisoner's cup – that spurred on many of these women to outwit and outshine the men around them. (Catherine de Médicis, for example, survived by deploying a 'flying squadron' of beautiful noblewomen, charged with extracting the secrets of their hapless male prey.)

It is not surprising, given their often unusual route to power, that mistresses, courtesans and outlaws frequent these pages. Some rose through brutal defiance of male domination, while others were more subtle, whispering policy into the ears of weak princes. Society offered these women little alternative. The luminous Marquise de Pompadour came to court as the mistress of the dull-witted Louis XV. The slave girl Roxelana was forced into service as a concubine, ensnaring the sultan as her route to power over the Ottoman empire. And in India, Nur Jahan sacrificed her beauty and brilliance to the drug-addled Jahangir to gain the Mughal empire as her prize.

Once in power, they were obliged to reassure their subjects that they would govern as men and surrounded themselves with male advisors; they were queens pretending to be kings. Three and a half thousand years ago in Egypt, Hatshepsut wore a false beard as part of her state costume. Three millennia later, her sister-queen, Elizabeth I, proclaimed to the world: *'I know I have the body of a weak and feeble woman, but I have the heart and stomach of a king, and of a king of England too.'*

As female rulers in an avowedly male world, they attracted, at best, suspicion and, at worst, visceral hatred. The chroniclers – mostly men – could be extraordinarily hostile. Many of these women were branded 'Jezebel', the evil 'whore' of the Bible. Lucrezia Borgia was reviled as 'the greatest whore there ever was in Rome', Isabella of France was a 'she-wolf … with unrelenting fangs' – while Catherine de Médicis was viciously denounced as 'the maggot from Italy's tomb'. As recently as the 1930s, Robert Graves accused the Empress Livia of poisoning not only her political rivals, but her husband and her son in his novel *I, Claudius*, drawing on the misogynistic prejudices and unproven accusations of the historian Tacitus.

How much has changed today? The advent of democracy and the seismic revolution in society's attitudes towards women have provided unprecedented opportunities for women to reach the pinnacle of power. But actual examples are still few and far between. Only in Asia has there been anything approaching a trend, beginning with Sri Lanka's Sirimavo Bandaranaike in 1960, the first-ever woman to be elected as head of government, and continuing with Prime Minister Indira Gandhi of India, President Cory Aquino of the Philippines, Pakistan's Prime Minister Benazir Bhutto, the two 'battling begums', Khaleda Zia and Sheikh Hasina Wajed, who alternated as prime minister of Bangladesh for sixteen years, and Aung San Suu Kyi, elected prime minister by the Burmese people in 1990 but under house arrest for most of the time since then. Even this phenomenon, however, is tempered by the fact that almost all of these women rose to power after their high-profile father or husband was assassinated. It seems, then – notwithstanding thousands of years of human civilisation – that we will have to wait a little longer for real change.

*Claudia Gold*
*London, 2008*

# HATSHEPSUT
## 15th Century BC
## Queen of Egypt

*Hatshepsut, Egypt's first female pharaoh, ruled more than 3500 years ago. Created co-ruler with her stepson Tuthmosis III, she usurped his rights after his father's death and reigned in Egypt for nearly 15 years. She was adored, worshipped and celebrated as a living god. Then, inexplicably, she disappeared. Did she die of natural causes, or did her stepson murder her?*

*Head detail from a carving of Queen Hatshepsut. During her reign she was often depicted wearing the false beard that signified kingship.*

Hatshepsut was the daughter of the mighty warrior-pharaoh Tuthmosis I (r. *c.*1506 – 1493 BC) and his principal wife, Ahmose. Tuthmosis, the third king of the 18th dynasty, ruled an empire at its peak; at the time, Egypt was the most powerful nation in the world. The young Hatshepsut grew up at Thebes, the vibrant, polyglot and wealthy capital on the banks of the River Nile.

### A CHILD BRIDE

Hatshepsut was still in her early teens when she was married to her half-brother, Tuthmosis (this was common practice in ancient Egypt); they shared the same father, but her brother-husband was the son of a concubine (or lesser wife) of the pharaoh, and Hatshepsut became his principal wife. Tuthmosis succeeded his father as pharaoh Tuthmosis II (r. *c.*1493–1479 BC) and ruled Egypt unremarkably while Hatshepsut played the part of the traditional, dutiful wife. However, on his death she immediately proclaimed herself regent for Tuthmosis' son and her stepson, Tuthmosis III (r. *c.*1479–1425 BC; Tuthmosis III was her brother-husband's son by a non-royal woman, Isis). A contemporary wrote:

> 'Having ascended into heaven, he [Tuthmosis II] became united with the gods, and his son [Tuthmosis III], being arisen in his place as king of the Two Lands, ruled upon the throne of his begetter, while his sister, the god's wife Hatshepsut, governed the land and the Two Lands were under her control; people worked for her, and Egypt bowed the head.'

Officially Hatshepsut and Tuthmosis III were co-regents, but Hatshepsut quickly disregarded her young stepson's claims and had herself proclaimed pharaoh. Although women had enjoyed power before – either as co-regents, behind the scenes or as the last female in a line that was dying out and desperate to preserve itself – Hatshepsut was the only woman to rule as pharaoh in her own right and to adopt full pharaonic ceremonial dress, including a false beard. Her name also appears in the official king lists. Hatshepsut gathered around her a coterie of powerful advisors – cultivated throughout her long years at the centre of government as the pharaoh's daughter, then wife – and loyal only to her.

## CLAIMS OF DIVINE DESCENT

Hatshepsut claimed divine authority to legitimize her rule. In the magnificent mortuary temple that she built herself at Dayr al-Bahri near Thebes soon after taking power, we see her to be a mistress of propaganda. The Egyptian pharaohs depicted themselves as the sons of Amen-Re – the principal deity in Egypt's vast pantheon of gods – and therefore semi-divine. Now the daughter of Tuthmosis I did the same. On the walls of her tomb she described her conception as a coupling between her mother, Ahmose, and Amen-Re:

> *'He [Amen-Re] found her ... as she slept in the beauty of her palace. She*
> *waked at the fragrance of the god, which she smelled in the presence of*
> *his majesty. He went to her immediately ... he imposed his desire*
> *upon her, he caused that she should see him in his form of a*
> *god. When he came before her she rejoiced at the sight*
> *of his beauty, his love passed into her limbs,*
> *which the fragrance of the gods flooded ... '*

*Colonnades and terraced porticoes of the mortuary temples of Hatshepsut (foreground) and Mentuhotpe (background), below the cliffs at Dayr al-Bahri near Thebes.*

*This carved statue shows Senenmut, Queen Hatshepsut's minister, kneeling behind a cobra – one of ancient Egypt's most powerful symbols. It dates from around 1490 BC.*

Ahmose replied: *'How great is thy fame! It is splendid to see thy front; thou hast united my majesty with thy favours, thy dew is in all my limbs.'* According to Hatshepsut, Amen-Re commanded that his daughter be made *'better than all gods; shape for me this my daughter whom I have begotten'.*

But Hatshepsut also justified her reign through the words of her earthly father, Tuthmosis I, who allegedly granted her his throne:

> *'Said his majesty before them* [the court], *"This is my daughter* [Hatshepsut], *who liveth, and I have appointed her … she is my successor upon my throne, she it assuredly is who shall sit upon my wonderful seat. She shall command the people in every place of the palace; she it is who shall lead you."'*

During Tuthmosis II's reign, brother and sister were depicted almost equally, and Hatshepsut exercised power as a priestess. Now she used that position to defend her right to rule.

Hatshepsut's funerary monument describes all the major events of her 'divine' reign – the monuments and temples she built and her celebrated trading expedition to Punt, a distant African land of immense riches. The expedition was a huge undertaking: wall paintings at Dayr al-Bahri show Egyptian sailors embarking on the journey up the Nile. The fleet returned with magnificent treasure: ebony, gold, incense, exotic animals, spices and perfumes. Her reputation as a great pharaoh spread beyond Egypt. But as a woman Hatshepsut was unable to lead her troops into battle as her father had done. Instead she concentrated on trade and ambitious building projects. In addition to her unsurpassable funerary monument, she also erected temples and numerous obelisks, such as those in the temple complex at Karnak.

## HATSHEPSUT AND SENENMUT

What was the nature of Hatshepsut's relationship with her minister Senenmut? Were they lovers? He rose from a humble background to be the most powerful man in Egypt. His official posts were numerous, and he was even honoured with the care of her daughter. She allowed him to build his own funerary temple underneath her own, and each commissioned numerous tiny statues of the other to adorn their tombs. Hatshepsut's stepson Tuthmosis III certainly despised Senenmut more than any of her other advisors.

Meanwhile, her nephew and stepson Tuthmosis III avoided the court, where Hatshepsut's powerful clique of acolytes held sway. Some scholars believe that Hatshepsut was grooming her daughter Nefrura – Tuthmosis III's half-sister – to be the next pharaoh. Hatshepsut appointed her favourite advisor, the wily Senenmut, as the girl's tutor. But Tuthmosis was no longer a boy. He joined the army, rose to lead it and bided his time.

## MYSTERIOUS DISAPPEARANCE

After a reign lasting 14 years, Hatshepsut suddenly vanishes from the historical records. Her mummy has never been discovered; nor is their any trace of Nefrura. Was the female pharaoh perhaps murdered by her nephew? Certainly, Tuthmosis III appears to have made strenuous efforts to expunge his stepmother's name from history. (Ironically, one such measure, the walls he built to immure her magnificent obelisks at Karnak only helped preserve the inscriptions on them for posterity.) Her funerary temple was raided and her advisors' tombs desecrated. The tomb of Senenmut suffered the worst indignity; its sculptures were defaced and its exquisite ceiling – a glittering map of the night sky – was destroyed. Tuthmosis III's revenge on those he thought had slighted him was complete: he removed from the tombs everything Egyptians believed they needed for the afterlife – everyday objects, food, pictures – so the spirits of his enemies would be unable to survive.

After Hatshepsut's disappearance, Tuthmosis III ruled as one of Egypt's greatest pharaohs for over 30 years. He sought to associate his reign with those of his father and grandfather. Hatshepsut was forgotten. On the wall of his tomb Tuthmosis had inscribed: *'I am his [Tuthmosis II's] son, whom he commanded that I should be upon his throne, while I was one dwelling in his nest, he begat me in uprightness of heart ... there is no lie therein.'* The power struggle was over.

Hatshepsut's colossal obelisk at the Karnak temple was originally covered with gold. Today only the granite remains, but we can read the inscription she left, telling of her tremendous achievements:

> *'And you who after long years shall see these monuments, who shall speak of what I have done, you will say "We do not know how they can have made a whole monument of gold as if it were an ordinary task". To gild them I have given gold measured by the bushel, as though it were sacks of grain. And when my majesty had seen the amount it was more than the whole of the Two Lands [Egypt] had ever seen ... When you shall hear this, do not say that this is an idle boast, but "How like her this was, worthy of her father!" ... '*

### TIMELINE

c.1493 BC Tuthmosis I dies; Hatshepsut is married to her half-brother, Tuthmosis II, and they succeed their father as co-rulers

c.1479 BC On the death of Tuthmosis II, Hatshepsut proclaims herself regent for Tuthmosis II's son, Tuthmosis III; soon after, she declares herself pharaoh and builds her funerary monument near Thebes

c.1473 BC Hatshepsut builds a colossal obelisk at Karnak

c.1470 BC Trading expedition to Punt in Africa (probably near present-day Somalia) returns to Egypt with magnificent treasure

c.1465 BC Hatshepsut vanishes; Tuthmosis reigns alone for another 33 years, hiding or destroying all records of his stepmother's existence

*'Her majesty became more important than anyone else. What was within her was godlike; godlike was everything she did; her spirit was godlike. Her majesty became a beautiful maiden, blossoming out ...'*

INSCRIPTION IN THE FUNERARY TEMPLE OF HATSHEPSUT

# NEFERTITI

## *14th Century* BC
## Queen of Egypt

*After Cleopatra, Nefertiti is Egypt's most famous queen. Her remarkable beauty and the mystery of her sudden disappearance have captivated people for centuries. But for nearly 3500 years she was invisible. Contemporary Egyptian historians obliterated her name from the list of kings, and her city of Amarna was swallowed by the desert. Nefertiti and her husband Akhenaten were branded heretics for their abandonment of Egypt's pantheon of gods in favour of only one – the Aten, or sun god. Nefertiti, one of the most influential women in the ancient world and revered for most of her married life as a goddess, was sentenced to the most dreadful fate ancient Egyptians could imagine: not to be remembered by posterity.*

*The painted stone bust of Queen Nefertiti, housed in the Altes Museum in Berlin, Germany, was only discovered in 1912. She is wearing her crown with the ureaus – the rearing cobra that symbolizes kingship.*

Nefertiti (literally, 'a beautiful one is come') was a daughter of the Egyptian élite. She lived during the late 18th dynasty and was born into the world's sole superpower at that time. Egypt – vast, wealthy and unchallenged, with its borders stretching from Nubia to Syria – was ruled by a strong, traditional pharaoh, Amenhotep III. The sophisticated court at Thebes attracted artisans, musicians, scribes and intellectuals from all over the empire; Egypt, with its population of 4 million, was an empire at its zenith.

Nefertiti was still only in her early teens when she married the pharaoh's second son, Amenhotep. By marrying her, the young prince Amenhotep followed the example set by his father. Rather than wed one of his numerous sisters or half-sisters (which was common practice in Egypt, to maintain the purity of the line) he chose instead, like his father, to marry a commoner.

*'She pure of hands, Great King's Wife whom he loves, Lady of the Two Lands Nefertiti, may she live. Beloved of the great living Sun Disc who is in jubilee ...'*

INSCRIPTION IN THE MANSION OF THE BENBEN-STONE, KARNAK

## TIMELINE

c.1353 BC Amenhotep III dies and is succeeded by Amenhotep IV

c.1348 BC Amenhotep IV takes the name Akhenaten and founds a new city, Akhetaten, dedicated to the worship of a single god

c.1341 BC Death of Nefertiti's eldest daughter; possible death also of Akhenaten's concubine, his mother and three of his daughters; about this time, Nefertiti disappears from the records

c.1336 BC Smenkhkare ascends the throne

c.1334 BC Smenkhkare is succeeded by Tutankhamen

c.1330 BC Tutankhamen returns the court to Thebes and obliterates references to the Aten

AD 1824 Egyptologists unearth the lost city of Akhetaten

1912 The bust of Nefertiti is found by German archaeologist Ludwig Borchardt

Amenhotep never expected to inherit the throne, but when his older brother, Tuthmosis, died he became his father's heir. During the last years of his reign the elderly and now feeble pharaoh handed government over to his wife, Tiy. It was interesting for her son to observe the 'King's Great Wife' emerging from the shadows to exercise unlimited power. Did she set a precedent for her daughter-in-law, Nefertiti? When the pharaoh died in about 1353 BC, Amenhotep took the throne as Amenhotep IV. His 17-year reign was to be the most controversial in Egypt's history.

## A SINGLE GOD

At his accession, Egyptians worshipped a pantheon of gods. Amen, or Amen-Re, was chief among them and the numerous gods and goddesses offered solace and spiritual relief. In the fifth year of his reign Amenhotep broke with 20 centuries of tradition. He abandoned the pantheon of gods in favour of one obscure god, the Aten, or sun god. Amenhotep took the name Akhenaten, meaning 'one useful to Aten', and abandoned Thebes for a glorious new city dedicated to the worship of his god. Traditional gods such as Amen, Mut and Khonsu were replaced by the triumvirate of Akhenaten, Nefertiti and the Aten. All references to Amen were ruthlessly obliterated. Scholars have ceaselessly debated Akhenaten's motives. Some see him as self-serving, using his new religion to divert funds from the old priesthood to finance his new city, while others see him instead as a great visionary – the world's first monotheist.

Akhenaten's new capital, Akhetaten – 'Horizon of the Aten' – is today known as Tell el-Amarna (or Amarna for short). Situated in the middle of Egypt on the banks of the River Nile, the site was not ideal, but for Akhenaten it was perfect because it was virgin land. This new city, 'the seat of the First Occasion', was to be Aten's city, dedicated to the new state religion. Did Nefertiti doubt the suitability of the site because of its distance from Egypt's major cities? A tomb inscription shows Akhenaten making a rare complaint about his wife: *'Neither shall the queen say unto me "behold there is a goodly place for Akhetaten in another place" … I will not say "I will abandon Akhetaten, I will hasten away and make Akhetaten in this other goodly place".'*

Despite Nefertiti's protests, when the construction of Amarna finally came to an end after five years, the result was magnificent. Its palaces, great houses, fragrant gardens and rich tombs reflected the wealth of the empire, and by the ninth year of the reign it had become Egypt's new capital. Resistance to the new religion was minimal, perhaps because of Akhenaten's firm control over the military. He is shown everywhere surrounded by soldiers sworn to protect the new religion and its 'high priest' – the pharaoh himself.

Akhenaten, who adored his wife, gave her the soubriquet *Neferneferwaten,* meaning 'Exquisite Beauty of the Sun Disc'. Nefertiti became the embodiment of Egypt's abandoned goddesses. In the monuments at Amarna we see her and her husband benefiting equally from the light of the Aten. In her flimsy, transparent robe with exaggerated hips and stomach, she is the personification of fecundity. The 'Great Royal Wife' had become semi-divine. The pharaoh's boundless love for both his wife and the

royal city he had built emerge clearly from a famous inscription on one of the boundary stelae at Amarna:

> '*A tomb shall be made for me in the eastern mountain of Akhetaten, and my burial shall be performed in it with a multitude of festivals which the Aten has ordered for me. If the Great Queen Nefertiti who lives, would die in any town of north, south, west or east, she shall be brought and buried at Akhetaten.*'

## FAMILY LIFE

The couple had six daughters, who are shown sitting on their parents' laps or playing together in the scenes of happy domestic life that abound in Amarna. Because Nefertiti's daughters ensured continuance of the royal line, the queen's status increased with each child she bore. Akhenaten himself married at least two of his own offspring in order to maintain the purity of his lineage. Nefertiti probably enjoyed an almost equal reign with Akhenaten. Her image is everywhere; in places it appears alongside that of her mother-in-law, Tiy, with the two queens often depicted as sphinxes annihilating Egypt's foes. Yet, while daughters were prized in Egypt, Nefertiti's lack of sons meant that she could only enjoy her power for a limited time. She would not be a queen mother and if she outlived her husband her influence would wane. Akhenaten had to look elsewhere for sons.

*This highly illustrative stone carving depicts Akhenaten and Nefertiti seated on stools with two of their children.*

## CONCUBINES, CELEBRATIONS AND TRAGEDY

The pharaoh maintained a large harem. One of his concubines whose name has come down to us was Kiya, who bore him at least one daughter and may well have been the mother of his two sons, Tutankhaten and Smenkhkare. Presently, to showcase his new city, Akhenaten organized a huge festival at Amarna, to which ambassadors from Libya, Nubia, the Near East and the Mediterranean islands were all invited. Vivid scenes of the event adorn the tomb of Nefertiti's steward, Meryre II. But this is the last time we see the family together. In the 12th year of Akhenaten's reign tragedy struck the royal family. Nefertiti's beloved eldest daughter, Mekataten, died when she was 12 years old. She was buried in her father's tomb, where the scenes that portray the event are laden with grief. At the same time we lose sight of Kiya, Tiy and the three youngest royal daughters. They probably died of the plague that devastated Egypt. Nefertiti also disappeared. There is no magnificent tomb to mark her passing to the land of the dead. What happened to the 'Great King's Wife', his co-regent and Aten's goddess?

*A carving of Kiya, one of Akhenaten's concubines, or 'secondary wives'. She is often called the 'Greatly Loved Wife' and probably held some power within the kingdom.*

Scholars have offered numerous theories: that the queen quarrelled with Akhenaten and, disgraced, disappeared into exile; that, grief-stricken, she abandoned the Aten in favour of Egypt's traditional gods; that Akhenaten married their daughter, Meritaten, who replaced her ageing mother as a symbol of fertility; or that Nefertiti changed her name and became an official king alongside her husband. She enjoyed unprecedented status in Egypt: never had a pharaoh's wife been so honoured, and it is possible that she succeeded Akhenaten to rule alone as pharaoh. Glimpses of an unknown woman appear throughout the decades in stone and statuary – she may have been Nefertiti. But we will never know.

## TUTANKHAMEN AND THE RETURN TO THEBES

Akhenaten had built a city to last forever, but it was only to survive for 30 years. After his death his son, Smenkhkare (some scholars believe this was actually Nefertiti who had risen to rule alone as pharaoh), briefly took the throne. But when he died his younger brother, Tutankhamen, succeeded him. If Nefertiti was still alive and living in retirement or disgrace she may have hoped her line would continue – the new pharaoh was married to her daughter and his half-sister, Ankhesenpaaten.

Tutankhamen soon abandoned Amarna and threw off the worship of the Aten. He changed his name (he had been born Tutankhaten, in honour of the Aten) and returned the court to Thebes. Ankhesenpaaten also changed her name to Ankhesenamen. In an attempt to disassociate himself from the 'heresy' of his father and Nefertiti, all references to the Aten were obliterated as Tutankhamen returned to the old beliefs and re-opened the temples. Tutankhamen wished to portray himself as a strong, traditional pharaoh:

*'When his majesty arose as king, the temples of the gods and goddesses, beginning from Elephantine down to the marshes of the Delta had fallen into decay, their shrines had fallen into desolation and become ruins overgrown with weeds, their chapels as though they had never been and their halls serving as footpaths. The land was topsy-turvy and the gods had turned their backs on the land.'*

Throughout his reign he associated himself with his grandfather, Amenhotep III, in an attempt to distance himself from his now universally unpopular father.

Tutankhamen and Ankhesenamen had two stillborn daughters. When the pharaoh died his elderly mentor, Ay, took the throne. Ay was succeeded by Tutankhamen's general Horemheb. Horemheb, who married Nefertiti's sister, Mutnodjmet, obliterated the names of Nefertiti, Akhenaten and his sons from lists of kings and wiped their names from temples and statues. It was as if 'the heretics' had not existed. They were forgotten for nearly 3500 years.

Nefertiti's name first became known to modern scholars from hieroglyphic inscriptions discovered in 1824 during excavations at the lost city of Akhetaten. On a later dig at the same site, German archaeologist Ludwig Borchardt unearthed the famous bust of the former queen, about which the historian J. Baikie wrote in 1926:

> 'The portraits of other queens of romance, such as Cleopatra and Mary of Scotland, are apt to leave one wondering where the charm came in, about which all men raved, but no one could question for a moment the beauty of Nefertiti. Features of exquisite modelling and delicacy, the long graceful neck of an Italian princess of the Renaissance and an expression of gentleness not untouched with melancholy make up the presentation of a royal lady about whom we should like to know a great deal and actually know almost nothing.'

## TUTANKHAMEN'S TOMB

Tutankhamen is Egypt's most famous pharaoh, not because of his deeds (his ten-year reign was unremarkable) but because of his magnificent tomb. This was discovered at Thebes in 1922 by the British archaeologist Howard Carter, having eluded grave robbers and remained intact for nearly 3500 years. The jewellery, amulets and everyday objects contained in the tomb offer an extraordinary insight into Egypt's 18th dynasty.

*A detail of Tutankhamen's richly decorated throne shows the young king with his wife, Ankhesenamen.*

# PUDUHEPA
## 13th Century BC
## Hittite queen

*Centred on Anatolia (modern southeastern Turkey), the ancient empire of the Hittites stretched from the Aegean Sea to the Euphrates and encompassed an immense swathe of Asia Minor. Puduhepa was its queen. She ruled with her husband, then with her son, and corresponded on equal terms with the kings of Assyria and Babylon and with Egypt's mighty pharaoh, Ramses II.*

The Hittite kingdom emerged at the beginning of the second millennium BC, nearly one thousand years before King David created his empire. The Bible describes the Hittites as a mighty power who dwell *'in the mountains'* and *'towards the north'* of Canaan. The most famous of them, Uriah, was the cuckolded husband of Bathsheba (see pages 26–29), murdered by King David, who coveted his wife. Puduhepa and her husband Hattusilis III ruled in the 13th century BC, during the golden age of the New Kingdom of the Hittites.

Puduhepa was a noblewoman, the daughter of a priest and a priestess in her own right. She was a Hurrian, from the south-eastern corner of the empire and was most likely born in the city of Kumanni. She served the most powerful deity in the Hittite pantheon, the sun-goddess Arinnitti.

### A MARRIAGE FORETOLD

Puduhepa first met her future husband as he passed through her city on his way back from war against the Egyptians – one of the many battles that the Hittites fought to maintain their regional ascendancy. A chronicler records that the goddess Ishtar, his guardian in battle, appeared to Hattusilis in a dream. Decreeing that they would enjoy *'the love of husband and wife'*, the goddess instructed him to marry Puduhepa.

For Puduhepa it was an advantageous match. Although her husband was physically frail, probably much older than her and already had numerous wives and concubines, Puduhepa became the first among his wives. Several years later, around 1286 BC, he ignited a civil war against his incompetent nephew, Urhi-Teshub, claiming the young man had failed to show him sufficient respect. He triumphed and took the throne as Hattusilis III (r. 1267–1237 BC). In a magnificent and protracted festival that lasted for five days, Puduhepa ascended the throne with him, becoming *tawananna*, or queen.

*A pendant in the form of a seated goddess, probably representing the all-powerful Hittite sun goddess Arinnitti. It dates from around 1400–1200 BC and was discovered in Turkey.*

## THE QUEEN'S STATUS

Hittite queens were not merely fecund and decorative – and Puduhepa enjoyed power equal to her husband's. She had the use of her own seal, controlled the domestic arrangements of the royal palaces and judged court cases. Even in the fulfilment of her religious duties, Puduhepa transcended the customary queenly role. Blending religion and politics, she reorganized the vast Hittite pantheon of gods and goddesses.

*Two carved stone lions guard a gateway in Hattusa, once the capital of the ancient Hittite empire.*

## RELIGIOUS REFORMS

Accordingly, the Hittite empire was known as *'the land of a thousand gods'* and worship was a fundamental part of life. Richly decorated temples and enormous statues plated with gold and other precious metals and studded with jewels were widespread throughout the land. The Hittites saw deities everywhere – but, as a society that depended on favourable weather to grow crops, none were more important than the gods of thunder, rain, earth, the sun, clouds and fire. Stories were told to explain the gods' existence. Fire, for example, was the son of the sun god; he *'slid into the dark night, and he coiled himself together like a serpent'*.

When Puduhepa and Hattusilis III took power, many of the gods had the same function; for centuries the conquering Hittites had added the deities of subjugated peoples to their own brimming pantheon. Now Puduhepa reformed this chaotic system, partly in a bid to unify the disparate peoples of the empire. She amalgamated the thousands of gods, fusing the many deities who represented thunder, for example, into one: the Hittite god Taru.

It was chiefly due to Puduhepa's influence that the pre-eminence of the sun goddess Arinnitti among the numerous deities was assured. King Hattusilis was often unwell and the queen prayed to Arinnitti frequently and publicly to restore her husband to health. She even offered the goddess a life-sized statue of her husband, plated in silver with golden hands and feet, if she would make him well. In a masterful public relations exercise, the queen thus ensured her favoured deity's prominence.

While religious duties were the traditional role of a Hittite queen, Hattusilis – whether as a result of ill-health or because he viewed their reign as an equal partnership – entrusted Puduhepa with far more responsibility. For example, it was she who was given the task of making peace with the Egyptian pharaoh Ramses II (r. 1279–1213 BC).

The Hittites calculated that an alliance with the mighty Egypt was vital to their interests; they needed the pharaohs to help stave off the Assyrian menace on their borders. Puduhepa succeeded in negotiating a mutually advantageous peace treaty, sealing the alliance by marrying her daughter to Ramses in about 1275 BC.

Hattusilis had numerous children with his many other wives and concubines. However, as chief wife and co-ruler, Puduhepa was responsible for the upbringing of all his offspring. In a letter, she describes family life at the royal residence:

> ' … *The daughters of the king whom I discovered when I came to the palace gave birth with my assistance, and I raised their children. I also raised the children who had already been born and I made them commanders in the army.'*

## GODDESS WORSHIP

Goddess worship is the oldest form of worship and has been practised for at least 20,000 years. By the time of the reign of Puduhepa and Hattusilis, the worship of female deities was being swiftly overtaken by reverence for a male god or gods.

Puduhepa's feat of advancing the sun goddess Arinnitti as head of the Hittite pantheon was extraordinary. Although male and female gods still held equal status in some contemporary societies, the worship of a goddess as chief deity among a host of gods had been abandoned nearly 1000 years earlier.

*' … Puduhepa … the Lady of the land, the servant of the goddess.'*

INSCRIPTION ON PUDUHEPA'S SEAL ON HER HUSBAND'S TREATY WITH RAMSES II, FROM THE WALLS OF THE TEMPLE OF AMEN AT KARNAK

Puduhepa was probably the mother of Manefrure (her Egyptian name), the Hittite princess married to Ramses. The marriage is recorded both in Hittite documents and in Egyptian temple inscriptions. The girl, who was given an enormous dowry of cattle, horses and sheep, became part of Ramses' vast harem.

## A PHARAOH'S ADMIRATION

Extensive correspondence bearing Puduhepa's seal survives between the Hittite queen and Ramses. The pharaoh evidently admired her authority and integrity, addressing her in his letters as an equal.

From the royal palace in the newly re-built capital city of Hattusa, Puduhepa used her sons and daughters as pawns to ensure Hittite ascendancy. This was a role that had never been performed by a Hittite queen before. She married her daughters and step-daughters to neighbouring kings to cement alliances and her sons and stepsons were given vice-regal posts throughout the empire.

Puduhepa had ascended the throne with her husband with the right to rule until her own death. When Hattusilis died, she continued to reign jointly, with her son Tudhaliya IV. While Tudhaliya's wife is simply called *'Great Princess'* or *'Dumu-Sal Gal'* in the sources, she is not mentioned by name. Only Puduhepa was deemed important enough to appear in the records; she was the last Hittite queen to be mentioned by name. After her death, so the Hittites believed, she was finally united with the sun-goddess she had served so faithfully in life. In modern Turkey, women still celebrate this iconic and independent queen.

The reign of Puduhepa and Hattusilis coincided with the golden age of the Hittite empire. However, the kingdom began to disintegrate after the destruction of the capital city, Hattusa, by fire at the beginning of the 12th century BC.

*A Hittite statue of a semi-nude goddess with long hair braids – the Hittites worshipped numerous deities. This figure is believed to date from around 2000–1500 BC.*

# DEBORAH

## 12th Century BC
## Judge and prophet

*Before the founding of a royal dynasty – the House of David – in Israel, the land was governed by charismatic leaders known as Judges. Deborah was unique among them, as the only woman ever to hold formal power. She inspired the Israelites to rise up against their Canaanite oppressors, released them from tyranny and ushered in peace in Israel for 40 years.*

The only place in which Deborah is mentioned in the Bible is in two brief chapters of the Book of Judges. The first chapter is a prose account of her battle against the Canaanites, while the second, The Song of Deborah (which may have been written by Deborah herself) treats the same battle in verse. Deborah was probably a 'witch' – meaning a wise woman, a soothsayer or an interpreter of dreams. She lived in the south of the country, in the hill country of the tribe of Ephraim, near Ramah, where she dispensed justice from beneath a palm tree. The Bible indicates this was a sacred site. We know very little about Deborah's family life except that she was married to one Lappidoth (though, since the word means 'torches', some have interpreted this merely as a metaphorical allusion to Deborah's passion for justice).

Deborah's story is told against the background of God's promise to the Israelites of a homeland in Canaan. After Moses' death Joshua had led the children of Israel into battle against the Canaanites. But the Bible tells us that the Israelites sinned against God; they intermarried and, tempted by the gods of the Canaanites and the Philistines, lapsed from monotheism into idolatry. The Israelites were locked in a cycle of sinning against God, suffering his retribution, penitence and forgiveness. When we meet Deborah they had endured 20 years of violent cruelty at the hands of the Canaanites and their mythical 900 chariots of iron.

### DEBORAH'S MESSAGE OF DELIVERANCE

Judges records that ' ... *the Israelites again did what was wrong in the eyes of the Lord, so he sold them to Jabin the Canaanite king, who ruled in Hazor'.* After years of oppression God heeded their pleas for deliverance, and the task fell to Deborah to save her people. Although Deborah lived in the south she sent for a northerner, Barak, to act as her general. She told him what God commanded: *'Go and draw 10,000 men from Naphtali and Zebulun and bring them with you to Mount Tabor, and I will draw all his rabble, and there I will deliver them into your hands.'*

*An 1866 engraving of Deborah by the French printmaker Gustave Doré in a scene from his sequence of illustrations for the* Bible.

*'Champions there were none,*

*none left in Israel,*

*until I, Deborah, arose,*

*arose, a mother in Israel.'*

THE SONG OF DEBORAH (JUDGES 5:7)

Barak agreed to help, although he had reservations: *'If you go with me, I will go; but if you will not go, neither will I.'* According to the Bible, Barak knew nothing about Deborah and when she told him to gather an army, he was acting blindly. Deborah had no military experience, the Canaanites were a formidable foe and Barak had no evidence of God's promise; he only had Deborah's word for it. Nor would he be hailed as the ultimate victor. Although they would command the army together, she told him *'this venture will bring you no glory, because the Lord will leave Sisera* [King Jabin's famous general] *to fall into the hands of a woman'.* Would that woman be Deborah?

Deborah and Barak mustered a vast force of 10,000 troops from nearly every tribe of Israel. When Sisera heard, he called up his men with their fearsome '900 chariots of iron'. Sisera must have been confident of victory despite the size of the opposing force; the Canaanites had tortured, enslaved and beaten the children of Israel for 20 years and now he would face a mere woman on the field. But, according to Judges, Deborah called to Barak: *'Up! This day the Lord gives Sisera into your hands. Already the Lord has gone out to battle before you.'*

## CANAANITES VANQUISHED

Barak and his army charged down Mount Tabor towards Sisera and the Canaanites at Taanach as a thunderstorm crashed around them. As the Kishon river burst its banks, the Canaanites were terrified. Their iron chariots stuck uselessly in the mud and they drowned in the Kishon in their thousands. The rest fled, pursued by Barak's army. Barak could not find Sisera, but he slaughtered the rest.

Sisera abandoned his horse and ran away on foot to the tent of a Canaanite ally, Heber the Kenite. Only Jael, Heber's wife, was there; she beckoned him in, tempted him to lie down and he slept. But Jael was anxious to avert the wrath of the victorious Israelites; she disregarded her husband's alliance with Sisera. She *'took a tent-peg, picked up a hammer, crept up to him, and drove the peg into his skull as he lay sound asleep. His brains oozed out on the ground, his limbs twitched, and he died.'* Deborah's prophecy was fulfilled: Sisera fell at the hands of a woman. When Barak finally passed in pursuit of Sisera, Jael called to him: *'Come, I will show you the man you are looking for.'* In The Song of Deborah Jael is praised for the murder: *'Blest above women be Jael ... blest above all women in the tents ... with the hammer she struck Sisera ... Where he sank down, there he fell, done to death.'*

The Israelites, spurred on by the victory over Sisera, pushed their triumph home and killed King Jabin of Canaan. Deborah, the 'mother of Israel', had united the

## JUDAH – THE TRIBE THAT REFUSED TO FIGHT

According to the Song of Deborah, the southern tribe of Judah was one of the few tribes not to join Deborah's battle. The Book of Judges offers an explanation: when the children of Israel went back into Canaan from Egypt, God commanded them to defeat the Canaanites so they would not be tempted by their false gods. Unlike the northern tribes who worshipped Canaanite gods, Judah fulfilled the command. They did not slip into apostasy. Because they obeyed God, no foe was sent to harass Judah.

bellicose and disparate tribes against a common foe. But her victory, although glorious, was finite. There are hints throughout the Book of Judges that the only way out of the cycle of apostasy and redemption is the coming of the Age of Kings. The sentence, *'in those days there was no king in Israel; every man did what was right in his own eyes'* is repeated over and over again. Only King David, through his commitment to God, his defeat of his enemies and his unifying of the disparate tribes of Israel, could lead the Israelites out of apostasy.

But The Song of Deborah, composed in the fever of victory, celebrated the Israelites' new freedom at the hands of their national heroine: *'So perish all thine enemies, O Lord; but let all who love thee be like the sun rising in strength.'* It claims the war as a woman's triumph and Judges tells us that Deborah's victory brought 40 years of peace before the Israelites sinned against God once more.

*A print by Gabriel Bodeneer (1673–1765) depicting Jael, wife of Heber the Kenite, greeting Barak and other soldiers after she has killed Sisera.*

# BATHSHEBA

## 10th Century BC
## Queen of Israel

*Bathsheba only appears in three brief stories in the Bible. The first account, in the Book of Samuel, represents her as a passive adulteress whom King David seduced and then married after murdering her first husband Uriah (probably with her complicity). The second, in the Book of Kings, shows her plotting with the prophet Nathan to usurp David's oldest surviving son Adonijah and place her own son Solomon on the throne of Israel. The final story recounts how, in her role as an influential queen mother, she intercedes with Solomon on Adonijah's behalf to get permission for him to marry a woman from David's harem.*

In his youth David was a ruthless warrior, the slayer of Goliath, and the king who united the tribes of Israel into the most powerful nation in the Middle East – the second and possibly the greatest king of Israel. He had many wives and concubines, whom he chose either for reasons of lust or out of political expediency. By the time Bathsheba, the beautiful daughter of Eliam (who was possibly one of the king's advisors; we do not know who her mother was), meets the king he is probably in his mid-fifties, an ageing lion.

### ADULTERY AND MURDER

Every afternoon the king liked to sleep on the roof of his palace. One afternoon he woke to see Bathsheba naked on the roof of the next house, taking a bath. David was besotted, summoned her and slept with her, although she was married to one of his soldiers, Uriah the Hittite. Bathsheba conceived a child on this first encounter; when she realized she was pregnant, David plotted first to deceive and then to murder her husband.

*Bathsheba striking a seductive pose in an 1832 painting by the Russian Romantic artist Karl Briullov (1799–1852). This work now resides in the State Russian Museum in St Petersburg.*

At the time, Uriah was serving under David's general Joab at the siege of the city of Rabbah in Jordan. David panicked and summarily recalled Uriah, giving him food and telling him to '*go down to thy house, and wash thy feet*' (a euphemism for having sexual relations with his wife), so that the coming child could plausibly be passed off as Uriah's and not the king's. But the cuckolded husband doggedly refused. '*My Lord Joab and the servants of my lord are encamped in the open fields; shall I then go into mine house to eat and to drink and to lie with my wife?*' he asked. David thereupon resolved that there was nothing for it but to have Uriah slain.

'But finally [King David] asked ... "What is the nature of the Lord?"
And [Bathsheba] answered at once from within her warmth and certainty,
"He is like me. He is exactly like me".'

TORGNY LINDGREN, *BATHSHEBA*

*David, the second king of Israel and the husband of Bathsheba. Detail from a painting by the Milanese artist Luigi Ademollo (1764–1849).*

David therefore sent him back to Joab with a letter ordering his death: *'Put Uriah opposite the enemy where the fighting is fiercest and then fall back, and leave him to meet his death.'* Uriah duly fell in battle and Bathsheba, now a widow, married the king.

How passive was Bathsheba? Some have speculated that David raped her during their first meeting, but she would have known that David slept opposite her house every day and that by bathing naked on her roof she was likely to attract his attention. Rather than being regarded as a victim and submissive beauty, then, she can be seen as an adulteress and seductress out to ensnare a king.

### 'SINS OF THE FATHERS'

According to the Bible, God punished David for his crime. Nathan, David's prophet, warned him that Bathsheba's unborn child must be sacrificed for his father's sins. The Second Book of Samuel (12:10) relates that God spoke the following chilling words to David through Nathan:

*'Now, therefore, since you have despised me and taken the wife of Uriah the Hittite to be your own wife, your family shall never again have rest from the sword … I will bring trouble upon you from within your own family …'*
After Bathsheba gave birth, the child duly died before he could be named.

Thereafter, Nathan's grim prophecy continued to be fulfilled. David did indeed no longer enjoy any peace within his household. When his son Amnon raped his half-sister Tamar, another of David's sons, Absalom, murdered Amnon and revolted against his father. The nation, so methodically united by David, was now plunged back into a civil war. In the midst of this chaos Bathsheba gave birth to a second son, Solomon. Solomon means 'his replacement' – did this signify the replacement of the dead child or an indication that one day it would be Solomon and not one of his many older brothers who would inherit David's kingdom?

## THE RAPE OF TAMAR

David's eldest son, Amnon, lusted after his half-sister Tamar. Feigning illness, he told David that he would only be cured if the lovely Tamar would come to his room and cook for him. When she arrived, he took hold of her and demanded, *'Come lie with me my sister'*. And she answered him, *'Nay, my brother, do not force me; for no such thing ought to be done in Israel'*. Amnon ignored her plea and raped her.

Unlike many of the surrounding nations – including Egypt, where brother and sister could marry – the Israelites did not practise incest. Absalom, David's third son and Tamar's full brother, murdered Amnon in fury. The author Torgny Lindgren (1905–84) suggests that Bathsheba was behind this act and that she subtly manipulated events in the hope of eliminating two of Solomon's rivals for the throne; there is no evidence for this in the Bible, however.

Bathsheba appears next towards the end of David's life, when the king is *'old and stricken'*. As a test of his virility (and hence his suitability to be king), his councillors sent a beautiful young woman, Abishag, to his bedroom to seduce him. (Bathsheba's thoughts about this are not recorded.) But King David was too old and sick to make love to her, and his oldest surviving son, Adonijah, proclaimed himself king. Adonijah surrounded himself with powerful supporters, including the general Joab. He even asked Bathsheba for her support, which indicates how influential she was, saying, *'You know that the kingdom was mine and that all Israel expected me to reign'.* Bathsheba did not challenge Adonijah immediately, but with Nathan's support she decided to instigate a coup on Solomon's behalf. First, however, she approached David.

## BATHSHEBA THE POLITICAL MANIPULATOR

Bathsheba persuaded David that he had promised her that Solomon would reign after him. This was probably a lie, in fact, but the frail and vulnerable king chose to believe her. Bathsheba convinced her husband of Adonijah's deceit in proclaiming himself king while his father still lived, and, incensed, David commanded Nathan to anoint Solomon king of Israel. Adonijah was forced to make way for his younger half-brother. This was David's final act of kingship before his death; he had reigned for 40 years.

As queen mother, Bathsheba wielded considerable power, unprecedented for a woman in ancient Israel. In Solomon's court *'a throne was set for the king's mother and she sat at his right hand'*.

The third and final time we meet Bathsheba, she intercedes with Solomon on behalf of Adonijah. Adonijah had approached Bathsheba with a strange request. He wanted to marry the beautiful Abishag, the woman sent to seduce David, and asked the queen mother to speak to Solomon. But Abishag belonged to David's harem and their marriage would have been tantamount to a claim to the throne. Solomon was perplexed, and asked: *'Why do you* [Bathsheba] *ask for Abishag ... as wife for Adonijah? You might as well ask for the throne ...'* Solomon duly executed his brother.

Why did Bathsheba make the request? Adonijah, Solomon and Bathsheba would all have been aware of the political ramifications. It is likely that, as a devoted mother, she manipulated the destruction of Adonijah and persuaded Solomon of the necessity of his murder to avoid a future threat to the stability of his rule. Solomon, possibly under instruction from his mother, also murdered Adonijah's supporters, including Joab, the general who had been the key to David's military success.

But Bathsheba's support for Solomon had fatal consequences: Solomon's favouritism towards the tribes of Benjamin and Judah led to the division of the kingdom after his death in 928 BC. The Assyrians overran the northern kingdom of Israel in 721. Judah, the kingdom of the south survived for another 135 years before it fell to the might of the Babylonian empire in 586 BC. This event was nothing short of catastrophic; the Israelites were deported to Mesopotamia (the Babylonian exile) and only returned after 50 years.

## TIMELINE

*c.*1035 BC David born

*c.*1006 BC David succeeds as king of Hebron

*c.*1000 BC David becomes king of all Israel

*c.*1000 BC Birth of Solomon to David and Bathsheba

*c.*970 BC Abishag is sent to tempt the ailing King David

*c.*967 BC David is usurped by Adonijah

*c.*967 BC Bathsheba persuades David to choose Solomon as his successor

*c.*965 BC Death of David

928 BC Solomon dies; Israel is divided

721 BC The northern kingdom of Israel is overrun by the Assyrians

586 BC Judah falls to the Babylonians

# QUEEN OF SHEBA
## 10th Century BC

*Sheba was whatever history wanted her to be. For nearly 3000 years Jews, Christians, Muslims, Arabs and Persians embellished her story. For the authors of the Bible, she enhanced the prestige of the great King Solomon. To the Muslims she was the Arabian princess Bilquis, and medieval Arab traders and storytellers wove her tale into their own traditions. For centuries her connection with the spice trade has symbolized eastern exoticism and has inspired artists, film-makers, composers and authors. Ethiopians claim her as the ancestress of their royal dynasty. But did she even exist?*

Sheba appears in only one short passage in the Bible, in the First Book of Kings, where she is mentioned in the context of a trade agreement between Solomon and an Arabian queen (although her story is later repeated in the Second Book of Chronicles). She is not mentioned by name. The queen, hearing of Solomon's wisdom, visits him *'to prove him with hard questions'* (that is, to ask him to solve riddles). She travels laden with the wealth of her country, at the head of a great caravan of spices, gold and precious stones. Solomon easily vindicates himself:

> *'And she* [the queen of Sheba] *said to the king, "It was a true report that I heard in mine own land of thy acts and of thy wisdom … the half was not told me: thy wisdom and prosperity exceedeth the fame which I heard … Happy are thy men … which stand continually before thee, and that hear thy wisdom."'* She gives the king *'a hundred and twenty talents of gold, spices in great abundance and precious stones. Never again came such a quantity of spices as the queen of Sheba gave to King Solomon.'* And then the king *'gave unto the queen of Sheba all her desire …'*

### OLD TESTAMENT 'SPIN'?

This cameo is the source of further legends about the mysterious queen. Fascinated, storytellers began to embellish the facts. Many interpreted her 'desire' as a sexual relationship with Solomon that resulted in a son. But it seems unlikely that Sheba even existed. No queens ever ruled the land modern scholars think she came from. Nor is there any evidence that the trade route she travelled was operating at that time. She was a beautiful piece of propaganda, created to lionize King Solomon, 400 years after his death.

Solomon, the builder of the first temple in Jerusalem, presided over Israel's golden age. God gave him *'wisdom and understanding beyond measure'*, which he used to

*Solomon receiving the Queen of Sheba by the Flemish painter Frans Francken the Elder (1542–1616).*

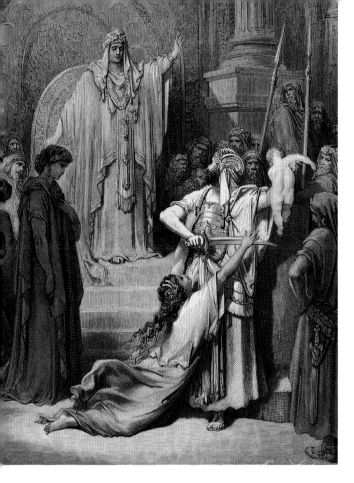

consolidate the empire created by his father David. The story of his meeting with the queen of Sheba proudly proclaims ancient Israel's sophistication, influence and affluence, largely the result of its extensive trade links: *'Thus King Solomon outdid all the kings of the earth in wealth and wisdom, and all the world courted him ...'*

The land of Sheba has been identified as most likely to be Saba, a former kingdom in modern-day Yemen, in southern Arabia. There were no queens in southern Arabia at that time – the monarchs were always male – although queens did reign in northern Arabia in later centuries. Could the queen of Sheba be a conflation of a northern queen from a southern land? Even if a southern Arabian queen did rule in the tenth century BC, it is highly implausible that she travelled all the way to Jerusalem, a huge distance across desert wastes and a dangerous journey even today. But Sheba, according to the propagandists of the Book of Kings, made the journey in deference to Israel's regional importance, and readily submitted to Solomon's superior wisdom and power. The story smacks of 'spin'.

*This 1866 engraving by the French illustrator Gustave Doré (1832–83) shows the famous* Judgement of Solomon.

## A METAPHOR FOR POWER

It is also unlikely that there was a spice trade between Israel and southern Arabia during the time of Solomon. When the Book of Kings was written, between the fourth and the sixth centuries BC – at least 400 years after Solomon's death – a trade route had been established. But there is no evidence to support its existence during Solomon's reign. Instead it seems likely that the authors of the Book of Kings use the story as a metaphor for the king's power: Solomon, ahead of his time, was trading with southern Arabia centuries before a trade route was established. And nearly 1000 years later the myth was flourishing. The Jewish-Roman historian Josephus (AD 37 – c.100) gave Sheba the epithet *'Nikaulis, the marvellous queen of Egypt and Ethiopia'*. The early Christians incorporated her story into the gospels, where Matthew and Luke tell us that *'she came from the ends of the earth ...'* and call her the queen of the South. Taking their cue from the religious texts, medieval Christian artists painted her repeatedly.

In Arabia, too, the tale of the queen of Sheba thrived. Storytellers and poets embroidered the biblical story before the rise of Islam in the seventh century AD. Some 1600 years after the supposed event, the first cohesive account in Arabic literature is found in the Qur'an. The story is based on the accounts in Kings, Josephus, and Arab and Jewish oral traditions and literature. The Qur'anic story claims that Solomon is told of her existence by a small bird, the hoopoe, which announces to him:

> *'I have ... come to you from Sheba with tidings true. Verily I have found a woman ruling over them, to whom everything has been given; and she has a magnificent throne. I have found that she and her people worship the sun, to the exclusion of God: for the devil has taken charge of their affairs ...'*

*'And King Solomon gave unto the Queen of Sheba all her desire, whatsoever she asked ...'*

I KINGS, 10, VERSE 13

## AN EPIC JOURNEY

Solomon gives the hoopoe a letter for the queen, commanding her to come to him. In recognition of his power she travels to Jerusalem, a journey that takes seven years. When she arrives she mistakes Solomon's glass floor for a pool of water and lifts her skirts, allowing the king to see her legs. *'Madam,'* he remarks, *'your beauty is feminine, but the hair on your legs is masculine. Well, hairy legs are fine for a man but revolting on a woman.'* Incensed, the queen poses riddles and is astonished to discover that he is cleverer than her. *'And so she praised and worshipped the One God, and after receiving all she most desired from Solomon she took her leave.'* Unlike in the biblical account, in the Qur'an, then, the queen embraces God and renounces paganism.

In the account above, the queen remains anonymous, but she is popularly known throughout the Muslim world as Bilquis, a third- or fourth-century AD princess of Saba. Arabian storytellers and historians gave her the identity of a real woman. Moreover, despite the enormous time discrepancy, the relationship between this princess and King Solomon was eventually accepted as fact. The southern Arabian kingdom of Saba became firmly identified as Sheba, and Bilqis became its queen.

Sheba also appears in Ethiopian tradition, where she is known as Makeda. Makeda bore the king of Ethiopia a son named Menelik I (r. *c.*204–179 BC), who became Ethiopia's first emperor. In 1960 Ethiopia's last emperor, Haile Selassie (r. 1930–74), visited Saudi Arabia. During his stay he claimed kinship with the Saudi royal family, based on Solomon's relationship with the queen of Sheba. It is true that in the fourth century AD Abyssinian kings commonly married Arabian princesses. Ethiopians had embraced the tradition that the queen of Sheba was Bilqis, an Arabian princess, and hence the ancestress of their dynasty.

We cannot detach the Sheba of history from the Sheba of legend. We do not know who Sheba was, or even if she can be identified with the southern Arabian kingdom of Saba. But the brief account in Kings of an unknown woman submitting to Solomon has captured imaginations for centuries. A slave to hagiographers who caught the whiff of immortality on the pages of her story, she has come to symbolize the mystery and allure of the ancient spice trade and is entwined with oriental exoticism.

*Italian film star Gina Lollobrigida as the queen of Sheba, photographed in 1959.*

## SOLOMON AND SHEBA AT THE MOVIES

Hollywood also tells Sheba's story. In 1959 the Italian actress Gina Lollobrigida starred opposite Yul Brynner as the queen of Sheba in the film *Solomon and Sheba*. She is portrayed as a Jezebel, determined to bring down Solomon and his God. She seduces Solomon, who is so captivated that he reintroduces idol worship to Israel. God retaliates by destroying the temple at Jerusalem. Having brought Solomon to the brink of destruction, the queen decides she loves him. She converts to Judaism and returns to Sheba [Saba?] pregnant with Solomon's child. Cinemas were even advised to emulate a scene from the film for publicity – they were encouraged to *'arrange for a local girl to sit in a warm bath of water coloured white by powder'.*

# Jezebel
## died c.843 BC
## Queen of Israel

*Villainesses throughout history have been dubbed 'Jezebels'. In literature and art a Jezebel is synonymous with all that is both wicked and female – she-devils, viragos and femmes fatales. The British writer Peter Ackroyd calls Jezebel 'the archetypal bad girl'. Her story, which is told in the Book of Kings, reads as a catalogue of sensational crimes against God, Israel and the prophets. She is notorious for idol worship, sorcery, witchcraft and promiscuity.*

The real Jezebel was a princess of the Phoenician empire (part of modern-day Lebanon), the daughter of Ethbaal the priest-king. She was brought to Israel in the ninth century BC as a wife for Ahab, king of Israel (r. *c*.874–853 BC). After the death of King Solomon, Israel had split into two nations – Israel in the north and the kingdom of Judah in the south – and Ahab was desperate to heal his fractured nation, which was still reeling from its division from Judah. Ahab wanted to foster trade and international relations with his powerful northern neighbour, but Jezebel's 'foreignness' immediately presaged trouble.

Jezebel's first crime was to bring the prophets of her false gods with her – 450 to worship the nature god Baal, and 400 to serve the Canaanite goddess Asherah. Baal was chief among the many gods the Phoenicians worshipped. If a prince or princess married a foreigner they were permitted to take their gods to their adopted homeland, but Jezebel's polytheism aroused the wrath of the prophet Elijah, who interpreted it as an affront to Yahweh. Elijah loathed the presence of the 'false' prophets at Jezebel's court and feared their impact on the fickle Israelite aristocracy. He therefore accused the queen of idolatry.

Jezebel's confrontation with Elijah, who wielded enormous power, had disastrous consequences. Elijah massacred the prophets of Baal – the 'pollutants' of Israel – and in response the furious Jezebel threatened to murder him. In doing so, she quite deliberately set herself up as his sworn enemy: *'If you are Elijah, so am I Jezebel.'* After she had the prophets of Yahweh murdered, Elijah fled in fear of his life.

### EVIL OR ROYAL PREROGATIVE?
Although Ahab was denounced as 'evil' for marrying a foreigner and permitting the worship of Baal, the Bible indicates he was a passive figure next to his queen. But how outrageous were Jezebel's actions? Was she simply exercising a royal prerogative?

*A meeting between Jezebel, Elijah and Ahab, depicted in
an 1862 painting by the British historical painter Frederic
Leighton (1830–96).*

'... *dogs shall devour the flesh of Jezebel* ... *her corpse shall be like dung
upon the ground* ...'

## TIMELINE

*c.*945 BC After Solomon's death, ten northern tribes split from Judah to form the kingdom of Israel, with Jeroboam as their king

*c.*870 BC Jezebel arrives at Ahab's court to be his wife; Elijah flees following his massacre of the prophets of Baal; Jezebel murders the prophets of Yahweh

*c.*860 BC Landowner Naboth is stoned to death on Jezebel's orders after he refuses to sell Ahab his vineyard

*c.*853 BC Ahab dies; he is succeeded by Ahaziah, with Jezebel as queen mother

*c.*850 BC After Ahaziah's death, Jehoram becomes king of Israel

*c.*843 BC Elijah appoints Elisha as his successor; Elisha anoints Jehu as king of Israel and incites him to kill the royal household; Jezebel is brutally murdered

721 BC Israel is conquered by the Assyrians

The Israelites were uniquely monotheistic, while Jezebel, as a polytheist, would have had no compunction in worshipping Yahweh as just another god in the pantheon. But his prophets fought to uphold Yahweh's exclusivity – idol worship was forbidden. Jezebel also grew up in a society where royal prerogative was paramount, which would have convinced her that Elijah should be forced to submit to royal power. Another of Jezebel's crimes was the incident of Naboth's vineyard. Ahab wanted to purchase the vineyard, but Naboth refused to sell. Ahab sank into depression and Jezebel intervened, maliciously framing Naboth. His townspeople accused him of blasphemy and he was stoned to death.

Once again Jezebel had acted according to her own tradition. Kings had rights above the common man and the vineyard was rightfully Ahab's. She had no qualms about having a man stoned to death to assert royal authority. Jezebel's immense power suggests that Ahab may have created her co-regent, an unprecedented position for a woman in ancient Israel. Elijah, who had since returned, was incensed by her high-handed actions; he met Ahab at the vineyard and cursed him and his house for what Jezebel had done.

## QUEEN MOTHER OF A POWERFUL REALM

Ahab died in around 853 BC, fighting the Assyrians, and for the next ten years Jezebel wielded power as queen mother to her two sons, Ahaziah and Jehoram. The alliance her marriage had created between Israel and the Phoenicians brought Israel immense economic and military success. But Elijah preferred spiritual purity to strength. The Book of Kings accuses Ahaziah of Baal worship: *'And he* [Ahaziah] *did evil in the sight of the Lord, and walked in the way of his father, and in the way of his mother … for he served Baal, and worshipped him, and provoked to anger the Lord God of Israel …'* After Ahaziah's death Jehoram took the throne; the Bible also accuses him of sinning against Yahweh.

Elijah was now the only buffer between the Israelites and their demise into idolatry. The Bible relates that the desperate Elijah approached Yahweh saying: *'The people of Israel have forsaken thy covenant, torn down thy altars and put thy prophets to death with the sword. I alone am left, and they seek to take my life.'* Yahweh told Elijah to anoint his disciple Elisha as his successor. In turn, Elisha made Jehu, a military commander and an enemy of Jezebel, king of Israel. Equally zealous in his hatred of the queen as Elijah had been, Elisha incited Jehu to massacre the royal household, but to leave Jezebel to him:

> *'You shall strike down the house of Ahab your master, and I will take vengeance on Jezebel for the blood of my servants the prophets and for the blood of the Lord's servants. All the house of Ahab shall perish … .'*

When Jehu murders Jehoram he expressly blames Jezebel: *'Do you call it peace while your mother Jezebel keeps up her obscene idol-worship and monstrous sorceries?'*

## A BLOODY END

Jezebel never neglected the trappings of queenship. After she was warned of her fate she dressed her hair, painted her face and waited for her murderer. She positioned herself at an upstairs window of her palace so she could see him approaching. When he appeared,

*In this 1866 woodcut by Gustave Doré, Jezebel is shown being hurled from a window on the orders of her assassin Elisha. Her body was subsequently eaten by dogs, fulfilling the prophecy of Elijah.*

she challenged him and tried to shame him by calling him an assassin. But Jehu showed no pity – he persuaded three of her eunuchs to throw her out of the window; her body was then crushed by horses as it lay on the ground below.

Jezebel's story, which was written 200 years after her death, denigrates her as a heinous criminal responsible for Israel's spiritual decline. But Jezebel was merely the scapegoat; as a foreigner she was perfect for the role. Many Israelites were practising idolatry before Jezebel's arrival. The despotic nature of Ahab's rule, Jezebel's influence over policy and her encouragement of idol worship led Elijah and Elisha to act against the ruling house to restore Israel to purity. Paradoxically, the purge led to Israel's eventual destruction. Jehu established a dynasty that endured for nearly a century, but Jezebel's death ended the crucial alliance with Phoenicia; Israel could not stand alone against the Assyrians and was conquered in 721 BC.

Elijah's bloody biblical curse was fulfilled: ' ... *dogs shall devour the flesh of Jezebel, and Jezebel's corpse shall lie like dung upon the ground ... so that no one will be able to say: this is Jezebel.'* When they finally came to bury Jezebel, all that was left were her skull, her feet and the palms of her hands.

## ELIJAH AND THE PROPHETS

The prophets of ancient Israel enjoyed exceptional status and wielded tremendous power. Not only did they have the ear of God, they were king-makers with the power to anoint the kings of Israel and Judah and to stage-manage coups. As Israel's moral compass they were both feared and revered.

# TOMYRIS
## 6th Century BC
## Queen of Massagetae

*In the mid-sixth century BC Cyrus the Great, king of Persia, assembled the disparate tribes under his command and set out on a campaign of conquest. Within 20 years he was master of vast territories stretching from the Indus Valley to the Aegean Sea. Cyrus was the undefeated 'Great King, King of Kings' and founder of the Achaemenian empire, which would endure until its defeat by Alexander the Great more than 200 years later. He is celebrated by Xenophon as an exemplary leader and revered in the Bible for freeing the Jews from their Babylon captivity. Given his enormous prowess, his defeat at the hands of a woman fascinated early historians.*

The Massagetae, an ancient warriorlike tribe, occupied a rough, hilly stretch of land to the east of the Caspian Sea. They were a nomadic people who did not cultivate the land, but who instead lived by cattle herding and fishing in the River Araxes. Herodotus, the fifth-century BC Greek historian, tells us in his writings that they were monotheists who worshipped the sun god. Their queen, general and protector was the widowed Tomyris.

Thrusting his way through central Asia, Cyrus (r. 559–529 BC) led his armies to the borders of Tomyris' kingdom. Flushed with success, he was certain victory was his. As a contemporary observer wrote, *'For wherever Cyrus directed his attack, that people could in no way escape'*. However, he did not immediately attack the Massagetae but first tried diplomacy, sending messengers with an offer, perhaps genuine, of marriage. Tomyris believed he only wanted her territory and refused, whereupon Cyrus prepared to invade.

### CYRUS MEETS HIS MATCH
Cyrus' plan of attack was hampered by the vast River Araxes. He ordered a frenzy of bridge-building, but the sensible queen suggested he desist: *'King of the Medes, cease to be so eager to do what you are doing ... Give it over and rule over your own people, and endure to look upon us governing ours.'* But, knowing her enemy, she conceded, *'Still, you will not follow this advice of mine, but will do anything rather than remain at rest'*. If he must fight, she said, then she would facilitate the clash. Either she would allow him to cross over in safety and they would battle in her kingdom, or she would come to him.

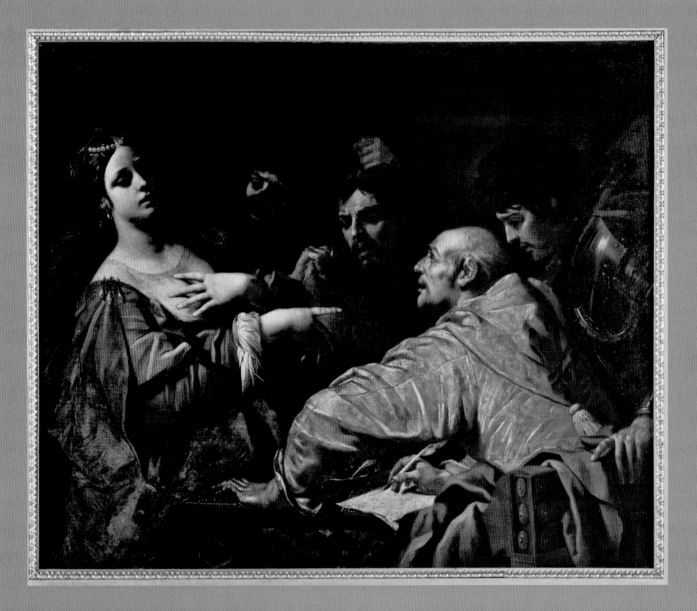

*The victorious Tomyris brandishes the head of Cyrus, which
she hacks from his dead body in revenge for the death of her
son. This painting, from about 1630, is by the Italian
Baroque artist Luca Ferrari (1605–54).*

'Tomyris, since Cyrus would not listen to her, gathered all her host together and
fought him. Of all the battles that were fought among the barbarians, I judge
this to have been the severest ...'

HERODOTUS

*'Cyrus ... started out with a little band of Persians and became the leader of the Medes ... he then conquered Syria, Assyria, Arabia, Cappadocia, both Phyrgias, Lydia, Caria, Phoenicia and Babylonia ... the tribes which he brought into subjection to himself were so many that it is a difficult matter even to travel to them all, in whatever direction one begins one's journey, whether towards the east or the west, towards the north or the south ...'*

XENOPHON I.I. 4–5

Cyrus consulted his council, the kings of conquered lands (now his loyal subjects), and all agreed – they would fight Tomyris on their side of the river. But Croesus the Lydian (r. 560–546 BC) proposed a duplicitous scheme, which Herodotus faithfully recounts. He suggested they inform Tomyris that they would battle on her side of the river. Cyrus and the greater part of his army would then secretly march away from the camp, leaving the weakest soldiers to fight the tribe. The Massagetae, having defeated Cyrus' feeblest troops and believing themselves victorious, would then feast on a magnificent banquet that Cyrus' cooks would prepare. The barbarian Massagetae were unfamiliar with good food and wine (they drank only milk), and the alcohol would intoxicate them. Cyrus and his army would then swoop on the unsuspecting – and drunk – tribe and murder them all.

Croesus' scheme violated all the rules of engagement of ancient warfare. Ancient Greek literature details the numerous codes, ethics and practices of combat – and drugging the enemy with wine was certainly not one of them. Uncharacteristically, Cyrus, benevolent conqueror of a mighty empire, approved the plan. His pride would not allow him to be thwarted by a woman.

Tomyris sent a third of her army to battle Cyrus' soldiers in good faith. Their general was her son Spargapises. As Croesus predicted, the Massagetae slaughtered the Persians, fell on the banquet and drank themselves into a stupor. Then Cyrus returned with his crack troops and murdered or imprisoned the entire Massagetae force. Prince Spargapises was among the prisoners.

The furious Tomyris sent Cyrus a message: *' ... you have overmastered my son by trickery ...'* and demanded, *'give back my son to me now and get out of our country ... If you do not so, I swear by the sun, the lord of the Massagetae that, for all your insatiability of blood, I will give you your fill of it.'* But Tomyris was too late with her ultimatum. When Spargapises realized his predicament, he killed himself.

## HERODOTUS – 'THE FATHER OF HISTORY'

The Greek historian Herodotus was active in the fifth century BC. His vast narrative of the contemporary Graeco-Persian wars has earned him the soubriquet 'the Father of History'. Herodotus travelled widely throughout the Persian empire and *The Histories* are founded on extensive interviews and first-hand accounts – his story of Tomyris and her defeat of Cyrus roughly 100 years after the Massagetae queen's death comes directly from the oral tradition of Tomyris' people.

## A MOTHER'S DREADFUL REVENGE

Tomyris hurled her army at Cyrus and, according to Herodotus, the battle that followed was the fiercest of all those fought among the 'barbarians'. First the two armies rained down arrows on one another. They then engaged in deadly hand-to-hand combat with spears and daggers. For a long while, neither side could prevail and thousands were slaughtered: *'Long they remained fighting …'* Finally the Massagetae gained the upper hand. They murdered all the Persian soldiers they could find. Cyrus, the *'Great King, King of Kings'* (as an Akkadian inscription on a cylinder-seal in the British museum calls him) was among the dead.

But Tomyris had not finished. She sought out his corpse on the battlefield, and when she found it she hacked his head from his body and thrust it into a wineskin filled with human blood, saying: *' … I am alive and conqueror, but you have destroyed me, all the same, by robbing me of my son by trickery. Now it is you and I; and I will give you your fill of blood, even as I threatened.'* The histories record that she kept the skin with her for the rest of her life in memory of her dead son.

Tomyris fascinated the ancient historians, particularly Herodotus. She was one of the only women to appear in his histories. He admired her – although she was a 'barbarian', she observed the rules of warfare and, unlike Cyrus, she did not resort to trickery. Yet today Tomyris is largely forgotten.

### TIMELINE

546 BC Persian forces led by Cyrus the Great conquer the Lydians, led by Croesus, at Sardis; Lydia comes under Persian control

539 BC Cyrus defeats the king of Babylon and destroys the city of Babylon

529 BC Cyrus attempts to conquer the Massagetae and reaches the River Araxes; a trick backfires and he is killed by Tomyris, avenging her son's death; Cyrus is succeeded by Cambyses II

*The remains of the tomb of Cyrus the Great in Pasargadae, Iran. The stone gateway to the tomb is seen on the left.*

# CLEOPATRA VII THEA PHILOPATOR

## 69–30 BC
## Queen of Egypt

*Cleopatra, queen of Egypt from 51 to 30 BC, was the last ruler of the Ptolemaic dynasty. Her reputation as a great seductress is largely the result of propaganda generated by an ambitious and vengeful Roman emperor. In reality, Cleopatra was both a competent queen and a pragmatic mother, anxious to protect the birthright of her children. By the end of her reign, she had managed to restore much of Egypt's wealth, which had been squandered by her father, Ptolemy XII.*

*The Roman dictator and general Julius Caesar was rumoured to have been Cleopatra's lover and possibly the father of her son, Ptolemy Caesar ('Caesarion').*

Cleopatra was born in 69 BC, a descendant of Ptolemy I (r. 323–283 BC), a Greek general of Alexander the Great (r. 336–323 BC), who ruled Egypt after the Macedonian ruler's death in 323 BC. By the time of Cleopatra's birth the once mighty Ptolemaic empire, which extended from Syria to modern-day Turkey, had diminished and was riven with corruption; only the land of Egypt remained in its sphere of influence. Egypt was a client kingdom of Rome, and Cleopatra's father, Ptolemy XII (r. 80–58 BC; 55–51 BC), was deeply in debt to the empire. In 58 BC he travelled to Rome to ask for military support against his nationalistic foes at home; the Ptolemaic dynasty had been imposed on Egypt and its scions did not even speak the native tongue, preferring to converse in Greek. He took Cleopatra with him, but while he was away, his eldest daughter, Cleopatra VI Tryphaena, took the throne and was promptly assassinated – possibly by her father's supporters.

Now another sister, Berenice IV (77–55 BC), seized power; her father deposed and executed her. But in 51 BC Ptolemy XII died and Cleopatra, his second daughter – now 18 years old – and her ten-year-old brother, Ptolemy XIII (r. 51–47 BC), inherited the throne in a dual monarchy. But they quarrelled; Cleopatra left Alexandria, the Egyptian seat of power, and Ptolemy XIII, supported by a powerful cabal of eunuchs, cut her out of the administration of the kingdom. She might then have languished in obscurity or been assassinated, but the young queen's political career was

saved by the arrival in Alexandria of the fabled Roman general – and soon to be dictator –
Julius Caesar (100–44 BC). He was in Egypt to try to collect Ptolemy XII's debt to Rome,
which was still outstanding. He had anticipated that his mission would be swift, but both
the familial politics that threatened to destabilize a wealthy client state and the inclement
weather that trapped his fleet in Alexandria harbour delayed his departure.

## A FATEFUL ENCOUNTER

The young pharaoh welcomed Caesar. Cleopatra also came to Alexandria to greet the
general, hoping that he would arbitrate in the dispute. We do not know if Cleopatra's love
affair with Caesar was the grand passion that history has portrayed. Political opportunism
may have formed the greater part of her desire, while Caesar was a notorious seducer of
queens. She became pregnant and in 47 BC gave birth to a boy – possibly Caesar's son –
whom she named Ptolemy Caesar (r. 44–30 BC). Caesar never publicly acknowledged the
child, and in his memoirs refers to Cleopatra only briefly, without sentiment.

He did, however, arbitrate a peace – Cleopatra and Ptolemy XIII would rule jointly in
Egypt and marry; incestuous royal marriages were Ptolemaic custom. But the peace
crumbled as the pair bickered. After a battle near Lake Mareotis, Ptolemy XIII drowned

*Detail from the painting
Cleopatra Testing Poisons
on Condemned Prisoners
(1887) by the French artist
Alexandre Cabanel
(1823–89). This portrayal
of Cleopatra as a languid
femme fatale is typical of
the way she has been
traduced by history.*

in the Nile. Caesar now insisted that his mistress marry her youngest brother, Ptolemy XIV (r. 47–44 BC). He was 12 years old and malleable. Effectively Cleopatra was sole ruler.

Two years later, Cleopatra travelled to Rome with her brother-husband; she was probably in the city when Caesar was assassinated by Brutus, Cassius and their cohorts in the Senate on the Ides of March in 44 BC. Caesar had gathered too much power to himself, and his murder ignited a new Roman civil war. Cleopatra returned to Alexandria and by the autumn she was sole queen in title; her brother was dead and she designated her small son, Ptolemy XV Caesar, her new co-ruler.

## EGYPT PROSPERS UNDER CLEOPATRA

Cleopatra soothed the nationalistic rumblings of her kingdom by being the first of her dynasty – according to the Roman historian Plutarch (46–122) – to speak Egypt's native language. She was an able ruler, and under her successful economic reforms Egypt prospered. But then the internal politics of Rome intruded on her state. Caesar's assassins were locked in a power struggle with the uneasy alliance of Mark Antony (83–30 BC) and Caesar's 19-year-old nephew and heir, Octavian (r. 30 BC–AD 14). Cleopatra, as ruler of the newly stable and rich client state of Egypt, was approached for financial support by all the protagonists; wisely she prevaricated.

In 42 BC, at the Battle of Philippi, the assassins of Caesar were defeated and the leaders killed themselves. Mark Antony, hoping to imitate Caesar's campaigning and in his own bid for glory, planned to invade Rome's *bête noire* – the Parthian empire. He needed funds and approached Cleopatra. They became lovers and Cleopatra gave birth to twins, whom she named Alexander Helios ('the sun') and Cleopatra Selene ('the moon'). But the lovers were only together briefly; it seemed a pragmatic, rather than romantic, alliance. Soon Antony left to participate in a rebellion against Octavian. They would not see each other again for nearly four years.

When Antony's wife Fulvia (77–40 BC) died, he decided to cement an alliance by marrying Octavian's sister, Octavia (69–11 BC). But in 37 BC he returned to the east to continue his glorious fantasy of subduing the mighty Parthian empire. Again, he wanted Cleopatra's money, and in return she asked for extensive territories in the east that were not in his gift. He launched his catastrophic attack on Parthia the following year.

## A REPUTATION BASED ON ROMAN PROPAGANDA

Meanwhile, his relationship with Octavian, never easy, crumbled as they jostled for power. Eventually, Antony left his wife to live with Cleopatra and their children – she had borne their third child, Ptolemy Philadelphus – in Egypt. Octavian could not tolerate such a naked threat to his authority and pride, and so mounted an aggressive propaganda campaign against the 'bewitched' Antony and his foreign whore. The Roman historian Dio Cassius (c.150–235) wrote of Antony, '*He gave not a thought to honour, but became the Egyptian woman's slave*'. Likewise, the earlier Greek historian and biographer Plutarch (c.46–120) offered the following damning assessment in his *Parallel Lives*:

*An undated portrait of Mark Antony. In his play* Antony and Cleopatra *(1606–7) William Shakespeare called him 'the triple pillar of the world transformed into a strumpet's fool'.*

*'Such was his passion … it was as if he were no longer the master of his own judgement but rather under the influence of some drug or magic spell.'*

Cleopatra was therefore a construct of Roman propaganda. We can distinguish two Cleopatras – the real one, a shrewd and competent queen; and the infamous harlot of myth. Like Zenobia in third-century Palmyra and Boudica in first-century Britain, Cleopatra threatened Rome and was maligned.

At an incredible ceremony in 34 BC, known as the Donations, Antony named Cleopatra *'Queen of Kings'* and Ptolemy XV *'Caesar, King of Kings'*. He also endowed their children with vast realms that already belonged to client kings of Rome. Most damagingly, he insisted that Caesarion, not Octavian, was Julius Caesar's heir. He then formally divorced Octavia. His styling of himself as an eastern potentate outraged Roman public opinion and lost him valuable support.

## DEFEAT AND DEATH

The inevitable war came slowly. Antony and Cleopatra constructed a fleet, equipped an army, and waited. When Octavian finally declared war, he did so not on Antony, but on the foreign *'prostitute-queen'* Cleopatra. In the spring of 31 BC the first blow was struck – Octavian's navy, under his friend Marcus Agrippa (*c.*63–12 BC), attacked the Egyptian fleet at Methone and cut off their supplies. On 2 September, at the Battle of Actium, the Egyptian fleet was captured, although Antony and Cleopatra escaped with their treasure; meanwhile their land armies began to defect to Octavian.

It took almost a year for the end to come. Both Antony and Cleopatra tried to strike a deal with the resurgent Octavian. Cleopatra offered to abdicate if her children were allowed to succeed her. For his part, Antony pledged to take his own life if Cleopatra were spared. Octavian ignored their parleys and at the end of July, 30 BC landed in Alexandria. The fleet and the army surrendered to him without a fight; Antony, apparently believing that the queen was already dead, stabbed himself and was carried still alive to Cleopatra. She was taken prisoner, and later took her own life. Legend has it that she died by clutching a venomous asp to her breast.

## WHAT BECAME OF THE CHILDREN?

Octavian murdered Cleopatra's oldest son Caesarion, her child by Julius Caesar. He would countenance no threat from a rival 'heir' to his great-uncle' Caesar's name and title. However, he spared her three children by Mark Antony, although the twins were taken to Rome for his victory triumph. Later, little Cleopatra wed a prince of Numidia in north Africa and her brothers lived with her.

# LIVIA

## 58 BC—AD 29
## Empress of Rome

*Livia is reviled as one of the most wicked women in history, an empress who stopped at nothing, not even murder, to promote the interests of the newly established imperial family and prevent the return of the Roman republic. When she was 17 years old and pregnant with her second child, Livia deserted her husband to marry Rome's rising political star, Octavian. Through Octavian, later known as Caesar Augustus, she controlled the Roman empire. Although she bore him no heirs, Livia exercised absolute power and helped to create a bureaucracy that ensured the empire's domination of the known world for 400 years. Our popular knowledge of the empress comes from Robert Graves' novel, I, Claudius, based on accounts by the usually reliable Roman historian, Tacitus. But Tacitus' hatred of Livia inspired a portrait of pure evil. The real Livia was a far more complex character, often admired by contemporaries – a woman who survived Rome's vicious political forum for over 60 years.*

Livia was born into an ancient Roman patrician family, the Claudians. According to legend, this aristocratic family yielded good and bad fruit, and Livia was one of the worst. When she was 15, her father married her to her cousin, Tiberius Nero (c.85–33 BC). At the time, Rome was embroiled in a civil war as Octavian (r. 30 BC–AD 14), Mark Antony (83–30 BC) and the assassins of Julius Caesar (r. 49–44 BC) all vied for control of the state. Nero was allied with the assassins against Octavian and, when Octavian emerged victorious, he was forced to flee Rome. After Octavian realized he needed the support of the aristocracy to legitimize his regime, the family was allowed to return.

When she was introduced to Octavian in 39 BC, Livia already had one son and was pregnant with her second child. Octavian instantly fell in love with her – Roman legend tells us that she was one of the two most beautiful women in the world (the other was Cleopatra, 69–30 BC). Octavian divorced his wife Scribonia (c.70–16 BC) on the very day she gave birth to his daughter, compelled Nero to do the same, and married Livia.

*This bust of Livia, one of the most influential yet vilified
women in history, was created in around AD 41–44.*

'The face of Poison was unmistakably the face of Livia.'

ROBERT GRAVES, I, CLAUDIUS

Perhaps Octavian was smitten, or perhaps his motivation was an alliance with the important Claudian family. In any event, the union thrust the ambitious and clever Livia into a position of immense power. She remained faithful to her new husband – who was honoured by a pliant senate with the name Augustus ('the illustrious one') – for 51 years. Augustus remained in thrall to her throughout their long marriage.

## THE MOST POWERFUL WOMAN IN THE WORLD

Livia became Augustus' most trusted advisor, an unprecedented position for a Roman woman. She directed policy and often acted as his regent. Tacitus (*c.*56–*c.*117) tells us that Livia exerted so much influence over Augustus that later, when most of the family were dead and few possible heirs remained, '*he exiled his only surviving grandson to the island of Planasia*'. Livia had no children by her second marriage. Instead, Augustus' daughter Julia (39 BC–AD 14) lived with them – he took her away from her mother, Scribonia, as soon as she was born – and he showered Livia's sons from her marriage to Nero (Tiberius, 42 BC–AD 16 and Drusus, 38–9 BC) with honours. Drusus was married to Augustus' favourite niece Antonia (36 BC–AD 37), the daughter of Mark Antony. Determined to make Tiberius Augustus' successor, Livia forced Tiberius to divorce his adored wife Vipsania (36 BC–AD 20) and marry Julia.

Contemporary sources accuse Livia of the murder of Marcellus (42–23 BC), Augustus' nephew and original heir, and of poisoning Julia's children by her second husband, Agrippa (*c.*63–12 BC), to clear the path to imperial power. Whether or not it was at Livia's hand, tragedy repeatedly struck the imperial family as all possible successors – including Livia's own son Drusus (who had republican sentiments) – died in mysterious circumstances. Although the emperor disliked Tiberius, Livia nevertheless persuaded Augustus to adopt this capable but surly soldier and to name him as his heir.

Augustus died in AD 14; in his will, he left Livia one-third of his property, adopted her into the imperial family and granted her the title Augusta, thereby allowing her to retain power. (Livia is even accused of murdering Augustus when he was no longer useful to her by brushing the figs of his favourite tree with poison.) But if Livia expected to rule through Tiberius, she was to be sorely disappointed. Her son loathed her for her overbearing manner and political ambitions. Some sources claim that he retired to Capri because he could not bear to be near her.

## AUGUSTUS' SHAMEFUL SECRET

The British writer Robert Graves offers his own interpretation as to why Livia and Augustus, despite having children with other partners, had none together. He tells us that Augustus desired Livia more than any other woman. But he was in such awe of her that he was unable to perform physically. To maintain her hold over him, Livia provided Syrian slaves, whom she selected herself from the slave market, for his bed (Augustus had a penchant for Syrians). These beautiful young women slipped quietly into his room and remained mute and pliant throughout the night. Livia never mentioned these encounters and Augustus was so grateful, while at the same time so ashamed of his inability to be a proper husband to her, that he allowed her to dominate him.

*An early first-century AD bust of Livia's second*
*and enduring husband, the emperor Caesar*
*Augustus, as Octavian.*

## TIMELINE

44 BC Julius Caesar assassinated

42 BC Livia's father hands her in marriage to her cousin Tiberius Nero

40 BC Octavian victorious; Livia and Nero flee from Rome

39 BC Livia returns to Rome and is introduced to Octavian; they both divorce their spouses and marry

23 BC Livia is accused of murdering Augustus' heir Marcellus

11 BC At Livia's command, Tiberius divorces Vipsania and marries Julia

9 BC Drusus' suspicious death

AD 4 Augustus adopts Tiberius and names him as his heir

14 Augustus dies; Tiberius becomes emperor

24 Livia is granted a seat among the Vestal Virgins

26 Tiberius retires to Capri; he is succeeded by his adopted grandson Caligula

29 Livia dies, aged 86; Tiberius denies her wish to be deified

41 Livia's grandson Claudius (son of Drusus) succeeds as Roman emperor

42 Claudius grants Livia the title Diva Augusta (the Divine Augusta)

Yet when Tiberius came to power, the rift seemed to be healed – he even passed a law making it a treasonable offence to speak against Livia and granted her a seat among the Vestal Virgins (the guardians of the sacred fire of Vesta, Roman goddess of the hearth). However, relations soon deteriorated. He may have become frustrated with her constant interference, or perhaps he still resented her for forcing him to divorce Vipsania. When Livia died in AD 29 at the age of 86, Tiberius did not attend the funeral and refused to honour her will. He also denied her last wish – she wanted to be a goddess. Graves tells us that she confided to her grandson, Claudius (r. 41–54), that she must be deified or she would suffer eternal damnation for her crimes. It would be another 13 years, when Claudius became emperor, before she was at last named the Divine Augusta.

## MONSTER OR MODEL ROMAN WIFE?

Livia certainly exerted extraordinary influence in Rome, but was she a power-hungry monster? She was the first European woman to be publicly represented in statues and portraiture and her image was portrayed throughout the Roman world. Yet because she was associated with a regime that ruthlessly curtailed the power and position of the educated élite to which they belonged, later Roman chroniclers – Tacitus, Suetonius, Dio and Seneca – were universally hostile. It was easy for them to paint Livia – a proud and ambitious woman – as the architect of Rome's (and the Julio-Claudian family's) misfortunes, and so they faithfully recorded all the sensational gossip and rumour that surrounded her.

But among ordinary Roman citizens Livia was popular. She was respected and admired as a model of Roman wifely virtue and as Augustus' prop and helpmeet. Her status was unmatched by any of her female successors and no Roman woman would ever achieve the level of power and status enjoyed by Livia. Livia's part in establishing the majesty and security of the new regime cannot be overestimated. Her assiduous efforts laid the foundations of Roman domination of the 'civilized' world for the next four centuries.

# BOUDICA
## died AD 60
## Queen of the Iceni

'A terrible disaster occurred in Britain,' *wrote the Roman historian Dio Cassius, 150 years after Boudica's death,* 'Two cities were sacked, 80,000 of the Romans and of their allies perished, and the island was lost to Rome. Moreover, all this ruin was brought upon the Romans by a woman, a fact which in itself caused them the greatest shame.' *This queen of the Iceni tribe is famous for having opposed the Roman occupation of Britain, laid waste to their largest cities and slaughtered thousands of her enemies before her humiliation and defeat on the fields north of London two millennia ago. But who exactly was she?*

The Romans invaded Britain three times. Julius Caesar (100–44 BC) brought his armies to the edge of the known world – only 'barbarians' lived beyond Rome's borders – in 55 BC and again in 54 BC. Nearly 100 years later, in AD 43, Emperor Claudius (r. 41–54) sent his armies back and this time they stayed for 400 years, creating a Roman province in the wastes of northern Europe.

### A PRAGMATIC ARRANGEMENT

The Iceni were one of many Celtic tribes that had inhabited Britain for over half a millennium. Their king, Prasutagus, and his wife Boudica initially acknowledged Rome's suzerainty, as an act of pragmatism, and became a client kingdom of Rome. (The Iceni were not alone; most tribes allied themselves to the empire rather than be annihilated.) But in 49 the Roman governor Ostorius Scapula (d. 52) humiliated the Iceni. He was suppressing the tribes to the west and north of the country and, distrusting the Iceni, disarmed them. Enraged, Prasutagus led a rebellion. When he was defeated, the Roman terms were generous, with the Iceni being allowed to retain their client status. We hear nothing more of Boudica and the Iceni until Prasutagus' death 11 years later. Then the Romans committed an outrage against Boudica and her daughters.

*'In stature she was very tall, in appearance most terrifying, in the glance of her eye most fierce, and her voice was harsh; a great mass of the tawniest hair fell to her hips …'*

ACCOUNT OF BOUDICA BY THE ROMAN HISTORIAN DIO CASSIUS

The wealthy Prasutagus had entrusted Boudica with the regency for their two young daughters and divided his lands and riches between his family and the emperor Nero (r. 54–68), hoping that bribery would ensure a smooth transition of power and continuing Roman indulgence. But Rome ignored the late king's will. The Roman historian Tacitus (c.56–c.117) tells us, '[they] *seized all the king's estate and the total of his treasure … kingdom and household alike were plundered like prizes of war, the one by Roman officers, the other by Roman slaves … his widow Boudica was flogged and their daughters raped …'.* It was a fatal error. Other tribes flocked to join what became a mass protest against Roman barbarism, allowing Boudica, queen of an obscure tribe, to muster a mighty army of Britons.

*Boudica was queen of the Iceni, whose lands covered Norfolk and part of Suffolk in eastern England. This bronze statue of Boudica and her daughters stands by the River Thames in London.*

## TIMELINE

55 BC First Roman invasion of Britain

AD 43 Roman armies under Claudius occupy Britain and create a province

49 Ostorius Scapula disarms the Iceni; a rebellion led by Prasutagus fails, but the Iceni retain their sovereign status

60 Prasutagus dies, leaving no male heir; ignoring his wishes, the Romans seize his lands and possessions and humiliate his family; Boudica leads an army and defeats the Romans at Camulodunum, Londinium and Verulamium before being vanquished by Suetonius

410 Roman withdrawal from Britain

## AN AVENGING FURY

According to Dio Cassius (*c.*150–235), on the eve of her first battle Boudica evoked the figure of the goddess Andraste (whom the historian Antonia Fraser believes was the war deity of the Iceni) with the following words: *'I thank thee, Andraste, and call upon thee as woman speaking to woman ...'.* Boudica then vented her fury on Camulodunum (modern Colchester), a city with no fortifications and few soldiers, inhabited by Roman veterans. The citizens begged the procurator Catus Decianus for help but, underestimating the ferocity of the British attack, he sent only 200 men. Camulodunum was soon overrun, as the population were put to the sword and all symbols of Roman imperialism smashed. Boudica then marched on the capital, Londinium (London).

Londinium was a thriving city of 30,000 people. Its merchants supplied soldiers, settlers and native Britons with goods from all over the empire. Yet the Roman commander Suetonius Paulinus surrendered it without a fight. Boudica's army massacred the population and torched the city. *'The enemy neither took nor sold prisoners nor indulged in any of the traffic incidental to ordinary warfare ... [they] massacred, hanged, burned and crucified with a headlong fury ...'.* The carnage is etched into London's foundations, as archaeologist Peter Marsden explains in his book *Roman London*: *'Far below the modern streets of the City of London the events of AD 60 are indelibly scorched on the soil as a red layer of burnt debris.'* This layer is 0.5 metres (20 in) thick.

This bloodthirsty rebellion left 70,000 dead and two cities in ruins. Writing many decades later for a Roman audience, Dio Cassius paints a scene of horror:

> *'Those who were taken captive by the Britons were subjected to every known form of outrage,'* he says. *'They hung up naked the noblest and most distinguished women and then cut off their breasts and sewed them to their mouths, in order to make the victims appear to be eating them. Afterwards they impaled the women on sharp skewers run lengthwise through the entire body. All this they did to the accompaniment of sacrifices, banquets and wanton behaviour ...'*

Whether or not Dio's account is accurate, it illustrates the sheer terror that the rebellion instilled in Rome.

Yet Boudica's fury was unquenched. She now marched on Verulamium (modern St Albans), a city whose inhabitants were British but loyal to Rome. Again, her army sacked the city and murdered the population. But at this point, the queen made a major error. Unskilled in military tactics, she did not pursue the fleeing commander Suetonius Paulinus and his army and neglected to take important forts and garrisons while her men plundered. Paulinus exploited her inexperience. He chose the place and the time of the final battle.

## THE FINAL SHOWDOWN

Boudica's army, now numbering a quarter of a million men (though this figure may be exaggerated to emphasize the eventual Roman victory) met Suetonius Paulinus' far smaller force – perhaps 10,000 strong – at an unknown site. The historian Suetonius called it *'a position in a defile* [a narrow pass] *with a wood behind him. There could be no enemy, he knew, except at his front, where there was open country without cover for ambushes'*. Women and children swelled the rebels' numbers by tens of thousands, as they brought their carts to the edge of the battlefield to cheer on their men. Dio Cassius described the scene as Boudica mounted her chariot with her daughters and called to her people:

> *'We British are used to woman commanders in war … I am descended from mighty men! … But now I am not fighting for my kingdom and wealth. I am fighting as an ordinary person for my lost freedom, my bruised body, and my outraged daughters. Nowadays Roman rapacity does not even spare our bodies. Old people are killed, virgins raped. But the gods will grant us the vengeance we deserve! … Consider how many of you are fighting – and why. Then you will win this battle, or perish. This is what I, a woman, plan to do! Let the men live in slavery if they will.'*

## BRITISH QUEENS AND THE ROMANS

Boudica was not the only British queen, but she was the only one who dared to rise up against Rome. Queen Cartimandua, ruler of the Brigantes, chose to co-operate. She delivered up to the Romans Caratacus, a brave warrior king who had led an uprising, to be taken to Rome in chains. When her husband Venutius revolted against her, Cartimandua turned to Rome to keep her throne, and remained their loyal puppet queen.

Brave words, but Boudica's massive *'unwarlike, unarmed …'* force (Suetonius) was no match for the well-drilled Roman army. The British went into battle naked or partially clothed, their weaponry was inadequate and their retreat was blocked by the onlookers. Some 80,000 Britons died here, while Rome lost barely 400 men. Roman vengeance was horrific. Suetonius Paulinus brutally suppressed all traces of the uprising. Thousands were slain and many more died from famine; Britons neglected to sow their fields while they fought with Boudica. We do not know exactly what happened to Boudica or her daughters. The chronicles tell us that the queen either poisoned herself or died of shock. Her daughters, meanwhile, faded into history; their fates are not mentioned. Boudica's uprising was the last significant threat to Roman rule in Britain until they quit the country in 410.

*This aquatint from* The History of Nations *depicts semi-naked Britons and Caledonians alongside Boudica – dressed as they might be when going into battle.*

# ZENOBIA
## 3rd Century AD
## Queen of Palmyra

*The Roman Senate begged the emperor to '… set us free from Zenobia!' This queen of Palymra in modern-day Syria carved out an empire from Roman territory – including its grain basket Egypt – before she was finally crushed by the brilliant emperor-general Aurelian.*

Palmyra was an exceptionally wealthy client kingdom of Rome. The 'City of the Palms' was at the centre of the Syrian caravan routes and also provided a buffer between the empire and its ancient enemy Persia. In return, the Palmyrene kings pursued their own interests unmolested, as long as they did not conflict with Rome's. When King Odenathus was assassinated in the summer of 267 or 268 – possibly at the instigation of the Romans, who feared his power – his beautiful second wife Septimia Zenobia became regent for their young son Vabalathus. The heir was styled 'Lord of Palmyra' and 'King of Kings'. However, Roman emperor Claudius II (r. 268–70) refused to recognize Vabalathus' succession to his father's position.

*A replica of an ancient bronze coin bearing the head of Queen Zenobia.*

Zenobia, the real power behind the throne, was not content to simply play the passive, grieving widow. An audacious and cunning warrior queen, she was determined that her husband's death should not diminish the might of Palmyra. And so, in 269, while Claudius II was engaged in staving off barbarian encroachment on Rome's northern borders, she went to war. She appointed her husband's general, Septimius Zabdas, as supreme commander of the Palmyrene army. Zenobia and Zabdas then proceeded to exploit the network of alliances so carefully constructed by Odenathus and gained control over the Arabian Peninsula. The Romans did little as Zabdas secured victory after victory in Arabia and Judea. Meanwhile, the inhabitants of northern Syria welcomed the Palmyrene army. Zenobia and Zabdas then turned their attention to Egypt, Rome's principal supplier of grain.

## MIGHTY ROME HUMBLED

Because the prefect of Egypt, Tenagino Probus, was absent, fighting with his emperor against the Goths, Zabdas found it remarkably easy to overrun the country. When Probus learned of its capture, he committed suicide. But Zenobia's Egyptian conquest coincided with the sudden death of Claudius II while on campaign and the succession of his gifted general Aurelian (r. 270–5).

The author of the late Roman collection of emperors' biographies known as the *Historia Augusta* describes the humiliation of mighty Rome: '*Now all shame is exhausted, for in the weakened state of the commonwealth … even women ruled most excellently*'. Zenobia was able to savour her victory for nearly two years. At the beginning of 272 the mints at Alexandria and Antioch provocatively struck coins proclaiming the ascendancy of Vabalathus and Zenobia (as Augustus and Augusta). But she had disturbed Roman

*The ruins of Palmyra, in the heart of the Syrian desert. This settlement covered an area of 2.3 square miles (6 sq km), and developed into one of the most important cities on the trade route from the Persian Gulf to Central Asia.*

*A portrait of the Roman general and emperor Aurelian, who crushed Zenobia when her activities threatened Roman interests.*

hegemony in the east and disrupted the empire's commerce. It was only a matter of time before Rome launched a counterattack. And indeed, no sooner had the barbarian threat in the north abated than Aurelian struck. First he sent his fleet to recapture Egypt and its vital corn supply. By the beginning of the summer it was under Roman occupation. He then led his armies into Asia Minor, where the principalities that had so readily supported Zenobia subjugated themselves once more to Roman control. Now only Syria, the centre of Zenobia's power, remained under Palmyrene control. Aurelian anticipated a bloody fight.

The armies met near Antioch. Aurelian's well-armed and well-drilled army cut Zenobia's force, including her famed cavalry and archers, to pieces. Zenobia abandoned Antioch and rode south, with Aurelian in pursuit. The armies clashed again near Emesa (Homs). Zenobia had assembled a force of over 70,000 men, but once again Aurelian outmanoeuvred it and crushed it. Zenobia no longer enjoyed regional support, as every town and village in Aurelian's path pragmatically capitulated to the emperor. The only option remaining to her now was to race back across the desert to her power base of Palmyra and prepare the city for a siege.

Although Zenobia's alliances had crumbled in the wake of Aurelian's victorious advance, she remained defiant within the city walls and refused the emperor's offer of peace. In desperation, she even considered an alliance with her enemy Persia against Rome. But Persia refused to accept appeals from her emissaries; Zenobia would have to go in person. She fled the city at night, in disguise, on a camel. However, Aurelian got wind of the plot and captured her.

## ZENOBIA AND CLEOPATRA

Roman propaganda painted Zenobia as a virago who, like Cleopatra, dared to challenge Rome and paid the price. But Zenobia actually courted comparison with the Egyptian queen, her predecessor and fellow enemy of the empire. During the period when she controlled Egypt, she encouraged the cult of Cleopatra and even claimed to be her descendant. She resurrected several monuments honouring her, while the *Historia Augusta* records that she made assiduous efforts to learn Egyptian (she was also fluent in Greek, Arabic and Latin).

## AURELIAN TAKES PALMYRA

When the Palmyrenes learned of their queen's capture they quickly surrendered and allowed Aurelian to enter the city. He exacted no retribution against its inhabitants, but Zenobia and her cohorts were escorted to Emesa, while much of Palmyra's extensive treasure was shipped to Rome. To forestall any further unrest in the east, Aurelian concluded a treaty with the Persians.

We do not know what happened to Zenobia's councillors, but it is likely that they were executed. The sources make no further mention of Zabdas either. As for Zenobia, she was spared, not because she was a woman, but because

Aurelian wanted to parade her as the centrepiece of his triumph in Rome. The captive Palmyrene queen was intended to symbolize his subjugation of the east. On the journey to Rome, she was chained and led on a camel through the cities of Syria. At Antioch she was put in stocks at the Hippodrome for three days while the population who had once supported her trailed past to witness her humiliation.

Meanwhile, with their queen in chains, the Palmyrenes staged another revolt. They proclaimed the five-year-old Septimius Antiochus – who in all likelihood was Zenobia's son (though not by Odenathus) – king and proclaimed their independence from Rome. This time Aurelian showed no mercy. The city was stripped of all its remaining treasure and never recovered, languishing henceforth as an obscure outpost on the edge of the Roman world. The remainder of the trade that it had once controlled now moved northwards to the cities of Mesopotamia. Aurelian considered Septimius Antiochus too insignificant to persecute and sent him into exile.

## CONFLICTING REPORTS

There is some disagreement over what happened to Zenobia when she arrived in Rome. One source, the fifth-century Greek historian Zosimus, claims that she committed suicide rather than accede to Aurelian's humiliating demands. Many other sources, however, state that the defeated Palmyrene queen was the triumph's main attraction. They describe how, accompanied by at least two of her sons, she was placed on a camel, bound in golden chains and forced to adorn her body with all the heavy jewels she had once so proudly worn.

## FOOLHARDY OR COURAGEOUS?

Was Zenobia foolish to have antagonized the mighty Roman empire? When she first took over as regent for Vabalathus, Rome was facing a deep crisis. If the emperor Claudius II had lived, she may have succeeded in keeping her eastern empire. But the accession of Aurelian sealed her fate. He could not afford to ignore Zenobia's lightning conquest of the east, with its huge negative impact on Roman trade and prosperity. Although the brilliant career soldier only survived for five years before the army who elevated him to the purple assassinated him, he certainly revived Roman fortunes.

The historical sources differ on the matter of Zenobia's ultimate fate. One claims she was executed, but others tell us that Aurelian, struck by her great dignity, pardoned her and allowed her to live in Rome for the rest of her life, contentedly married to a Roman nobleman. The *Historia Augusta* claims that she was given a villa at Tibur (Tivoli). Perhaps she did have children with her unnamed senator husband – the historian Antonia Fraser suggests that Zenobius, the fifth-century bishop of Florence, may have been her descendant.

*'How, O Zenobia, hast thou dared to insult Roman emperors?'*

ROMAN EMPEROR AURELIAN

# THEODORA
## *c.497—548*
## Empress of Byzantium

*The daughter of a bear-keeper at the legendary circus of the Hippodrome at Constantinople, Theodora rose to become the most influential woman in the history of the Byzantine empire. Her beauty and intelligence attracted the attentions of Justinian, heir to the throne of the Roman world, who made her first his mistress, and then his wife.*

Sixth-century Constantinople was a dynamic, frenetic and glorious city, the capital of the eastern Roman empire and a world of gods and circuses. Encircled by the Sea of Marmara and the Golden Horn, it was known as 'the Queen of Cities'. The games at the Hippodrome were a national obsession and supporters of the two great circus parties, the Blues and the Greens, were fanatically loyal to their chosen 'club'. The parties organized chariot races, acrobatics and other entertainments.

Theodora's family probably came from Cyprus or Syria and belonged to the lowest level of Byzantine society. Theodora's father, Akakios, had a job with the Green party as a bear-keeper. He died when she was aged just five, and without his income the family – Theodora, her mother and her two sisters – were poverty-stricken. In desperation, her mother remarried, hoping that her late husband's job would pass to her new husband. But another man secured the post. Frantic, Theodora's mother appealed to the crowd. She and her three young daughters begged them to be generous. However, it was the Blues, wanting to antagonize the Greens, who finally offered Theodora's stepfather a job. Theodora never forgave the Greens for their treachery.

### RISING STAR

When Theodora was seven her sister Comito began a career at the circus as a singer and dancer, with Theodora as her dresser. But by the time she was 15 it was Theodora who was established as the Hippodrome's rising star. She could neither sing, dance nor act, but was so exquisite and such a wonderful comic (and mimic) that the crowds adored her. She was the queen of the striptease, and her act became famous throughout the city. Her contemporary, the scholar Procopius (*c.*500–65), who loathed her, reported that her party trick was to lie naked on her back while a goose pecked at grains of corn secreted between her thighs.

Theodora supplemented her income from the striptease by working as a prostitute and an escort. She had such allure that even Procopius conceded: *'To express her charm in words*

*The court of Theodora, from a sixth-century mosaic in the Basilica of San Vitale at Ravenna in northern Italy. Theodora was no silent consort; ruling as Augusta, Justinian's co-monarch, she was responsible for upholding the majesty of Byzantium.*

'No one has ever been such a total slave to sexual pleasure and indeed to all forms of pleasure as she was.'

PROCOPIUS OF CAESAREA, *SECRET HISTORY*

or to embody it in a statue would be, for a mere human being, altogether impossible.'
Since Roman law forbade actresses or prostitutes to marry into the nobility, the best that
a stripper, however beautiful, could hope for was to ensnare a generous lover. Theodora
knew that if she stayed in the circus she would be on the scrapheap by 25. So when she
met Hecebolus, the governor of Pentapolis (a minor Byzantine province in North Africa),
she immediately left the Hippodrome and followed him to Africa.

Despite her beauty, Hecebolus found her wilful and opinionated and threw her out.
Destitute and far from her homeland, Theodora turned to prostitution to earn her passage
home. On the way she spent time in Alexandria. It was here, under the influence of
Timothy, patriarch of Alexandria (d. 535), that she took the Monophysite Christian faith.
(The Monophysites maintained Christ was wholly divine, contrary to the state-sanctioned
orthodoxy, which stated that Christ was both human and divine.)

## PLUCKED FROM OBSCURITY

Back in Constantinople, Theodora did not return to the circus but instead took a small
house near the palace and spun wool for a living. Yet she was not destined to live in
obscurity for long. At the age of 25 she first encountered Justinian (c.482–565), who at
40 was 15 years her senior. Cool, reserved and ambitious, he was heir to his uncle, the
emperor Justin (r. 518–27). As a patrician and consul he supported the Blues, and it was
through them that he met Theodora. He was instantly smitten and took her as his mistress.
They are thought to have had a daughter together, though the child did not survive.

Justinian saw Theodora as the perfect foil to his personality. He was brilliant, calculating
and patient, and a great strategist, but tended to lose faith in his decisions. The fearless
Theodora provided the antidote to this flaw and came to enjoy his complete trust. Deeply
in love, they decided to wed, but found themselves thwarted by the ruling that senators
could not marry actresses. Accordingly, in 524 Justinian persuaded his uncle to enact an
astonishing edict, which stated that reformed actresses who held high rank (Theodora had
been raised to the rank of patrician by Justin) could marry into the nobility.

The couple were married in 525 in the magnificent church of Santa Sophia in
Constantinople. In 527 the ailing Justin made Justinian co-emperor. He crowned his
nephew and Theodora emperor and empress, and the new rulers of the Roman world
greeted the crowds in the Hippodrome, where Theodora had once performed. Although
she was never formally created co-ruler, Justinian came to rely on her completely. Her
signature appears alongside Justinian's on numerous state documents, and she met
independently with visiting dignitaries. She was blindly loyal and her capacity for
vengeance was notorious.

## A BLOODY REVOLT

It was Theodora who saved the empire during the so-called Nika revolt. *Nika*, meaning
'win,' was the slogan chanted by Blue and Green supporters when urging on their teams.
In 532 these sworn enemies united against the government, established their own puppet

## TIMELINE

*c.*512 Theodora begins to
attract audiences at the
Hippodrome

*c.*522 Having returned
from Alexandria, where she
adopts Monophysitism, she
meets Justinian; they
become lovers

524 Justin I publishes an
edict allowing high-ranking
former actresses to marry
into the nobility

525 Justinian and Theodora
marry at Santa Sophia

527 Justin names Justinian
co-emperor; Theodora is
crowned with him and
becomes known as Augusta

532 Nika revolt almost
topples the empire;
Theodora advises Justinian
to stand firm

533 Theodora succeeds in
ending the persecution of
the Monophysites

537 Dedication of Santa
Sophia church in
Constantinople

548 Theodora dies

565 Death of Justinian

emperor and staged riots throughout the city. Justinian's advisors told him his cause was lost and counselled flight. Theodora alone insisted that he stay and fight. Having remained silent while her husband and his advisors argued, she finally rose to her feet and proclaimed:

> *'I think that flight, even if it brings us to safety, is not in our interest. Every man born to see the light of day must die. But that one who has been emperor should become an exile I cannot bear. May I never be without the purple I wear, nor live to see the day when men do not call me Your Majesty.'*

The events that followed were among the bloodiest in Byzantine history. Justinian's general Belisarius (*c.*505–65) shepherded the 30,000 rioters into the Hippodrome, where he and his German mercenaries slaughtered them.

During her 20 years in power Theodora fought for the rights of women, introducing laws to protect prostitutes, achieving greater equality in the divorce courts and prohibiting the trafficking of young girls. She persuaded Justinian to change the law to allow lower-class women to marry noblemen, encouraging social mobility – a marvellous innovation in sixth-century Constantinople. Yet although Theodora got her way in most things, the emperor never recognized the Monophysites, the 'heretical' Christian sect inhabiting most of the eastern provinces, over the orthodoxy of Byzantium. Despite Theodora's intervention, their repression contributed to the steady growth of Islam in Egypt and Syria, as Muslim forces began their inexorable conquest of the Middle East.

## PROCOPIUS, THEODORA'S CHRONICLER

Procopius, the Byzantine historian and Theodora's contemporary, was advisor to the military commander Belisarius (c.505–65). His notorious *Secret History* was ferocious in its attack on the ruling élite, particularly Belisarius and his wife Antonina (Theodora's friend), as well as on Theodora and Justinian themselves. Procopius hated and feared Theodora and she bore the brunt of his venom. His book was so incendiary that it was not published until 300 years after his death.

*Sarcophagus of Theodora, who died of cancer in 548. She was buried in the Church of the Apostles and, when Justinian died 17 years later, he was buried alongside her. They had no children, and Justinian's nephew Justin II (r. 565–78) succeeded him.*

# WU HOU

## 625–705
## Empress of China

*Wu Hou was the only woman in Chinese history to ascend the throne of the emperors; legend tells us that two prophecies predicted her reign. The first was told to Wu's father, who tried to trick the astrologer by presenting his daughter in boy's clothes. The astrologer, confused, declared, 'If this is a girl, she will be the ruler of the empire'. The second was revealed to the emperor himself by the Grand Astrologer: '… the One in question is actually living in Your Majesty's palace and is one of Your household. In no more than 40 years from now this One will rule the empire and will almost exterminate the House of Tang. The portents show that this cannot be avoided … the Decree of Heaven cannot be set aside by men … .'*

Wu was born into a minor aristocratic family. Her father, a successful general, was ennobled for his services to the emperor. When she was only 13 years old the great Tang emperor Taizong (r. 626–49), unifier of China, heard of her beauty. He summoned her to the imperial palace and in 638 she entered its closed and regimented society. In this febrile atmosphere 122 women – all potential rivals – were officially ranked. At the apex stood the empress. (She died before Wu entered the palace.) Directly below her were four women of the First Grade and nine women of the Second Grade. Still lower down the hierarchy were 27 'wives', sub-divided into nine grades. Wu was designated a 'wife' of the third class and was awarded the title 'Elegant'. These women existed for the emperor's pleasure and many bore him children – Taizong already had 14 sons. The chosen women received an education and carried out household chores. Theoretically the emperor was the only man they saw. Male palace servants were eunuchs, and sons left mothers for their own households as soon as they came of age.

The elderly emperor was captivated by his low-grade concubine, calling her 'Beauty Wu'. She was not afraid to show her ambition. After his death she recalled:

> *'Taizong had a very wild horse whom no-one could master. I was then a Palace Girl, and standing by his side, said, "I can control him, but I shall need three things; first, an iron whip; second, an iron mace; and third, a dagger. If the iron whip does not bring him to obedience I will use the iron mace to beat his head,*

*Empress Wu Hou, from an 18th-century album of portraits of 86 Chinese emperors in the British Library.*

*This drawing of 706, which is entitled* Palace Ladies, *comes from the tomb of Princess Yung T'ai.*

*and if that does not do it I will use the dagger and cut his throat." Taizong understood my meaning.'*

But Wu also clearly recognized that she was of little importance. When an emperor died, tradition dictated that his concubines be sent to a convent for the rest of their lives. Wu was determined to avoid this fate, and so she entranced his heir, the weak, stupid and lascivious crown prince Li Zhi (the future emperor Gaozong; r. 649–83).

### An incestuous affair
Wu and Gaozong first met during the emperor's last illness; Wu's detractors claimed they began their incestuous relationship even before Taizong's death. They told how Gaozong had visited his father on his sickbed and had left the room to relieve himself. He returned to find Wu kneeling before him offering a bowl of water. As he was washing his hands, he

*'The whole sovereign power of the empire passed into her* [Wu Hou's] *hands; life or death, reward or punishment, were decided by her word. The Son of Heaven* [the emperor] *sat on his throne with folded hands, and that was all. Court and country called them the Two Holy Ones.'*

FROM THE ZIZHI TONGJIAN (*COMPREHENSIVE MIRROR FOR AID IN GOVERNMENT*) , AN 11TH-CENTURY HISTORY OF CHINA

inadvertently splashed water on Wu's face and, seeing he had spoiled her powder, apologized. She replied, *'Dew from Heaven has conferred Grace upon me'*. Wu's biographer, C.P. Fitzgerald, reveals that this sentence has a double meaning in Chinese and could have been construed as a sexual invitation. It was from this point, her critics claimed, that they became intimate.

Despite her relationship with Gaozong, however, when the Taizong emperor died in 649 Wu was sent to the Buddhist convent of Kan Yeh with her fellow concubines. Here, the women were ordered to shave their heads and resign themselves to a life sentence. Wu was only 24 years old. It is unlikely Gaozong would have saved her if his wife, the empress Lady Wang (d.655), had not intervened.

The childless Lady Wang had adopted the son of one of Gaozong's concubines, and the boy became heir to the throne. But Gaozong's favourite concubine, Xiao (d.655), also had a son and Lady Wang feared that her husband would favour this child instead. Lady Wang had heard of her husband's affair with Wu; in desperation, she sent a message to the convent, advised Wu to grow her hair, and persuaded her husband to allow his former mistress to return to the palace. By reinstating Wu, the empress hoped to usurp her rival.

## WU OUTMANOEUVRES HER RIVALS

As it turned out, Wu would be rid of them both. Many objected to her as the concubine of the former emperor, but Wu cultivated support. She was submissive to the empress, who became her friend and encouraged her promotion. Wu rose to the rank of Concubine of the Second Grade with the title 'Luminous Demeanour'. Now the empress became alarmed. Both she and her rival Xiao were neglected as the emperor continued his infatuation with Wu, and so they began to conspire against her. But Wu had been careful to befriend those whom the arrogant empress had offended, making the other concubines her spies and confederates. Accordingly, whenever Lady Wang and Xiao complained about Wu to the emperor, he did not believe them.

In 653 Wu gave birth to the first of her five children, a son, Li Hong (653–75), and the following year to a daughter. It was at this point that her critics accused her of a terrible crime. To rid herself of the empress, they alleged, Wu had murdered her own daughter and tried to pin the blame on Lady Wang. The emperor was in no doubt as to who was guilty, deposing his wife and imprisoning her in the palace. In December 655 Wu joined the imperial family as empress, a position she would occupy for the rest of her life.

Wu persuaded her husband to name her own son successor, exiled her opponents and secured positions of honour for her friends and family. She reserved a hideous fate for her two former rivals, Lady Wang and Xiao. They were beaten and their hands and feet were lopped off before they were thrown into a brewing vat. Wu reputedly scoffed, *'Now those two witches can get drunk to their bones'*. When the unfortunate women eventually perished, their corpses were hacked to pieces.

## TIMELINE

**638** Wu is admitted to the emperor's harem

**640s** Wu begins an affair with the emperor's heir, Gaozong

**649** Taizong dies; Wu is sent to a convent

*c.*651 Lady Wang has Wu brought back to the palace and plots against Xiao

**653** Wu's first child by Gaozong is born

**654** Wu implicates Lady Wang in the death of Wu's daughter; she is deposed and imprisoned

**655** Wu becomes empress to Gaozong; Lady Wang and Xiao are murdered

**660** Gaozong's illness forces him to rely on Wu to rule

**675** Wu's first son dies in suspicious circumstances

**683** Gaozong dies

**684** Wu's second son dies; Zhongzong becomes puppet emperor until Ruizong takes the throne

**690** Wu becomes empress

*c.*697 Zhang brothers exert influence over Wu

**698** Wu reinstates Zhongzong as crown prince

**705** A coup led by Zhongzong forces Wu to abdicate; Wu dies the same year

*A painting (c.618–907) from caves at Dunhuang in China, depicting Zhang military forces. The Zhang brothers exerted great influence over Wu until they were overthrown by forces under Zhongzong.*

## CHINA'S EXCEPTIONAL MISTRESS

In 660 the emperor suffered a stroke. Although he lived for another 20 years, his physical impairments forced him to rely on Wu completely. She was present at all audiences with the emperor and displayed such a high degree of competence that Gaozong increasingly entrusted her with most of the business of the empire. The ministers who had opposed her were in exile and she faced no opposition. She implicated the ex-crown prince in a plot to undermine her and allowed him to commit suicide. The power of the empire now lay with Wu.

Wu proved an excellent ruler. She was courageous and decisive, and pursued a successful foreign policy in subduing Korea. China was at peace and grew prosperous. Then, in 675, a powerful enemy arose from within her own family – her eldest son Li Hong. Now 24, he often disagreed with his mother but showed the makings an excellent emperor. When the young man died suddenly at the summer palace Wu's detractors accused her of poisoning him. Whether or not she committed the crime, the most obvious threat to her power was removed at a stroke.

Wu's second son, Li Xian (653–84), now became crown prince. But he probably believed the rumours that he was Wu's nephew, and not her son. (Gaozong had taken Wu's half-sister as a concubine and when she gave birth to a son, Wu claimed the child as her own.) Wu's fortune-teller, Ming, predicted that Li Xian would never be emperor and when the fortune-teller was murdered, Wu blamed her son and exiled him. It was now the turn of her next son, Zhongzong (r. 684; 705–10), to take the poisoned chalice of crown prince and after Gaozong died in 683, he became emperor. But Wu, in her new role of dowager empress, continued to control the throne. Gaozong's will instructed Zhongzong to refer all business to his mother; the new emperor, weak like his father, was unable to oppose her.

Yet Zhongzong's wife, the infamous Wei, was ambitious and grasping. She persuaded her husband to offer her father a powerful position, which so enraged Wu that she deposed her son and exiled him, accusing him of wanting to give the empire away to a stranger. He had been emperor for only two months. Wu's next son, Ruizong (r. 684–90; 710–12) ascended the throne.

Wu had deposed an emperor; now she ruled through his brother. No-one protested. She had been mistress of China for 30 years and her ministers preferred to support the unprecedented rule of an able woman rather than accept her weak sons. Then, in September 690, unopposed, she

## THE CALAMITY OF WU AND WEI

Chinese orthodox historians are equally hostile to Wu and to her daughter-in-law, the empress Wei. They refer to their grip on imperial power as 'the calamity of Wu and Wei'. The emperor Zhongzong, in thrall to his wife, allowed her to rule through him during his five-year reign. She was ruthless, cunning and cruel, yet neither as brilliant nor as capable as her mother-in-law. Some historians believe that she poisoned her husband.

usurped the throne. She changed the name of the dynasty from Tang to Zhou, elevated 23 of her Wu relatives to princely rank and proclaimed herself empress. Fifty-two years after entering the palace, she was no longer consort or regent but held power in her own right.

Wu had no interest in the succession – she did not care what happened after her death. She let her Wu nephews fight with the Tang faction for control of the throne, but in the end she was forced to capitulate in favour of the Tang. In 698 she recalled her son Zhongzong from 15 years of exile and made him crown prince, though he was as weak and foolish as ever.

## DECEIVED AND FORCED TO ABDICATE

Wu was finally undone by outsiders. When she was 72 years old the Zhang brothers – two handsome, travelling musicians – appeared at court. Wu was infatuated and for the first time in her life allowed herself to be exploited. The Zhangs used Wu to wield power and promote their family. She allowed no criticism of them, even from her own grandchildren; when they protested, they were forced to commit suicide. Some historians claim they were her lovers, that she *granted them both her favour*, but they were loathed by a court who feared they may prevent Zhongzong from succeeding after Wu's death.

In 705, the last year of Wu's life, Zhongzong, together with Wu's generals and ministers, stormed her apartments. They demanded the execution of the Zhangs, and Wu's abdication. Wu was forced to retire in favour of Zhongzong, and the heads of the Zhang brothers were exhibited on the Bridge of the Foot of Heaven. The name of the dynasty reverted to Tang and Wu spent her final months as a political outcast, exiled to a palace on the edge of the imperial park. She died in December, aged 80.

Wu left behind a united, prosperous and powerful China. She had pursued power for its own sake, but she was an exceptional ruler. She laid the foundations of the glorious reign of her grandson Xuanzong (the 'Brilliant Emperor'; r. 712–56) who presided over China's golden age. The Tang dynasty would endure for another 200 years.

*These stone attendants stand watch before a burial mound honouring Empress Wu, at Qianxian in Shaanxi province, China.*

# MATILDA
## 1102–67
## Claimant to the English throne

*By the tender age of 11, Matilda – a scion of the Norman conquerors and the ancient Saxon kings and the ancestress of the Angevin empire – was empress of the Holy Roman Empire. But despite styling herself 'Lady of the English' (Domina Anglorum), she never ruled in her own right and was never crowned queen of England. She fought and lost a bloody civil war for the English throne against her cousin Stephen, but won the peace, with her son becoming one of England's greatest kings – Henry II.*

Matilda was the daughter of Henry I of England (r. 1100–35) and Matilda of Scotland (c.1080–1118). She was born at the beginning of the 12th century, less than 40 years after the conquest of England by her grandfather William, duke of Normandy (r. 1066–87). Princess Matilda was a rich prize. When she was only eight years old she was betrothed to the king of Germany, later the Holy Roman Emperor Henry V (r. 1111–25), and her father sent her to live at her fiancé's court. Her future husband was hardly the playmate she might have hoped for, being 20 years her senior.

*Henry I of England, portrayed on an illuminated manuscript. With a sombre expression, he is shown mourning the loss of his only legitimate son, William, who drowned in 1120 on board the White Ship.*

### 'MATILDA THE GOOD'
The pair married when Matilda was 11 years old. Despite her youth, encouraged by her experienced husband, she threw herself into the business of government and became an able and enthusiastic administrator, acting as his regent in Italy. Her German subjects adored her – she was beautiful, with her Norman red hair, and she had a vivacity that won their affection – they called her 'Matilda the Good'. However, in 1125 the emperor died and Matilda suddenly found herself childless in a foreign land. She could either remain in Germany – and be at the mercy of her husband's family, to be married to a candidate of their choice – or she could return to England and her father's court. With no stake in the throne, she went back to the land of her birth. But she would retain the title of empress all her life.

When Matilda arrived in England, the country was embroiled in a succession crisis. Henry I, charismatic, sensuous and attractive, was the father of over 20 illegitimate children, but had only one legitimate son: William (1103–20), heir to the throne.

*This illumination from the Golden Book of St Albans (1380) shows a seated Queen Matilda holding a charter. Matilda was a benefactor of St Alban's Abbey.*

In 1120 William drowned while crossing the English Channel in the *White Ship*. (Some chroniclers accused the young prince of being drunk and contributing to the accident.) Henry swiftly took a second wife – Adela of Louvain (1103–51) – in the hope that she would bear him legitimate sons. But the marriage was barren and by 1127 the elderly king was forced to consider Matilda, his only surviving legitimate child, as his heir. Although there was no law barring female succession in England, neither was there any precedent, and the great barons were reluctant to support a woman.

On Christmas Day, 1127 Henry coerced his nobles into accepting Matilda as his successor, as 'lady of England and Normandy'. In return he promised not to marry her off without their approval. But Henry broke his promise and married his daughter to Geoffrey (1113–51), heir to the count of Anjou. The dukes of Normandy and the counts of Anjou were ancient enemies, and the union of Matilda and Geoffrey was designed to secure a lasting peace. But Henry's Norman barons were furious. They feared rule by a foreigner, particularly an Angevin, and Henry never made his intentions clear. After his death, did the king intend Matilda to rule alone, that Geoffrey should rule in Matilda's

*Geoffrey, count of Anjou – an engraved, gilded and enamelled portrait on copper from c.1151. He was buried in the Cathedral St-Julien at Le Mans, France, where this portrait also resides.*

place, that it should be a joint monarchy or that his daughter should act as regent until any male grandchildren were old enough to rule? And for Matilda, now aged 26, the marriage was less than ideal – her future husband was only 14 years old.

## PRELUDE TO CIVIL WAR

Matilda was livid. She had been an empress; now she was a mere countess. Her husband, though handsome (he was known as *Geoffrey le Bel*), was arrogant and Matilda considered him unworthy. Their marriage collapsed and the bride fled back to England, only to be forced by her father to return to Geoffrey. Despite their mutual detestation a son, Henry, was born in 1133, swiftly followed by another boy in 1134. But King Henry continued to ignore the succession problem and when he died in 1135 at supper (he collapsed after eating too many lampreys, an eel-like fish he loved) it was still unresolved. And by establishing potential rivals to Matilda – perhaps unintentionally – he laid the ground for civil war.

Matilda's rivals for the English throne were Stephen of Blois (*c.*1096–1154), Henry's nephew, and Robert of Gloucester (*c.*1090–1147), Henry's illegitimate son. Stephen was Henry's favourite nephew. He had grown up at the English court and the king had showered him with favours, lands and a rich wife, Matilda of Boulogne (1105–52). Equally, by marrying Robert to Mabel (d.1156), the fabulously wealthy Gloucester heiress, Henry had set up another powerful contender for the throne.

## HENRY II AND BECKET

Henry uncharacteristically failed to follow Matilda's advice when she refused to support his choice of his greatest friend, Thomas Becket (c.1118–70), as archbishop of Canterbury. Matilda foresaw the inevitable clash between the zealot Becket and her headstrong son. The murder of Becket in Canterbury Cathedral by four rogue knights, possibly acting on the king's orders in 1170, haunted the rest of Henry's reign. Had Henry listened to Matilda's advice, could one of the most notorious murders in English history have been avoided?

Although Robert supported his half-sister, initially she did nothing to secure her throne. Matilda – fiery, proud and vocal – saw Henry's kingdom as her birthright and her inaction was out of character. Why did she fail to claim her inheritance? The reason was probably her poor state of health. Matilda had almost died in childbirth in 1134, and was still too weak to undertake the journey across the English Channel. Her enforced inaction enabled her cousin Stephen to seize the throne. The archbishop of Canterbury crowned him king of England at Westminster in December 1135, and Matilda, sick in Anjou with her baby sons, was powerless to prevent it.

When Matilda recovered she begged Geoffrey to help her take the English throne. He refused, preferring to claim his wife's inheritance in Normandy, and sent his men to harass the border towns instead. For the rest of her inheritance, Matilda was forced to wait until 1139 when Robert of Gloucester gave her an army. With it she started a war that would last for more than a decade.

## THWARTED AMBITION

Within two years Matilda was confident of victory. She captured Stephen at the Battle of Lincoln in 1141, imprisoned him at Bristol and expected to be crowned queen of England. She was recognized as queen at Winchester and travelled to London, joyfully anticipating her coronation. Its citizens welcomed her, but she soon alienated them, styling herself 'empress', 'queen' and 'lady of the English', appointing earls and levying taxes. Gerald of Wales wrote that: *'she was swollen with insufferable pride by her success in war, and alienated the affections of nearly everyone. She was driven out of London.'* Stephen's wife, Matilda of Boulogne, raised an army and Matilda was forced to flee to Winchester. All hopes of coronation were lost.

When Stephen's wife captured her ally, Robert of Gloucester, Matilda agreed to an exchange of prisoners. Stephen was released and the war dragged on for another seven years, with neither side achieving a decisive victory. The misery of war was exacerbated by anarchy, mass looting and famine. Later chroniclers dubbed it *'the anarchy'* and wrote bitterly that during Stephen's reign *'Christ and His saints slept'*. By 1148 both Matilda and England were exhausted and 'the empress' at last relinquished her claim in favour of her eldest son, Henry. His father had given him Normandy and when Geoffrey died in 1151, Henry was proclaimed count of Anjou. A year later, he married the legendary heiress Eleanor of Aquitaine (1122–1204), who divorced the king of France to wed him. Matilda's son now had the resources to claim the throne of England and bided his time.

Stephen died in 1154. Henry launched his invasion and was crowned King Henry II of England (r. 1154–89). He met little resistance: Stephen's son, Eustace, was dead and Stephen had formally acknowledged Henry as his heir anyway. Despite Matilda's abilities, her pride and her sex damned her in the eyes of her contemporaries. Henry, acknowledging his debt to her, sought her counsel until her death at Rouen 13 years later. The chronicler Walter Map (*c.*1140–1210) recorded her words to her son:

> *'I have heard that his mother's teaching was to this effect, that he should spin out the affairs of everyone, hold long in his own hand all posts that fell in, take the revenues of them and keep the aspirants to them hanging on in hope; and she supported this advice by an unkind analogy: an unruly hawk, if meat is often offered to it and then snatched away or hid, becomes keener and more inclinably obedient and attentive.'*

Matilda died on 10 September, 1167 and was buried at Bec Abbey in Normandy. Her son wrote her epitaph: *'Here lies Henry's daughter, wife and mother; great by birth – greater by marriage – but greatest by motherhood.'*

## TIMELINE

**1110** Matilda is betrothed to Henry of Germany

**1114** Henry and Matilda marry; Matilda becomes empress

**1125** Henry dies; Matilda returns to England to face a succession crisis

**1127** Henry I names Matilda as his heir

**1128** Matilda is married to Geoffrey of Anjou

**1133** Matilda gives birth to Henry, future king of England

**1134** A second son is born

**1135** Henry I dies; Stephen seizes the throne while Matilda remains in Anjou

**1139** Matilda starts a ten-year civil war

**1141** Matilda captures Stephen at the Battle of Lincoln; later, Stephen's wife forces Matilda to flee

**1148** Matilda relinquishes her claim to the throne and retires to Normandy

**1151** Geoffrey dies; Henry becomes count of Anjou

**1152** Henry marries Eleanor of Aquitaine

**1154** Stephen dies; Henry invades England and is proclaimed king

**1167** Matilda dies in Normandy

# ELEANOR OF AQUITAINE

## 1122 – 1204
## Queen of England and France

*With her frenetic energy, her rare beauty and her glorious sense of adventure, Eleanor is one of the most vivid figures in history. She is the only woman to have been both queen of France and queen of England. Married at 15 to the dull Louis VII of France, she taunted him with her sexual infidelities and insisted on accompanying him on crusade – some sources claim she rode into Jerusalem bare-breasted. She left Louis for the 19-year-old Henry of Anjou, Europe's rising star. The political ramifications of their union continued to make themselves felt in Europe for several decades, even centuries, thereafter.*

Born in 1122, Eleanor was the eldest daughter of Duke William X of Aquitaine (1099–1137) and Aenor of Châtellerault (c.1103–30). The duchy of Aquitaine, an extensive region in the far southwest of France bounded by the Atlantic Ocean and the Pyrenees, was the home of the troubadours and the heartland of courtly love, and Eleanor grew up in a rich, sophisticated and erudite court. This was a society in which women were able to hold power independently. And so, when William died in 1137, Eleanor became the duchess of Aquitaine, one of the largest and richest domains in Europe.

### A BEAUTY AND A TRUE PRIZE
The rulers of Aquitaine were among the most powerful vassals of the French kings. Eleanor was a marvellous prize in the dynastic marriage market of medieval Europe. Not only was she one of the wealthiest women on the continent; she was also a tall, enchanting beauty with flaming red hair. William believed that in the event of his death his daughter would need an alliance to safeguard her inheritance, so he arranged her marriage to the son of the strongest man in France, King Louis VI ('the Fat' r. 1108–37).

*The painted stone effigy of Eleanor of Aquitaine atop her
tomb in Fontevrault Abbey, France.*

'… [a queen] *who surpassed almost all the queens
of the world.'*

THE NUNS OF FONTEVRAULT

*This detail from a 19th-century French stained glass window depicts Louis VII 'taking the cross' for the Second Crusade in 1146.*

Young prince Louis (r. 1137–80) was nothing like his father – he was weak and almost monastic in temperament. But Eleanor, according to the deceased William's wishes, married the 16-year-old prince in the summer of 1137. A month later Louis VI died; the young couple were now the king and queen of France.

The marriage was a disaster from the very outset. Where Eleanor was dazzling, Louis was passive. Although Louis adored Eleanor – contemporaries said he loved her *'almost beyond reason'* – they rarely made love. Louis was too pious to take pleasure in their congress, and Eleanor was vocal in her disappointment. But despite the infrequency of his conjugal visits, she still bore him two daughters, Marie (1145–98) and Alix (1151–98).

## ELEANOR THE ADVENTURER

In 1147 Louis joined the Second Crusade. Eleanor, desperate for adventure, insisted on accompanying him to the Holy Land. Observers at court speculated that Louis could not bear to leave her in Paris to enjoy the attentions of other men. By the time the crusading army arrived in Antioch, however, relations between king and queen were so bad that Eleanor had an affair with her uncle Raymond of Poitiers, Prince of Antioch (*c.*1115–49). The virile and worldly Raymond, whose nickname was 'Hercules,' provided the perfect counterpoint to her stale marriage.

Eleanor begged Louis for an annulment, claiming that she had *'married a monk, not a king'*. Despite her infidelities he refused, and their marriage plodded on. Further tension between them arose from her failure to produce a male heir. It was not until Eleanor found an incentive to leave that she pressed for an annulment in earnest. That incentive came in the form of Count Henry of Anjou (1133–89).

### ELEANOR'S LOVERS

We know that Eleanor had an affair with her uncle, Raymond of Poitiers, Prince of Antioch. But her most notorious relationship was with her future father-in-law, Geoffrey of Anjou. They met during the period before Eleanor went on crusade, when Geoffrey was seneschal of Poitou. The count, who was estranged from his wife Matilda of England (1102–67), must have seemed very dynamic to Eleanor, especially compared to the dreary, sexless Louis. Geoffrey was probably Eleanor's first extra-marital affair, and ten years later he begged his son not to marry her. If their affair became public, the marriage would be deemed incestuous and hence invalid.

Henry was the grandson of Henry I of England (r. 1100–35) and heir to the English throne. Although not conventionally handsome, contemporaries tell us he was the most vital, driven man of his age. He was short with a stocky build, bright red hair and an unquenchable thirst for power and knowledge. Henry was curious about everything and his energy and brilliance matched Eleanor's. He had ambitious plans to forge a vast empire out of England, Normandy and Anjou.

## A POWERFUL ATTRACTION AND A FORMIDABLE UNION

Eleanor and Henry first met in Paris, when she was 29 and he was 18. The attraction was instantaneous. The pair probably made secret plans to marry immediately, despite warnings from Henry's father, Geoffrey (*c.*1113–51), who had briefly been Eleanor's lover. In 1152, Louis eventually agreed to Eleanor's demands for an annulment – she did not tell him why – and she walked away from her marriage, leaving her daughters but with her territories intact. If the naïve Louis had any inkling of her plans, would he ever have let her go?

When Louis discovered that Eleanor and Henry had married later that year, he was devastated. The unification of Eleanor's lands with Henry's considerable territories created the vast Angevin empire – an area which, after Henry inherited the throne of England, stretched from the borders of Scotland to the Pyrenees. It was ten times the size of France and its threat to the French kingdom was to have disastrous consequences for the peace and stability of Europe.

*Eleanor:*
*'Henry was eighteen when we met, and I was queen of France. He came down from the north to Paris with a mind like Aristotle's … and a form like mortal sin. We shattered the commandments on the spot.'*

JAMES GOLDMAN, *THE LION IN WINTER*

When King Stephen of England (r. 1135–54) died in 1154 Henry and Eleanor were crowned king and queen at Westminster Abbey. The intense physical attraction between them did not preclude this from being a working marriage. They spent long spells apart, with Henry fighting to defend or expand his territories, and Eleanor frequently acting as regent in his absence. But despite her abilities Eleanor was the junior partner to her dominant husband. He did not rely on her counsel and was unfaithful to her, although she probably remained faithful to him. She bore him eight children over 14 years.

## REBELLION AND IMPRISONMENT

By 1165 the marriage had cooled and Eleanor set up court at Poitiers, accompanied by her third and favourite son, Richard (1157–99). Despite the separation, relations with Henry were cordial – for now. But when in 1173 their sons – the young Henry (1155–83), Richard and Geoffrey (1158–86) – rebelled against Henry, demanding power as well as money and lands, Eleanor took their part. Was she influenced by the murder of Thomas Becket (*c.*1118–70), archbishop of Canterbury, a crime that all Europe blamed on Henry? In any event, the rebellion marked her final break with the king.

*This 13th-century illuminated manuscript shows the English kings Henry II (top left), his sons Richard the Lionheart (top right) and John (bottom left), and John's son Henry III (bottom right).*

The rebellion nearly lost Henry his empire, but Eleanor and the boys were eventually defeated. Henry forgave his sons, but Eleanor's punishment was imprisonment. He even tried to have their marriage annulled; he was sleeping with Alys (1160–*c.*1220), King Louis' daughter by his second marriage, and she had already borne him at least one child. Alys had been betrothed to Richard when she was a child and had been brought up in England as Eleanor's daughter. Devastated by the rebellion, Henry fantasized about founding a new dynasty with the woman Eleanor believed had betrayed her. But the marriage was not to be and the annulment came to nothing.

Eleanor remained in captivity until Henry's death in 1189. She had been in prison for 16 years and was now 67 years old. The young Henry had died in 1183 and Eleanor's beloved Richard was now king of England (r. 1189–99). His first act as monarch was to release his mother, and his reign coincided with the happiest and busiest period of Eleanor's life.

Richard relied on Eleanor completely. He is known to history as the 'Lionheart', but he turned out to be a poor king of England, spending only ten months of a ten-year reign in the country. Four years alone were taken up by Richard's involvement in the Third Crusade and its aftermath. On his return from this adventure, which succeeded in capturing Cyprus but not Jerusalem, Richard was taken captive and held hostage by Duke Leopold V of Austria (who accused him of arranging the murder of his cousin) for over a year.

Throughout his entire reign, Eleanor was Richard's co-ruler and regent. During his captivity in Austria, she worked tirelessly to raise the ransom for his release – a huge sum that amounted to around three times the annual income of the English Crown at that period. Eleanor had negotiated her son's ransom by travelling in person to central Europe. The money was eventually amassed through taxation revenue and confiscation of Church property. Even when Richard married Berengaria of Navarre (1165/70–1230), Eleanor played the dominant role, protecting the Angevin empire from the threat of France.

## RETIREMENT BUT NO REST

Towards the end of the 12th century Eleanor attempted to retire to the abbey of Fontevrault. But Richard I's death in 1199 while fighting in France catapulted her out of retirement. Her younger son, John 'Lackland' (r. 1199–1216), was incapable of ruling alone; once again the empire needed her.

One of her final acts was to negotiate a peace treaty with France. In 1200, to cement the deal, she travelled over the Pyrenees in winter to Castile to fetch her granddaughter, Blanche (1188–1252), and bring her back as bride to the 12-year-old Louis, heir to the throne of France (Louis VIII, r. 1223–6). Although she was by now aged 77, Eleanor stood up well to the hardships of this long journey, including being ambushed and held captive for a while en route by a disaffected nobleman. Blanche and Louis had 12 children and their union made Eleanor the matriarch of European royalty. Her descendants would occupy the thrones of France, England, Castile and Jerusalem; one of her grandsons would be a Holy Roman Emperor and two of her descendants saints.

In 1202 Eleanor attempted once more to retire to Fontevrault. Meanwhile, John's disastrous foreign policies led to the loss of Anjou, Brittany, Maine, Normandy and Touraine. Despite Eleanor's efforts, by 1204 all that remained of the Angevin empire in France were Aquitaine and Poitou. Eleanor could see the empire she and Henry had built unravelling, but she was too exhausted to do more. She died at Fontevrault in April 1204 at the age of 82.

## TIMELINE

**1137** Eleanor becomes duchess of Aquitaine; she marries Prince Louis and they become king and queen of France

**1147–52** Louis and Eleanor go on crusade; Eleanor has an affair and presses Louis for an annulment

**1152** Eleanor meets Henry of Anjou; Henry and Eleanor marry, creating the Angevin empire

**1154** Death of Stephen; Henry and Eleanor become king and queen of England

**1165** Eleanor and Richard set up court at Poitiers

**1170** Thomas Becket is murdered; King Henry is implicated

**1173** With Eleanor's backing, three of Henry's sons rebel against him over the allocation of territories

**1174** Henry makes peace with his sons; Eleanor is imprisoned

**1189** Richard gains the throne of England; Eleanor is released to again control the Angevin empire

**1200** To secure peace with France, Eleanor arranges the marriage of her granddaughter to Prince Louis

**1202** Eleanor retires to Fontevrault

**1204** Eleanor dies, aged 82

# Blanche of Castile

## 1188 – 1252
## Queen of France

*Blanche was the daughter of Alfonso VIII of Castile and the granddaughter of Henry II of England and Eleanor of Aquitaine. She was married to the heir to the French throne at the age of 12, and it was at her instigation that her husband Louis VIII led a crusade against the Cathars in the south of France. When her husband died of dysentery fighting these 'heretics', she became regent for her young son, the future Louis IX (Saint Louis). Was Blanche a fearless heroine, a warrior queen who helped forge France into the strongest state in medieval Europe? Or was she a religious zealot, bent on rooting out heresy in southern France?*

In 1200 Blanche left her parents' court at Castile with her grandmother, Eleanor of Aquitaine (1122–1204). Eleanor had come to collect Blanche for her wedding to the 12-year-old Louis (r. 1223–6), heir to the French throne. Their marriage, arranged by Eleanor and Blanche's uncle, King John of England (r. 1199–1216), was intended to cement a truce between the warring nations. The French court, Blanche's new home, was dominated by the forceful personality of her father-in-law. Philip II Augustus (r. 1180–1223) was the son of Eleanor of Aquitaine's first husband, Louis VII (r. 1137–80), but he had nothing in common with his ineffectual father. Loud, blustering, a brilliant statesman and soldier, he vastly increased France's territories and pulled the quarrelsome barons into line. Under Philip Augustus France had never been so large or powerful – he had recently conquered the English territories of Normandy and Brittany.

Blanche and Louis were still children and they grew up together. Like all courts of the time, the French court was itinerant. Blanche and Louis resided with Philip Augustus at Paris, Fontainebleau, Melun, Étampes and Orleans. In Paris they lived at Philip's favourite residence, on the Ile de la Cité. The king was undertaking vast improvements to his capital. He paved the streets of Paris and embarked on ambitious building projects, including the cathedral of Notre Dame.

## A LOVE MATCH

The young couple fell in love and consummated their marriage in 1205 (when Blanche was 17), but their heir, the future Louis IX (r. 1226–70), also known as Saint Louis, was not born until 1214. Before Louis, Blanche gave birth to at least three other children who died, and the couple's eldest son, Philip, died when he was only nine.

In 1216 Blanche began to flex her political muscles when her father-in-law encouraged her to push her claim to the throne of England. Her uncle, King John, had lost most of his continental possessions to Philip and was unpopular in England, so much so that the English barons offered the throne to Louis and Blanche. Louis took the opportunity to invade England on Blanche's behalf. The invasion force was welcomed and Blanche

*This 19th-century painting on glass shows Blanche with her husband, Louis VIII. Unusually for a royal medieval marriage, Louis was faithful to his wife.*

waited in Paris, expecting that she would soon be crowned queen of England. But it was not to be. In a shocking move, the pope deposed John and placed England under the protection of the Holy See. Baronial support for the French withered, and when John died his courtiers supported the coronation of his nine-year-old son, Henry III (r. 1216–72).

When Philip Augustus died in 1223 Louis and Blanche, now 35, were crowned king and queen. It had been 23 years since their marriage and Blanche had had ample opportunity to learn statecraft from her father-in-law. Now she could practise her talents. Louis was devoted to his wife and everyone knew that if they wanted something from the king, they should ask the queen. (Even the pope approached Blanche before Louis.) Thanks to his father, Louis VIII was master of an expanded and powerful France. Known as 'Louis the Lion' because of his skill on the battlefield, he had been left a secure legacy.

Blanche and Louis now had five sons: Louis, Robert, John, Alphonse and Philip. The chroniclers tell us Blanche was *'well endowed in body, in carriage, in beauty, rich with nature's noblest gifts …'*. Even Matthew Paris (c.1200–59), an acerbic English chronicler who loathed the French, called her 'the magnificent queen'.

## 'GOOD QUEEN BLANCHE'

The 'good queen of France' gave lavishly to charity. Even in an age renowned for its religious fanaticism, Blanche was notable for her extreme piety. She became convinced of the evil of the Cathars (meaning 'pure'), or Albigensians, a Christian sect that spread throughout southern France in the 12th and 13th centuries. The Cathars railed against the wickedness of the material world and attacked the corruption and venality of the Church. Their uncompromising stance led orthodox Christianity to unite against them and declare them heretics, and in 1226 Louis, encouraged by Blanche, heeded the pope's call to arms. Summoning all the great lords of France, he led them on a crusade against the Cathars. In the course of the campaign, however, he suffered a fatal attack of dysentery. By November the king was dead; he had ruled France for only three years.

Blanche was devastated, but she did not allow herself the indulgence of mourning. Baronial plots to wrest the throne from her young son were already stirring. Louis IX's coronation took place three weeks after his father's death. The new king of France, the third in three years, was just 12 years old. How could his mother protect him from the powerful nobles who clustered threateningly around his throne?

## A WOMAN AT THE HELM

France's lords had only been kept in check by two powerful kings, Blanche's father-in-law and her husband. Philip Hurepel (1200–34), Philip Augustus' illegitimate son and leader of the rebellion, believed that it would be easy to take the crown from a boy and a woman. But he underestimated Blanche. The dowager queen had spent years studying warfare and now put Philip Augustus' lessons to use. For four years she successfully fought both the usurpers and an English invasion force, leading Louis' troops into battle – formidably dressed in white and riding a white horse.

*An early 15th-century illuminated manuscript showing Louis IX, later to be canonized as Saint Louis, seated on a throne surrounded by dignitaries and his mother, Blanche.*

When Louis came of age they ruled together. In 1234 she chose a bride for him, Margaret of Provence (1221–95), daughter of Raymond Bérenger, count of Toulouse (c.1199–1245). The count had four daughters, all of whom made illustrious marriages. Eleanor (1223–91), Margaret's sister, was the bride of Henry III of England. Louis, now 20, and the 13-year-old Margaret were married at Sens Cathedral.

The dowager queen was not an ideal mother-in-law; as far as Blanche was concerned, Margaret was simply a vessel to secure the royal line. Blanche resented the time Louis spent with his new wife, believing that it distracted him from the business of government. Even when Margaret fell desperately ill after giving birth, Blanche pulled Louis away from her side. At this, Margaret finally lost her composure, crying, *'Alack, you will not suffer me living or dead to see my lord'*.

When Louis vowed to go on crusade against the Muslim infidel, Blanche was dismayed. She was 60 when her son left in 1248 and she never saw him again. Exhausted by years of working to secure France's power, she suffered from a weak heart and she had hoped to retire to a convent, but Louis left both the kingdom and his children in her care.

By the time Louis returned she was dead. Her last wish was to wear the habit of a Cistercian nun but her courtiers compromised – she was dressed in her royal robes, with a nun's veil on her head topped by her crown. In 1297 Louis IX was canonized. Had she been alive to witness it, Blanche would surely have seen this as her greatest achievement.

## BLANCHE AND THE STUDENTS

Although she was a consummate politician, Blanche misjudged the gravity of a clash in 1229 between students at the Sorbonne and a tavern owner. Parisians immediately took the innkeeper's side and the scuffle turned into a riot. Blanche supported the Parisians. The students and masters responded by threatening to strike for six years and to desert the Sorbonne for Rheims, Orleans, Angers and Toulouse. Henry III gleefully offered them sanctuary in England. To Blanche's dismay, the pope insisted that she apologize and reaffirm the students' rights. Even so, they still stayed away from Paris for four years.

# ISABELLA, 'THE SHE-WOLF'
## 1296 — 1358
## Queen of England

*By St Matthew's Day 1327, Edward II of England had been imprisoned in Berkeley Castle in Gloucestershire for five months. That night, as he slept, two assassins entered his cell. Pinning the king to his bed, they inserted a red-hot iron into his anus. Edward died of horrific internal injuries, but no mark was left on his body to implicate his murderers or their paymasters: Roger Mortimer and his lover Isabella – Edward's wife. Isabella is the 'she-wolf' of myth. Aside from this heinous murder, she is remembered for her denunciation of her sisters-in-law, her adultery and her conquest of England. Her legacy was destruction on an unprecedented scale.*

Ironically, Isabella was born to be a peacemaker. As the only daughter of Philip IV of France (r. 1285–1314), her union with Edward II (r. 1307–27) was designed to revive friendship between two ancient enemies. They were wed in 1308, when she was only 12, at the church of Notre Dame in Boulogne. She was already exceptionally beautiful – tall, slender and fair. On seeing her in her scarlet wedding gown, the chronicler Geoffrey of Paris (d. *c.* 1320) called her a *'beauty of beauties'*.

### BANISHMENT OF GAVESTON
Yet this was no love match; Edward had for eight years been the lover of a young Gascon nobleman, Piers Gaveston (*c.* 1284–1312). Edward's infatuation with Gaveston infuriated both his nobles and Isabella. She demanded that her father intervene and Philip insisted that Piers be exiled. Edward, typically, bowed to this pressure; unlike his father Edward I (r. 1272–1307), the merciless 'Hammer of the Scots', he was not a warrior king. Rather, Isabella's husband was a weak and self-indulgent man, influenced by whoever was closest to him. But Isabella manoeuvred herself into the position of royal favourite.

This was the first period of happiness in her marriage, but it was shattered when Piers returned in 1312. This time Edward's nobles, led by Thomas of Lancaster (*c.* 1278–1322),

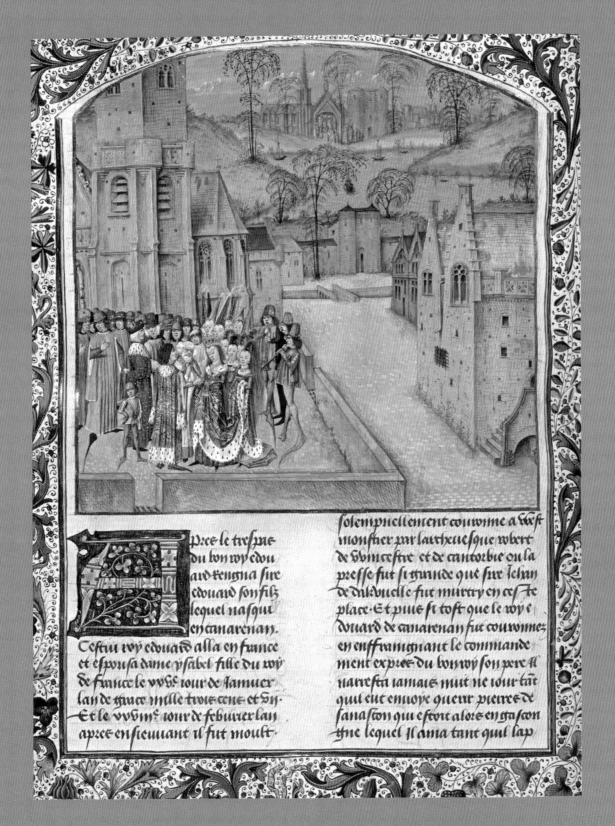

*The marriage of Isabella to King Edward II is shown in this
illuminated manuscript from the* Chronique d'Angleterre,
*dated around 1470–80.*

*A 19th-century oil on canvas by the artist Marcus Stone entitled* Edward II and his Favourite *depicts the ultimately doomed relationship between the king and his lover, carried on openly here in the presence of courtiers.*

dealt with him. Lancaster captured Piers and ordered his execution. Gaveston's final request was, apparently, a plea that *'because of his good looks his head not be cut off '*. Edward was devastated, but no revenge was taken. Instead, he turned to Isabella for consolation. In the autumn of 1312, she gave birth to the future Edward III (r. 1327–77). For Isabella, the birth of their son ensured her position in Edward's affections.

## THE 'SHE-WOLF' BARES HER FANGS

In 1314 Edward asked his now 18-year-old queen to be his ambassador to her father's court. Isabella arrived to find Paris in turmoil. Her father, Philip, wanted to steal the fabulous wealth of the Order of the Knights Templar and had sentenced the Grand Master to death on trumped-up offences. Amid the chaos, Isabella told her father that her sisters-in-law Marguerite and Blanche were cuckolding their husbands with two knights. The girls were imprisoned and died. Their 'lovers' were executed at Montfaucon, site of the royal gallows in Paris.

Why did Isabella destroy her sisters-in-law? Her motives were probably political: Isabella, the only child of Philip to have a male heir, wanted to install her son on the throne of France and this atmosphere of accusation and paranoia was the perfect opportunity. For the first time – and not in England, but in France – the 'she-wolf' bared her fangs.

Isabella began to gather power. In England she was the smiling face between the king and the nobility. The chroniclers gushed over her diplomatic skills and watched as she discarded the traditional queenly role to become the central political figure of the age. She had more children: John, Eleanor and Joan. But Edward's homosexuality shattered their marriage for a second time.

*'She-wolf of France, with unrelenting fangs That tear'st the bowels of thy mangled mate.'*

THOMAS GRAY, 'THE BARD', 1757

## LANCASTER BEHEADED

In 1318 the king fell in love with Hugh Despenser, lord of Glamorgan (c.1287–1326). Together they went to war against Lancaster, and their success was swift and brilliant. Lancaster was captured and imprisoned, and on 22 March, 1322 Edward watched as Piers' murderer was beheaded at his own castle, Pontefract.

Isabella hated Hugh. In 1318 her status was absolute; four years later it was in tatters. Hugh taunted the queen and demanded that Edward choose between his lover and his wife. Again Isabella was discarded, but now she was in a dangerous position. Despenser was a shrewd and malicious opponent and Isabella believed he would try to have her killed.

Who would champion her? She chose Roger Mortimer, earl of March (1287–1330), a battle-hardened nobleman from a famous family. Moreover, he hated Hugh Despenser. It was while he was in the Tower of London, incarcerated for fighting against the king in the barons' rebellion of 1322, that Isabella took him as her lover. In 1324 Isabella engineered Mortimer's escape from the tower. He fled to the court of Isabella's brother, Charles IV (r. 1322–8). In England, Edward continued to humiliate Isabella. She was now desperate to escape to France and her opportunity came from an unexpected source.

*Thomas of Lancaster, who had earlier executed Piers Gaveston, met his own fate by beheading in 1322, as shown in this contemporary illumination.*

## ISABELLA DENOUNCES HER HUSBAND

Charles IV demanded Edward's presence in France to pay homage for the English territory of Gascony. Hugh persuaded Edward they would be murdered if they parted and instead sent Isabella. It was a deadly error. Isabella left in March 1325 and fulfilled her mission perfectly. Charles again summoned Edward to Paris, but Isabella convinced her brother to accept her 13-year-old son, Prince Edward instead. In September the prince left for Paris accompanied by Despenser's supporter, the bishop of Exeter. The bishop insisted Isabella return to England immediately. In response she publicly abandoned her husband, saying:

> *'I protest that I will not return until this intruder is removed but, discarding my marriage garment, I shall assume the robes of widowhood and mourning until I am avenged of this Pharisee.'*

This was treason punishable by death. Isabella had brought the situation to a head. If she failed to depose her husband she could suffer the same fate she visited upon her sisters-in-law 11 years before. She courted English expatriates, set up an alternative government in exile, lived openly with Mortimer and dressed as a widow.

## KING PHILIP IV AND THE KNIGHTS TEMPLAR

When Isabella arrived in Paris her father was embroiled in the most notorious crisis of his reign. Desperate for funds to maintain French hegemony in Europe and his own authority at home, he had decided to annihilate the fabulously wealthy Order of the Knights Templar and to steal its property.

He falsely accused the Order of sorcery, devil worship, bestiality, sodomy, intercourse with devils and trampling on the cross; in the horrific climax of the affair, he commanded that the Grand Master of the Order, Isabella's godfather, Jacques de Molay (1244–1314), be burned at the stake.

De Molay shouted his innocence from the flames and, according to legend, cursed Philip and the pope. The 'curse' bore fruit: the pope was dead within days and Philip by the autumn. And, as de Molay apparently foresaw, Philip's three sons, Louis, Philip and Charles, all died young, leaving only daughters. In 1328 the French throne passed from the Capetian line to the Valois.

Isabella brought other charges against Despenser, so grave that the sources do not mention them by name. Writer Paul Doherty argues it is likely that the charge was rape and, whether or not it had a basis in fact, she was believed. She had the support of her son, the king of France and the pope, and she resolved to invade England.

## ISABELLA'S REVENGE

On 24 September, 1326 Isabella's army landed at Suffolk. She was hailed as a liberator and, after a frantic chase, her husband and his lover were seized. Edward was imprisoned in Berkeley Castle and Hugh was sent to Isabella. She executed him as a traitor, having him hanged, drawn and quartered in Hereford's market square. Isabella installed her son as a puppet ruler and, with the agreement of Parliament, decided to depose the king.

Edward II fainted on hearing the news and wept piteously. When his staff of office was symbolically broken, Edward ceased to be king of England. But Isabella was convinced

*The execution of Hugh Despenser in 1326, from Chronique d'Angleterre. Isabella is shown in the foreground, with the army camp behind her.*

that so long as he remained alive, Edward would pose a constant threat. And so, by 1327, the former king's fate was sealed. He was placed in the custody of two relatives of Mortimer, Thomas Berkeley (c.1293–1361) and John Maltravers (c.1290–1364). The *Brut Chronicle* describes the ghastly murder that ensued in unsparing detail:

> '*Roger Mortimer sent orders as to how and in what manner the king should be killed … And when that night the king had gone to bed and was asleep … [they] went quietly into his chamber and laid a large table on his stomach and with other men's help pressed him down. At this he awoke, and in fear of his life, turned himself upside down. The tyrants, false traitors, then took a horn and put it into his fundament as deep as they could, and took a spit of burning copper, and put it through the horn into his body, and often-times rolled therewith his bowels, and so they killed their lord, and nothing was perceived* [as to the manner of his death].'

The dreadful deed was done. With the king dead, Isabella now had control both over the boy-king and over England. But after the triumph came the fall. The same characteristics that had brought success now wrought catastrophe: Isabella succumbed to greed, and Mortimer to power.

In 1330 Mortimer ordered that he was to be obeyed over and above the king. Rumours circulated that Mortimer wanted to usurp the throne, so Edward III decided to act. The lovers were taken at Nottingham Castle in October 1330. As Mortimer struggled, Isabella cried out to Edward, '*Fair son, have pity on gentle Mortimer*'. She was placed under guard in her chamber. There was no mercy for Mortimer. He was hanged naked at Tyburn. Isabella was luckier. Edward forgave her and sentenced her to luxurious captivity at Windsor Castle, while the chroniclers took their lead from the king. Isabella's crimes were laid firmly at Mortimer's door.

## A LEGACY OF WAR

Isabella survived her paramour Roger Mortimer by three decades. She died on 22 August, 1358, while her son was embroiled in the Hundred Years' War, a desperate struggle with the Valois kings for the throne of France. (This, the final tragedy in the cataclysmic 14th century, was precisely what Isabella's marriage to Edward II had been designed to avert.) Instead, she now actively fomented the conflict, dazzling her son with the splendour of the French court and inculcating in him the belief that he, the only grandson of Philip IV, should rightfully rule France. So, throughout his reign Edward III exhausted England's wealth and the blood of its men fighting to wrest the French crown from his Valois cousins. This war, plus the first legal deposition of an English king – a precedent for the later overthrow of Richard II (r. 1377–99) and Charles I (r. 1625–49) – were her bequests. Isabella had a curious final request. She was buried in the same church as Mortimer, with the heart of Edward II in her coffin.

A final twist in the tale of this extraordinary woman; Edward II may not have been murdered after all. A number of historians have recently argued convincingly that the deposed king may in fact have been secretly smuggled out of England.

### TIMELINE

**1307** Edward II ascends the throne of England following the death of Edward I

**1308** The 12-year-old Isabella marries Edward II

**1311** Isabella has Edward's lover Piers Gaveston exiled

**1312** Lancaster arranges Gaveston's execution; the future Edward III is born

**1314** Isabella visits the French court and denounces her sisters-in-law; their alleged lovers are executed

**1318** Edward begins an affair with Hugh Despenser

**1321** Edward exiles Despenser, but he returns later the same year

**1322** Edward and Despenser capture and execute Lancaster

**1324** Isabella helps her lover Mortimer escape from the Tower of London

**1325** Isabella goes to the French court; she sends for her son, Edward, and refuses to return to England until Despenser is removed

**1326** Isabella's army invades England; Despenser is executed and Edward imprisoned

**1327** Isabella arranges for her husband's assassination; Edward III becomes king, but Isabella and Mortimer are effectively in control

**1330** Mortimer moves to usurp Edward; Mortimer is hanged; Isabella is spared

**1337** Start of the Hundred Years' War

**1358** Death of Isabella

# MARGARET I
## *1353—1412*
## Queen of Denmark

*Margaret, whose popular name was the 'Prancing Charger,' was acclaimed by the Danes and Norwegians as 'Dame of our Kingdoms, Master of our House, Mighty Guardian'. Elected queen of Denmark, Norway and Sweden, she fashioned a vast kingdom on Europe's northernmost periphery. As the first woman to rule in Scandinavia in her own right, amidst the viciousness of medieval power politics in that region she carved out an empire that would last for more than a century.*

Margaret was the daughter of King Valdemar IV of Denmark (r. 1340–75) and his queen, Helvig (d.1374). The *Chronicle of Zealand* records her birth: *'In the year 1353 the queen gave birth to a daughter … and she was called Margrete.'* Of her parents' six children, only three survived infancy: Prince Christoffer (1342–63), her father's heir; Ingeborg, who was married to the son of Albrecht II (1318–79), the warlike duke of Mecklenburg; and Margaret. As the youngest female child, it is surprising her birth was recorded at all.

Fourteenth-century Scandinavian politics were characterized by shifting alliances and internecine feuding within ruling families. When Margaret was born, Denmark was still relatively weak; the country had fragmented under the inept reign of her grandfather, Christoffer II (r. 1319–26; 1330–32), and when Valdemar came to the throne in 1340 only a quarter of the country belonged to the crown. The king fought heroically to recover those fiefdoms the Danish lords had sold to German and Holstein nobles and after 20 years of war and diplomacy he succeeded; Denmark was reunited. Meanwhile Sweden and Norway had been united under one ruler, King Magnus Eriksson (r. 1319–74).

### 'SOLD' FOR MILITARY AID
In 1343 Magnus split his kingdom between himself and his two sons, Haakon (1340–80) and Erik (1339–59). Magnus would rule Sweden with Erik, while Haakon was given charge of Norway. But when Magnus and Erik quarrelled and went to war, Magnus sought a defensive alliance with Denmark. To seal the peace, his younger son Haakon was betrothed to the six-year-old Margaret in return for her father's military aid.

*Margaret I, queen of Denmark. After the death of her husband, King Haakon, she ruled the kingdom with her son, Olav, but finally she became the reigning monarch in her own right.*

They were married in magnificent splendour at Copenhagen in the spring of 1363. Margaret, now aged ten, found herself queen of both Sweden and Norway. (Erik was dead and Haakon had inherited his lands.) The new queen required a suitable education and so was placed in the care of Merete Ulvsdatter (d.1415), a noblewoman and the daughter of the future Saint Birgitta of Vadstena. Her upbringing was harsh, and the chronicler of the Vadstena convent tells us that she was *'often whipped … '*. Birgitta, writing to the pope of her disapproval of a marriage in which *'worldly honour is sought hereby and not Christian law …'* included a startlingly accurate prediction in her complaint: *'… from this marriage there will come troubles and no health to the kingdom* [of Sweden]. *Nor shall its seed become firmly rooted, and the inhabitants shall not rejoice over an heir.'*

The same year brought a crisis in the Danish succession, which the Mecklenburg family exploited to superb advantage. In 1363 Margaret's 21-year-old brother Christoffer, the heir to the Danish throne, died. The question was, who would succeed – the children of Ingeborg, or the children Margaret might have? Initially Ingeborg had the stronger hand – her father-in-law, the duke of Mecklenburg, demanded that on Valdemar's death the throne should pass to his grandson, Albrecht. The Danish king, harried by his powerful neighbour, was forced to agree that *'if We resign or die without a male heir … then nobody shall gain the kingdom of Denmark and hold it as a king with all royal rights except the son of* [the] *duke … and Our eldest daughter Ingeborg'*. Accordingly, from this point on, the young Albrecht styled himself *koning der Denen* ('king of the Danes').

*Akershus Castle, on the waterfront in Oslo, Norway, where Margaret and Haakon took refuge for several years when Haakon and his father Magnus were deposed by the Swedish nobility.*

## PENURY IN NORWAY

Meanwhile King Haakon and his father Magnus were deposed by the Swedish nobility, who offered the throne to Ingeborg's husband. Margaret and Haakon were forced to flee to Norway, where they spent the next few years in desperate financial hardship at the castle of Akershus. When she was 17, Margaret wrote to her husband, '*... that I and my servants suffer great need for food and drink ... and therefore We ask You, my dear Lord, that You will find a way to improve the situation in order to prevent them from leaving me because of hunger ...*'. In 1370 Margaret gave birth to a son, Olav (r. 1376–87). He was named after an 11th-century Norwegian king and saint and he was to be her only child. It was with Olav's birth that Margaret became politically ambitious.

She was also lucky. When her father Valdemar died in 1375, the Danish nobility had still not ratified the treaty confirming Ingeborg's son as king of the Danes. Margaret, the stronger partner in her marriage, took the opportunity to usurp her young nephew's rights. Seeking the protection of the powerful Hanseatic League (an international federation of predominantly German merchants), who had no wish to see Mecklenburg control both Swedish and Danish trade, she had her own son named as Valdemar's successor.

We do not know how Ingeborg felt about the appropriation of her son's rights. Margaret and Haakon were proclaimed Olav's regents, but in 1380 Haakon died. Now Margaret ruled both Denmark and Norway on behalf of her young son – queen regnant in all but name. She was such an exceptional ruler that a Hanseatic merchant described the Danish nobility's '*respect for that lady's wisdom and authority, so that they offered her their services*'. Olav also inherited his father's rights to Sweden, and Margaret ferociously pursued that claim against the Mecklenburg dukes. The House of Mecklenburg was increasingly unpopular in Sweden, and a Swedish chronicler antipathetically recorded that, '*The Germans sat on the mountain tops like birds of prey and tyrannized the country*'. Margaret fostered the discontent. But in 1387 tragedy struck the queen; Olav died suddenly on 3 August at the castle of Falsterbo. He was 17 years old.

## THE 'LADY KING'

Now Margaret had no right to rule in Sweden, Denmark or Norway – she had reigned or pursued claims only in the name of her son. However, within a week of Olav's death, the Danes, impressed by Margaret's political skills and impelled by their dislike of the Mecklenburg interlopers, acclaimed her as '*Almighty lady and husband and guardian for the whole kingdom of Denmark*'. The following February, the Norwegian magnates followed suit by proclaiming her their '*mighty lady and master*'. Similarly the Swedes, desperate to be rid of the Germans and knowing Margaret's reputation as a leader of astonishing ability, invited her to rule. She was duly affirmed as their '*sovereign lady, master, and guardian*' in March 1388.

### THE PIRATE KING

Eric of Pomerania did not enjoy Margaret's diplomatic success; he failed to quash an uprising in Sweden, which spread rapidly, and unchecked, to Norway. The nobility, unhappy with his less than brilliant yet autocratic style, forced him to abdicate. He took off the crown saying, '*I do not intend to be your yes-master*'. Eric, driven from his kingdom, spent his remaining days as a pirate.

In February of the following year she marched out against the duke of Mecklenburg and, united with the Danes, routed him at Falköping in Västergötland. He was imprisoned. All Sweden – except Stockholm, which resisted for nine more years – was now under her control. In his *History of the Kingdom of Denmark*, written between 1732 and 1735, the Danish historian Ludvig Holberg applauds Margaret's talents as a ruler. The Union, he says, attested to:

> *'the skill of the great queen and constituted an ornament to Danish history ... in everything she always appeared to govern with ... more than a man's courage and heart ...'*

Margaret, the 'Lady King', chose the grandson of her sister Ingeborg, Eric of Pomerania (r. 1397–1439), as her heir. He was crowned king of the Nordic Union of Sweden, Denmark and Norway in 1397, but he was a figurehead, a male cipher of female rule. Even when he came of age in 1401, it was Margaret who continued to hold the reins of power. The Kalmar Union marked the unification of the three Scandinavian kingdoms, and Margaret reigned with Eric for the rest of her life. She controlled one of the largest united landmasses in Europe, second only to the vast dual kingdom of Poland–Lithuania. In 1412 Margaret, now nearly 60, journeyed to pursue her claims to Slesvig (Schleswig) in northern Germany. While on board ship in Flensborg harbour she died, possibly a victim of the Black Death.

*'It happened then*

*That the Swedes paid homage to a Danish woman.*

*She was named Queen Margareta.*

*Indeed one would have to look far*

*To find a person who with such prudence*

*Was able to unite these kingdoms.*

*Very seldom is such a woman born ...'*

THE SWEDISH *RHYMED CHRONICLE* (OR *KARL'S CHRONICLE*), c.1440

## TIMELINE

**1340** Valdemar inherits the throne of Denmark

**1343** Magnus, with his son Erik, rules Sweden; he gives Norway to his son Haakon

**1359** Magnus and Erik go to war; Magnus seeks an alliance with Denmark

**1360** Valdemar captures Scania and reunites Denmark

**1363** Margaret is married to Haakon; Margaret's brother Christoffer dies, causing a succession crisis

**1364** Haakon and his father are deposed; Haakon retains the throne of Norway, and he and Margaret flee there

**1370** Margaret gives birth to her only child, Olav

**1375** Valdemar dies; Olav is elected to the Danish throne

**1380** Haakon dies; Denmark and Norway ruled by Margaret in her son's name

**1387** The Danes affirm her status as ruler of Denmark

**1388** Norway and Sweden declare Margaret to be their sovereign

**1389** Margaret defeats the duke of Mecklenburg at Falköping, bringing all of Sweden except Stockholm under her control

**1397** Eric of Pomerania is crowned king of the Nordic Union; Margaret effectively rules

**1412** Death of Margaret

**1430** Eric is deposed in Sweden and Denmark; Norway remains loyal, but he refuses the throne and withdraws to Gotland

# MARGARET OF ANJOU

## *1429–82*

## Queen consort to Henry VI of England

*Margaret of Anjou was Shakespeare's queen with a 'tiger's heart wrapped in a woman's hide'. Married to the pitifully weak and periodically insane King Henry VI of England, she led his Lancastrian forces into battle against his Yorkist cousins in a deadly struggle for the throne. Fifteenth-century English history is dominated by a long-running conflict with France – the Hundred Years' War – and a series of battles between the descendants of Edward III for the throne of England – the Wars of the Roses. This bloody civil war lasted for 30 years; fiercely ambitious for her young son Edward, prince of Wales, Margaret was one of the conflict's major protagonists.*

*Margaret of Anjou is best remembered for igniting the bloody Wars of the Roses between the houses of York and Lancaster.*

Margaret was born in Lorraine in March 1429, the daughter of René I of Anjou (1409–80), the impoverished king of Sicily, Naples and Jerusalem, and Isabella of Lorraine (1400–53). Margaret was also the niece by marriage of the French king Charles VII (r. 1422–61).

When she was 13 years old, Margaret was sent to the French court, where she shone. A Burgundian chronicler wrote, admiringly: *'There was no princess in Christendom more accomplished than my lady Margaret of Anjou. She was already renowned in France for her beauty and wit and her lofty spirit of courage.'*

When her marriage to English king Henry VI (r. 1422–61; 1470–1) was mooted, René was delighted. He was titular ruler of Anjou only – the territory was occupied by the English – and, by securing this match for his daughter, he hoped to regain his lands.

*A 19th-century print depicting King Henry VI and
Queen Margaret of Anjou in about 1455.*

*An engraving of a portrait of Henry VI from about 1445. His inglorious reign ended with his murder in 1471.*

## A TRUCE

Henry obtained a portrait of Margaret before marriage negotiations began; he began to speak of her as *'the excellent, magnificent and very bright Margaret'*. Margaret had only a tiny dowry and both René and Charles VII demanded the return of Anjou and Maine, while England would keep Aquitaine and Normandy. The match would be extremely unpopular in England as Henry, then 23, agreed to relinquish territories that had been bitterly fought for. But the king was so enraptured that he even agreed to pay for the wedding.

The Treaty of Tours was signed on 22 May, 1444 and they were married by proxy at Nancy in March 1445; they still had not met. After a week of sumptuous feasts Margaret, now 15, left for England. She was escorted by 600 archers and travelled in luxury accompanied by 56 ships sent by Henry – but her personal dowry consisted only of bolts of golden cloth and pieces of fur.

Henry and Margaret were married on 23 April, 1445 in a quiet ceremony at Titchfield in Hampshire and then spent their honeymoon at the abbey there. The marriage may not have been consummated immediately. The devout and weak-willed king was in thrall to his confessor, William Ayscough, Bishop of Salisbury (d.1450), who instilled in Henry the belief that sexual intercourse was solely for the purpose of procreation. Otherwise, the bishop told his monarch, he should not *'come nigh her'*. As a result, Margaret and Henry would not have a child for eight years. Despite Henry's protestations of love, theirs would remain a predominantly sexless marriage.

A month later Margaret was crowned at Westminster Abbey. The queen, all the sources agree, was very beautiful with pale skin and long dark hair. The Burgundian chronicler Georges Chastellain (d.1475) described her as *'… a very fair lady, altogether well worth the looking at, and of high bearing withal'*. Charles, duke of Orléans (1394–1465) praised her beauty as well as her character: *'… this woman excelled all others, as well in beauty as in wit, and was of stomach and courage more like to a man than to a woman.'*

## SHREWD BUT UNPOPULAR

Henry and Margaret were fatally mismatched. Henry VI was nothing like his father, the warrior King Henry V (r. 1413–22), whose great triumphs had justified the 'usurper' Lancastrian claim to the throne. Henry VI was suggestible and vacillating and, despite having been king of England from the age of nine months, always submitted to his powerful nobility. Margaret was arrogant, overbearing and stubborn, and far cleverer than her husband.

But Margaret was also disliked by her subjects. For the English population, who wanted to see a return to the days of the bloody glories and conquests of Henry V, the haughty

Queen Margaret represented an unwanted truce with France. Furthermore the king allowed her to 'meddle' and she thrust herself into the political fray of the kingdom. Henry's nobility was split between those who had supported the marriage and those who wanted to continue the war. Margaret, still young and naïve, allied herself with the pro-French faction at court; together with the leading magnates, the queen, now 18, controlled Henry VI.

Her error was to alienate Richard, duke of York (1411–60). He was Henry's cousin, and by the laws of primogeniture he had a better claim to rule. But the Lancastrian dynasty was firmly established and York – although he thought the court faction corrupt, was anti-French and advocated reform – did not covet the throne. Nevertheless, he wanted recognition of his status as the most powerful man in the land, after the king. But Henry, encouraged by Margaret, treated him as an enemy.

## MARGARET BEARS AN HEIR

In 1453, after eight years of marriage, Margaret finally conceived. Her pregnancy coincided with Henry's first bout of mental instability. The chronicler John Whethamstead wrote that *'a disease disorder of such a sort overcame the king that he lost his wits and memory for a time, and nearly all his body was so uncoordinated and out of control that he could neither walk nor hold his head up, nor easily move from where he sat'*. Margaret, as politically naïve as she had been at her marriage, now had sole control of government. The king was still incapacitated when she gave birth to a boy, Edward (1453–71), on 13 October, 1453.

With motherhood Margaret became more paranoid about the duke of York. She was appalled when the duke – now allied to one of the most powerful magnates in the land, Richard Neville, earl of Warwick (1428–71; popularly known as the 'Kingmaker') – was created regent by parliament in March 1454.

*'She-wolf of France, but worse than wolves of France,*

*Whose tongue more poisons than the adder's tooth –*

*How ill-beseeming is it in thy sex*

*To triumph like an Amazonian trull*

*Upon their woes whom fortune captivates! …*

*Women are soft, mild, pitiful, and flexible;*

*Thou stern, obdurate, flinty, rough, remorseless.'*

THE DUKE OF YORK TO MARGARET OF ANJOU, BEFORE SHE STABS HIM
WILLIAM SHAKESPEARE, *HENRY VI*, PART III, 1.4

## TIMELINE

**1399** Henry, duke of Lancaster usurps the throne of England

**1444** Under the Treaty of Tours, Henry VI returns Maine and Anjou to France in return for Margaret's hand

**1445** Margaret and Henry are married, securing a truce in the Hundred Years' War

**1453** Margaret gives birth to a son, Edward

**1455** York wins the opening battle of the Wars of the Roses at St Albans

**1456** Henry dismisses York, who remains on the Council

**1459** Henry moves the seat of government to Coventry

**1460** Yorkists capture the king; Margaret and Edward flee; parliament disinherits the prince of Wales in favour of York; Richard and his eldest son are killed; his second son, Edward, becomes heir

**1461** Edward, duke of York defeats the king's forces and is proclaimed king; Margaret and her son flee to France

**1470** Warwick briefly restores Henry to the throne

**1471** Warwick dies; Margaret and Prince Edward arrive in England; the prince is killed; Henry is murdered; Margaret is imprisoned

**1476** Louis XI pays a ransom to release Margaret

**1482** Death of Margaret

**1485** Henry Tudor defeats Richard III at Bosworth Field, ending the civil war and restoring the monarchy to Lancastrian rule

York only enjoyed his regency for nine short months. On Christmas Day 1454 Henry emerged from his incapacitating mental stupor. He enthusiastically acknowledged his son (although it is claimed that he said that the boy *must be the son of the Holy Spirit*) and politely dismissed York. From now on Henry would turn to Margaret to govern his kingdom as he found solace in religion. Margaret, suspicious and wrathful, convinced an ailing Henry that York meant to take his throne. York never wanted war, but fearful that Margaret intended to influence the king to imprison him and his allies, he and Warwick raised an army.

## HOSTILITIES COMMENCE

The first battle took place at St Albans in Hertfordshire in May 1455. York won a startling victory and the king was forced to appoint him as his chief political advisor. In February of the following year Henry, at Margaret's insistence, dismissed the duke, but in a conciliatory gesture allowed him to remain on the Council. Meanwhile Margaret became extremely unpopular, particularly in London, as she rode roughshod over the citizens' privileges.

She therefore persuaded Henry to move the seat of government to Coventry in the Midlands, with disastrous consequences. Government was disrupted and – ultimately – the king lost the capital. As Henry withdrew further into himself, Margaret, fearing he was no longer a potent figurehead, begged him to abdicate in favour of their son. He refused. All Margaret could do was continue to gather her forces for the inevitable fray.

The king's allies met York again in July 1460, at Northampton. The result was a catastrophe for Henry: the Yorkists captured the king. Margaret and her son sought refuge in Scotland where she accepted help from England's ancient enemy (on condition that she would surrender the long-contested border town Berwick-upon-Tweed). Henry was still nominally king, but parliament, lobbied by the Yorkists, disinherited Edward, prince of Wales. Henry VI would reign for his lifetime, then the throne would pass to York. When Margaret heard, she was apoplectic. She raised a massive force and marched towards London.

## LANCASTER VERSUS YORK

Contemporaries called the Wars of the Roses *'the cousins' war'*. The Lancastrians took power when Henry, duke of Lancaster ordered the murder of his weak and dissipated cousin King Richard II (r. 1377–99) in 1399 and usurped the throne as Henry IV (r. 1399–1413). Lancaster's father, John of Gaunt (1340–99), was the third son of Edward III (r. 1327–77); Henry IV and his son Henry V (1413–22) were extremely able and popular kings. While the country prospered under excellent leadership and glorious victories against the French, the English were prepared to overlook the usurpation. But Henry VI's weak rule prompted the resurrection of the Mortimer claim – the right of the duke of York to inherit the throne through the female descendants of the second and fourth sons of Edward III – and provoked civil war.

## A NEW KING

The duke rode north to meet Margaret's army and on 30 December, outside the city of York, he was murdered in a skirmish, alongside his eldest son. The duke's second son, Edward (1442–83), was now his father's heir. The new duke of York first engaged the king's forces in battle on 2 February, 1461 at Mortimer's Cross, a hamlet near Ludlow in Shropshire. The 18-year-old was victorious and was proclaimed Edward IV (r. 1461–70; 1471–83) at Baynard's Castle on 27 February. The terrible rout at the Battle of Towton in Yorkshire the following month

marked the end of Lancastrian rule. Margaret and the young prince fled to exile in
France. Henry remained in hiding until he was betrayed four years later.

In 1470, Margaret and her son (now as vengeful as his mother), allied with a disillusioned
Warwick and financed by the new French king, Louis XI (r. 1461–83), launched an
invasion against Edward IV. Henry briefly sat on the throne again, while Margaret and
the prince waited in France for favourable weather to allow them to cross the Channel.
On landing they learned of Warwick's death and the loss of his army.

## DEATH AND DEFEAT

Prince Edward raised an army and met Edward IV's forces on 4 May at Tewkesbury near
the Welsh borders. It was the 17-year-old boy's first battle. But despite the Lancastrians'
superior numbers, they were routed and the prince was killed. Henry VI, in captivity
again, was murdered that night. Edward IV brought Margaret to London in an open cart
and she remained his prisoner for five years. In 1476 Louis XI ransomed Margaret for
50,000 crowns and she spent the rest of her life in poverty in France.

If anyone was to blame for igniting the Wars of the Roses, it was Margaret of Anjou.
But her party ultimately triumphed in 1485 with the defeat of the Yorkist Richard III
(r. 1483–5) – Edward IV's brother – by Henry Tudor (r. 1485–1509) at the Battle of
Bosworth Field. Henry's victory marked the end of the civil war and heralded over a
century of strong Tudor-Lancastrian rule. But by the time victory came, Margaret had
been dead for three years.

*A 19th-century painting
entitled* Margaret of Anjou
Taken Prisoner after the
Battle of Tewksbury. *This
battle, in 1471, saw the
capture of both Margaret
and Henry and the death of
their son, Edward. However,
the Wars of the Roses were
to continue intermittently
until 1485.*

# ISABELLA

## 1451—1504
## Queen of Castile

*She was the most Catholic of monarchs who, together with her husband Ferdinand II of Aragon, embarked on a religious crusade against the Moors and the Jews; she expelled them from Spain and created a unified Christian kingdom. She was the driving force behind the Spanish Inquisition, a movement that relentlessly rooted out heresy, and she supported Columbus in his mission to discover the New World. Many believed this crusading warrior queen to be more pious than the pope; Isabella was popularly known as the 'athlete of Christ'.*

Isabella was not destined to be queen. She was born in the spring of 1451 at Madrigal de las Altas Torres, the daughter of John II of Castile (r. 1406–54) and his second wife, Isabella of Portugal (1428–96). John already had a son and heir, Henry, by his first marriage, and the birth of Isabella's younger brother, Alfonso (1453–68), effectively eliminated Isabella from the succession.

When she was three years old Isabella's father died and her older brother became Henry IV (r. 1454–74). He was desperate for an heir and repudiated his wife of 13 years to marry Juana of Portugal (1439–75). When a princess – also named Juana (1462–1530) – was born, she was immediately proclaimed Henry's heir. But scandal surrounded her birth. Rumour-mongers gossiped that Henry was impotent and that the girl's mother had a lover, Beltrán de la Cueva (1443–92). Henceforth Juana was known as *la Beltraneja* – a reference to her allegedly shameful origins.

Isabella's early life was spent quietly with her widowed mother. She was not trained to rule and received little formal education. But when Alfonso died in 1468 Henry named Isabella his successor, ignoring the rights of his own daughter. Perhaps he believed the gossips. Isabella, now 17, was thrust into the thorny political arena.

### A PRAGMATIC MARRIAGE
The young heiress conducted herself with the integrity and foresight of a much older woman. She successfully fended off marriage proposals from princes of France and England – she wanted nothing to jeopardize her succession as queen of Castile – and chose her husband herself. He was Ferdinand of Aragon (r. 1479–1516). Castile was

*A portrait of Isabella, queen of Castile, by Juan de Flandes.*
*It is believed to have been painted c.1496–1519.*

'... *the most feared and respected queen that ever was in the world* ...'

ANDRES DE BERNALDÉZ, CONTEMPORARY CHRONICLER

The Surrender of Granada in 1492 (1882), a highly romanticized painting of the capitulation of the last Moorish stronghold in Spain by the artist Francisco Pradilla y Ortiz (1848–1921). Isabella is seen seated on the white horse.

vast compared with the much smaller Aragon, but Isabella believed that a union of the two kingdoms would greatly benefit Castile. Accordingly, she married him without her brother's consent.

Henry was furious and cut Isabella out of the succession; *la Beltraneja* found herself back in favour. But when Henry died in 1474 Isabella took power, proclaiming herself 'Queen Proprietress' of Castile. She held her coronation without waiting for Ferdinand, who was still in Aragon. Contemporaries were shocked and Ferdinand said, *'I have never heard of a queen who usurped this male privilege'*. Despite this poor beginning, Ferdinand was convinced he could control Isabella and that he would rule in Castile. A chronicler recorded that Ferdinand *'felt certain he would triumph through satisfying assiduously the demands of conjugal love, with which he could easily soften the intransigence that bad advisors had planted in his wife's mind'*. He would love her into submission.

But it was Isabella who reigned in Castile, with Ferdinand as her king consort. Although the two kingdoms were ostensibly united, they retained their separate administrative machines. Isabella had persuaded Ferdinand to relinquish his tenuous claim to the throne of Castile in favour of their daughters and she worked hard to defer to him whenever possible, particularly in public. Ferdinand sulked, but was slightly mollified when the couple adopted the motto, *'Tanto monta, monta tanto, Isabel como Fernando'* ('to stand as high, as high to stand, Isabella as Ferdinand').

However, the 12-year-old Juana disputed Isabella's seizure of the throne. She had powerful friends, not least her uncle Alfonso V of Portugal (r. 1438–77), who decided to marry his much younger niece and claim Castile in her name. The country was subjected to five years of civil war. Isabella eventually triumphed in 1478 for two reasons: she gave birth to a son and heir, and the pope rescinded the dispensation he had granted to Alfonso and Juana to marry. Alfonso abandoned his fiancée and she was forced into a convent; she believed herself the rightful queen of Castile until the day she died.

## ISABELLA THE CRUSADER

The defining event of Isabella's reign was the *Reconquista* – the drive to expel the Moors from Spain and to Christianize the entire peninsula. She and Ferdinand fought together, *'she with her prayers, he with many armed men'*. Seven hundred years earlier the Moors had conquered most of Spain, but throughout the Middle Ages the Christian princes had slowly driven them south. Now their only possession was the kingdom of Granada, and Isabella was determined to wrest it back. Spain would be united under the joint kingdoms of Castile and Aragon. Encouraged by her confessors, she embarked on holy war.

Isabella claimed that *'the desire which we have to serve God and our zeal for the holy Catholic faith has induced us to set aside our own interests and ignore the continual hardships and dangers to which this cause commits us'*. Moorish strongholds fell steadily to the crusading Christian army and with each victory the jubilant Isabella raised the flag of St James, the patron saint of her crusade. Victorious *Te Deums* marked the fall of Ronda and Málaga in 1485 and 1487 respectively. But Granada did not fall for ten years, despite divisions amongst the Moors. Late in 1491 the Christian army, headed by Ferdinand and accompanied by Isabella in her armour astride her horse, encircled the last Muslim stronghold in Spain. The city surrendered to Isabella's triumphant warriors of Christ on 2 January, 1492.

Isabella's peace terms were generous and the conquered Muslims initially enjoyed religious tolerance. But Isabella's confessor, Francisco, Cardinal Jiménez de Cisneros (1436–1517), demanded forced conversions. In 1499 the Muslims rebelled and faced the choice of conversion or exile. Most converted (they were known as *moriscos*), but they remained a separate community viewed with suspicion by the host Christian population.

## THE NOTORIOUS INQUISITION

The Jews of Granada, who had lived peacefully alongside the Muslims for centuries, were given three months to leave Spain. In 1492, 170,000 people were forced into exile. The chronicler Andrés Bernáldez (1450–1513) wrote, *'They* [the Jews] *went out from the land of their birth boys and adults, old men and children, on foot, and riding on donkeys and other beasts and in wagons … And so they went out of Castile …'*. The Borgia pope, Alexander VI (r. 1492–1503), welcomed those Jews who fled from Spain. He appreciated the economic advantages they would bring to Rome and organized a mass public conversion of 300 Jews in St Peter's Square. Sultan Bayezid II (r. 1481–1512) also granted the refugees from Spain – Arabs and Jews alike – the right to settle in the

## TIMELINE

**1454** John II dies; Isabella's half-brother succeeds as Henry IV

**1462** Juana is born

**1467** Jews in Toledo are victims of a pogrom

**1468** Isabella's brother, Alfonso dies; Henry names Isabella as his heir

**1469** Isabella marries Ferdinand of Aragon; Henry revokes Isabella's right to succeed, in favour of Juana

**1473** Pogrom against the Jews of Córdoba

**1474** After Henry's death, Isabella seizes the crown

**1475** Alfonso of Portugal becomes betrothed to Isabella's rival, Juana

**1478** Isabella gives birth to a son, settling the war of succession in her favour

**1479** The death of Ferdinand's father gives Ferdinand and Isabella the title king and queen of Aragon, uniting the kingdom of Aragon and Castile

**1480** The Inquisition is established in Spain

**1482** Start of the *Reconquista*

**1487** Málaga is captured by the Christian crusaders

**1492** The surrender of Granada marks the end of the *Reconquista*; the Jews are expelled; Christopher Columbus, sponsored by Isabella, sails to the New World

**1504** Isabella dies and is succeeded by her daughter, Juana

*A contemporary illustration showing some of the devices of torture used by the Inquisition to extract confessions of heresy.*

Ottoman Empire and become Ottoman citizens. Now, once again acting on the advice of her fanatical confessors including the notorious Inquisitor General, Tomás de Torquemada (1420–98), Isabella pursued a vicious internal crusade against those Jews who had converted to Christianity – the Spanish Inquisition.

These 'New Christians' had been the target of hatred and envy from the 'Old Christians' for centuries. They were known as *conversos* (converts) or *marranos* (swine). Anti-semitism had been common in Christian parts of the Iberian Peninsula since the Black Death of 1348–9, and the 'New Christians' of Jewish extraction were victims of pogroms in Toledo in 1467 and Cordoba in 1473. But for *conversos*, conversion brought all the advantages of access to Christian society. One of Isabella's confessors, Hernando de Talavera (1428–1507), the first archbishop of Granada, was a *converso*, and Tomás de Torquemada was from a *converso* family. Isabella's inquisition was undertaken to investigate the sincerity of the conversions. She set up an independent body to inquire into the nature of a man's faith. A man's actions did not count; unlike Elizabeth I of England (r. 1558–1603), Isabella wanted proof of the purity of his soul.

Isabella was applauded for her actions against heretics and infidels – the expulsion and the Inquisition – and her zeal earned her the praise of contemporaries, who compared her with the Virgin Mary. But 1492 not only saw the incorporation of Granada into Castile and the expulsion of the Jews; it was also the year of the exploration of the New World by Christopher Columbus (1451–1506). His sponsor was Isabella.

### COLONIAL AMBITIONS

Columbus's plan to sail west around the globe was seen as extraordinarily foolish and had already been rejected by Portugal. But Isabella wanted colonial possessions for Castile and was envious both of Ferdinand's achievements in Italy and the Mediterranean, and of Portugal's inroads into Africa and India. She therefore decided to invest in Columbus' expedition. After he returned for the first time, in 1493, the pope issued a bull stating that all lands discovered 100 leagues – roughly equivalent to 350 miles (560 km) – west of the Azores would belong to Castile. Portugal, dismayed, brought pressure to bear and, in the Treaty of Tordesillas signed by the two countries in 1494, the line of demarcation was moved to 170 miles (270 km) west of the Azores, enabling the Portuguese to claim Brazil. But it made little difference to the vast wealth that flowed into Castile.

Isabella's religious fervour extended to her possessions in the New World, where she enthusiastically welcomed converts. She died in 1504 at the age of 53, in the knowledge that she had unified Spain under a Christian

## ISABELLA AND THE CHESS QUEEN

In her book *Birth of the Chess Queen* the author Marilyn Yalom argues that Isabella was the inspiration for the queen as the most powerful piece on the chess board. The poem 'Love Chess', written in the late 15th century, stated that there could only be one queen on the chess board at any one time, in other words, that no queen could be pawned until the original had been taken. This could be a reference to Isabella's battle with her niece Juana for the throne of Castile. This restriction, however, does not survive in today's game.

The Reception of
Christopher Columbus by
Ferdinand II of Aragon and
Isabella of Castile *by the
French Romantic painter
Eugène Devéria (1808–65).*

kingdom and that her faith would extend to vast territories abroad. By upholding her
right to rule in Castile and denying Ferdinand, she ensured the throne would pass to her
daughter Juana. Prince John (Juan) had died in 1497, her daughter Isabella, queen of
Portugal, in 1498; Catherine was in England, hoping to marry Prince Henry, the future
Henry VIII (r. 1509–47). Juana, mother of the Holy Roman Emperor Charles V (r. 1519–
56), was mentally unstable and would become known as *Juana la Loca* ('Juana the Mad').
This athlete of Christ had been austere in life; at her request her funeral was simple.

Today the Vatican is considering the canonization of Isabella.

*'To whom, then is the title Catholic Monarchs [Reyes Católicos] better suited than
to your majesties [Isabella and Ferdinand], who continually strive to defend and
enlarge the Catholic faith and the Catholic church?'*

POPE ALEXANDER VI

# CATERINA SFORZA
## 1462–1509
## Regent of Forlì and Imola

*By 11 January, 1500 Caterina Sforza had been under siege at her fortress at Forlì for six weeks. The town had already surrendered and she was faced with the might of Cesare Borgia's army, funded by his father the pope and bolstered with 14,000 French troops. Caterina's courage was no match for Cesare's forces: the fortress fell, she was raped and taken prisoner, and her lands were absorbed into the independent state that Cesare had long sought to establish in northern Italy. Her son, Ottaviano, showed no desire to regain his inheritance; he preferred to stay in Rome looking for a rich wife. How did Caterina, daughter of a duke and famed throughout Italy as a valiant warrior-queen, come to be imprisoned and violated by the pope's son?*

*Caterina Sforza in 1498, from an oil-on-wood portrait by the Forlì artist Marco Palmezzano (c.1460–1539).*

Caterina was the illegitimate daughter of Galeazzo Maria Sforza (1444–76), the duke of Milan – one of the most powerful of the 15th-century Italian city-states. When she was ten her father betrothed her to Girolamo Riario (1443–88). Riario, anxious to form an alliance with the mighty Sforza family, was the nephew of Pope Sixtus IV (r. 471–84) and ruler of Imola. They were married when Caterina was 14, and the new countess of Imola moved to Rome.

Caterina quickly realized her husband was weak. He relied on favours from his uncle who granted him the strategically important town of Forlì. But his weakness worked in Caterina's favour. It allowed her to develop her skills as an independent ruler.

In 1484, when Caterina was 24, Pope Sixtus died. Despite being seven months' pregnant at the time, it was Caterina and not her husband who immediately marched on Rome to safeguard the family's possessions. She took the Castel Sant'Angelo and declared that she would not leave until a new pope had been elected and she had been assured that her husband would retain his territories. Caterina's tenacity won the day; a contemporary observer described her thus:

> 'wise, brave, tall, fine-complected, well-made, speaking little, she wore a dress of satin with a train of two-arms' length, a black velvet hat in the French fashion, a man's belt and a purse full of gold ducats, a curved falchion at her side; and among the foot soldiers and the horsemen she was much feared because, when she had a weapon in her hand she was fierce and cruel.'

## DEFIANT IN ADVERSITY AND RUTHLESS IN VICTORY

Three years later Caterina again defended the family's interests. When the fortress at Forlì was captured, the governor wrote to Caterina, not Girolamo, begging her to come. Although heavily pregnant once more, she captured the fortress within three days.

*Caterina's fortress at Forlì. It was here that she eventually succumbed to the forces of Cesare Borgia, who was intent on stealing her lands for the pope and himself.*

'[Caterina] *defended her fortress better than her virtue.*'

CESARE BORGIA AFTER RAPING CATERINA

In 1488 Girolamo was stabbed to death by members of a rival Forlì family; Caterina and her children were taken prisoner. But the conspirators underestimated the esteem in which Caterina was held, and the people of Forlì refused to surrender to the murderers. The wily countess convinced her captors to let her enter the citadel to negotiate its handover. But once inside she screamed abuse from the battlements. She was unmoved when the conspirators threatened to murder her children in front of her eyes. Instead, she lifted up her skirts to show them her genitals, declaring that she cared little as she could bear more children. Niccolò Machiavelli (1469–1527) recorded the event.

Caterina triumphed and the children survived. She then set about hunting down her enemies. They were captured and executed, and their heads displayed throughout the city. The pope, Caterina's overlord since Forlì and Imola were part of the Papal States, ratified her regency for her eight-year-old son, Ottaviano. Caterina Sforza was in the ascendancy.

## SEXUAL SCANDALS

Caterina was a popular, if uncompromising ruler. She cultivated mutually beneficial relationships with the neighbouring states of Florence and Milan. But presently things began to go awry for Caterina – her reputation among her contemporaries changed from one of an able, respected leader to that of a virago and predator, *'a daughter of iniquity'*. The reason was sex.

A year after her husband's death, when she was 26, Caterina took her first lover – Antonio Maria Ordelaffi (1460–1504), whose family were former rulers of Forlì. The liaison was popular with the people, who hoped for a marriage. But Caterina's family destroyed the relationship, fearing that she would be influenced against their interests. Ordelaffi was exiled to Venice.

Next she created a scandal through her relationship with Giacomo Feo (1468–95), the 22-year-old brother of one of her military commanders. A contemporary reported that she was completely subservient to Feo's will:

> *'they* [Caterina and Feo] *will bare any fate, and Madonna will sacrifice her friends and children and property; they will give their souls to the devil and the state to the Turk before abandoning one another or being separated from one another.'*

This was an unfair criticism. Caterina was never influenced by her lovers and was fiercely protective of her son's interests. In 1495 Feo was assassinated and Ottaviano was among those who ordered his death. Although the scandal reverberated throughout the peninsula, she managed to hold on to her territories. She then hunted down all those responsible for the murder – except, of course, her son.

The following year Caterina began her most notorious relationship, with Giovanni de' Medici (1467–98). Contemporaries were particularly vicious – one wrote that the relationship was *'to satisfy her appetite'*. Notwithstanding the fact that she was widowed, as a woman Caterina was expected to remain celibate. Although male rulers openly kept mistresses, Caterina was vilified for taking lovers. The couple were married sometime before the birth of their son in 1498 although they kept it secret – Caterina could not risk endangering her regency.

## CATERINA'S REPUTATION AND LANDS UNDER THREAT

Meanwhile Pope Alexander VI (r. 1492–1503) and his son, Cesare Borgia (1476–1507), were casting greedy eyes towards her lands. The pope pushed for an alliance between his daughter Lucrezia and Ottaviano but Caterina resisted, unwilling to relinquish her regency; instead she fortified her cities. When Louis XII of France (r. 1498–1515) invaded Italy, the crisis came. Louis and the pope made a pact: in return for Alexander's support Louis would ensure that control of the Papal States reverted to the papacy – Caterina's lands in Imola and Forlì were part of the deal. The pope cited Caterina's 'immorality', branded her *'a daughter of iniquity'* and despatched Cesare to steal her property.

Cesare tried to negotiate with Caterina. His terms were good – he promised safety for her and her seven children, a lucrative pension and the return of her possessions after a period of time. But Caterina refused. She shouted to him from the battlements of her fortress at Forlì:

> *'Signor duke, fortune helps the intrepid and abandons cowards. I am the daughter of a man who did not know fear. Whatever may come, I am resolved to follow the course until death.'*

Caterina's allies swiftly fell in the face of the combined French and papal armies. It is quite probable that she tried to poison the pope, sending him letters either dipped in poison or infected with the plague, but failed. Although she declared *'if I have to lose I want to lose in a manly way'*, Caterina could not withstand the strength of the opposing army. The fortress fell and Cesare viciously tortured and murdered his prisoners. The most humiliating punishment was saved for Caterina herself. Cesare raped her and held her captive for nearly two months before taking her triumphantly to Rome.

After 12 years in power Caterina was forced to relinquish her regency. She received no support from her children who were anxious to exchange papal promises of preferment for their lands. While they grew rich and fat in Rome, she spent nine desperate and heartbroken years trying to regain her property. Caterina died in Florence in 1509.

*Giovanni de' Medici, from a bust made by Mino da Fiesole around 1480. Despite public disapproval he and Caterina were lovers – even secretly marrying.*

## CATERINA'S VENGEANCE

Caterina made her lover Giacomo Feo – whom she may have secretly married – the new castellan of the fortress of Ravaldino, but the people of Forlì feared him for his cruelty. After his assassination a vengeful Caterina ruthlessly hunted down his murderers and killed them all, including their wives and their children.

# JUANA THE MAD

## *1479—1555*
## Queen of Castile

*The daughter of Isabella of Castile and Ferdinand of Aragon, Juana of Castile – commonly known as Juana la Loca ('the mad') – was heir to her mother's vast dominion. She married Philip of Burgundy, son of the Holy Roman Emperor, but the couple's passionate union disintegrated into antipathy, as Philip's infidelities drove her to wild acts. But was Juana really 'mad' or was she a highly strung young woman whose own needs were never recognized – the pawn of her mother, her father, her husband and finally her son, who all sought to render her an ineffectual queen?*

Juana was never meant to be a queen. She was born in November 1479 at Toledo, the third child of 'the Catholic Monarchs', Isabella I of Castile (r. 1474–1504) and Ferdinand II of Aragon (r. 1479–1516). Her older brother, Juan (1478–97), was her parents' heir; she also had an older sister. As a result, Juana was never trained to rule. Juan, by contrast, received the full benefit of Isabella's wisdom. He was allowed his own 'practice' court to prepare him for leadership, whereas his sister's education was more appropriate to a princess who would be a mere consort – decorative, charming and useless.

In 1496 Juana, now 17, left her parents' austere and devout court to marry Philip 'the Handsome' of Burgundy (1478–1506), son of Maximilian I, the Holy Roman Emperor (r. 1508–19) and Mary of Burgundy (1457–82). Their marriage sealed an alliance between Spain and the Holy Roman Empire against the expansion of their common foe, France. Juana sailed to Flanders to meet her 18-year-old bridegroom in splendour, accompanied by 133 ships and 15,000 men. She was astonishingly beautiful and, the chroniclers tell us, Philip could not wait to sleep with his bride – he insisted the wedding take place immediately.

### SIGNS OF MENTAL FRAILTY
However, it was not long before the marriage began to deteriorate. Juana was wildly jealous of Philip's infidelities. She even attacked one woman she supposed to be his mistress with a pair of scissors. It is from this time that her detractors begin to mention her 'madness'. Throughout her long life exorcists and physicians would try to cure her malady. In 1497, Prince Juan died. Hopes for the succession now lay with Ferdinand and Isabella's eldest daughter, Princess Isabella (1470–98), queen of Portugal. But she died in

*Juana, painted in 1500.
Like her sisters, she was
never trained to rule, which
is odd, considering how
deeply her mother Isabella
resented her lack of a
relevant education.*

childbirth, while the son she gave birth to only survived for two years. The future of the
Catholic monarchy of Spain now rested entirely with the fragile Juana.

## HEIR PRESUMPTIVE

She was named as her parents' successor in 1500. Her son, the future Holy Roman
Emperor Charles V (r. 1519–56), was born in the same year. Isabella and Ferdinand
begged her to come to Castile immediately, but Philip began to play power games with his
wife's parents – he coveted the throne she was to inherit. He delayed, despite Juana's
feeble attempts to assert herself. The couple only left Burgundy in 1501 and, at Philip's
insistence, they made their way leisurely through France. At the French court, Juana
once again made an ill-conceived gesture of defiance. She refused to pay homage to King
Louis XII (r. 1498–1515) and was forced to her knees by an apoplectic Anne of France
(1477–1514).

When the couple finally arrived in Castile in 1502 Juana was formally declared her mother's successor and Philip her king consort. She was also recognized as Ferdinand's heir in Aragon. Juana, pregnant once more, stayed behind with her parents while Philip left for Burgundy. But the perfidious Philip immediately betrayed Juana and her parents by negotiating a treaty with the French king. Isabella and Ferdinand were furious, but Juana was more distraught at her separation from her husband. She left her parents' court to rejoin Philip, abandoning her newborn son.

Philip's actions dismayed Isabella and she was deeply concerned about Juana's mental health. She altered her will. Juana was to be crowned queen of Castile at her death, but Philip would be powerless to intervene in Castilian government – she specifically stated that no foreigner could be appointed as an advisor. Furthermore, if Juana decided not to rule, the regency would bypass her husband in favour of Ferdinand. If Juana's health ever prevented her from fulfilling her duties as queen, Ferdinand was to act as regent until Charles, her son, *'shall be at least twenty'*. But Isabella's wishes did little to protect her daughter. When the queen died in 1504 Juana was unprepared for the treachery that was to follow, as her father and husband became locked in battle for possession of her throne.

## FERDINAND ASSUMES POWER

Juana, now queen of Castile, was also mistress of much of Spain, Naples, the Americas and Sicily. Philip was anxious to assert his own rights, however, and immediately declared himself king. But Juana, overcome with grief at her mother's death, locked herself away and Ferdinand took the opportunity to assume power in Castile. He used his daughter's anguish to try to declare her unfit to rule. Neither her husband nor her father showed any concern for her wellbeing. Philip attempted to grab the regency from Ferdinand, but Ferdinand manipulated his daughter and tried to persuade her to show her support for him in a letter. Philip, furious at this, wrote the letter himself and either forced Juana to sign it or forged the signature. The letter read:

> *'Since they want in Castile to make out that I am not in my right mind, it is only meet that I should come to my senses again … Tell everybody* [in Castile] *… that, even if I was in the state that my enemies would wish me to be, I would not deprive the king, my husband, of the government of the realms, and of all the world if it were mine to give.'*

Juana's purported support for her husband destroyed Ferdinand's hopes of a smooth transition of power and he looked for another route to the throne – pursuing a marriage with Isabella's niece, Juana la Beltraneja (1462–1530), who had an excellent claim to rule in Castile but had been usurped by Isabella. The marriage negotiations came to nothing and instead, in an attempt to win over the king of France against Philip, he married Louis' niece.

## BETRAYED BY FATHER AND HUSBAND

Despite Philip's rage, Juana refused to denounce Ferdinand's actions. She tried again to resist his hold over her, but was increasingly powerless. In 1506 they went to Castile, but

Philip refused to let her see her father. The battle for control of the throne had reached deadlock. Then Philip and Ferdinand entered into an unholy pact against Juana. They drew up a document that was tantamount to declaring her insane:

> '[Juana] on no account wishes to have anything to do with any affair of government or other things … and even if she did wish it, it would cause the total loss and destruction of these realms, having regard to her infirmities and passions which are not described here for decency's sake.'

But Ferdinand obviously had second thoughts. He repudiated the document and vowed to liberate his daughter from her husband. Then the Castilian nobility intervened. Distressed at Juana's treatment, the Admiral of Castile demanded a meeting with his queen. After seeing her he declared her sane and recognized her as queen with Philip as her consort. But Philip enjoyed his new powers for less than a month; the prince over-indulged at a banquet and by the next morning was dead. A chronicler wrote, *'through bad government he passed from this lifetime to the next'*. Ferdinand's rival was removed forever.

Juana was distraught with grief and went into seclusion for three months, just as she had after the death of her mother. She refused to have Philip's corpse buried and kept it with her at all times on her long, macabre journey with his body to Granada. Some contemporaries claimed that she kept opening his coffin to kiss his feet.

Ferdinand used her behaviour as evidence of his unfortunate daughter's mental instability and seized power. Juana's father-in-law, the emperor Maximilian, took control of her children, although she was allowed to keep as her companion her last child, Catalina, who was born in 1507. The pair were locked up in the fortress of Tordesillas. This was to be Juana's home for the rest of her life.

*Philip of Burgundy, from a 15th-century painting. His infidelities and scheming were to strain his marriage with Juana and may be the reason for her supposed 'madness'.*

## THE MADNESS OF DON CARLOS

If Juana was mad, did she pass on her malady to her great-grandson, Don Carlos (1545–68) of Spain? Schiller's play and Verdi's opera *Don Carlos* tell the tale of unrequited love between Don Carlos, son of Philip II (r. 1556–98), and his young stepmother, Elisabeth of Valois (1545–68). But the real Don Carlos was a vicious lunatic who loved to torture animals and the palace servants. Philip was forced to incarcerate him in an attempt to curb his increasingly violent behaviour and to stop him giving away state secrets. Although he conceived an obsessive love for Elisabeth and thought that his father was keeping them apart, the queen did not reciprocate.

When Ferdinand died in 1516 her son, Charles, came from the Netherlands to assume the regency in his mother's name. The Habsburgs would rule Spain for 200 years. Once again the queen of Castile had no voice in government. Growing ever more pious, she retreated into her own dark and cloistered world. Juana died in 1555 at the age of 76. She had been a prisoner, first of her father and then of her son, for nearly 50 years.

# LUCREZIA BORGIA
## *1480—1519*
## Duchess of Ferrara

*For over 500 years, the name of Lucrezia Borgia has been synonymous with incest, vice and evil. She is tainted by her family's crimes, with historians accusing her of complicity in their political machinations and assassinations. Nobody, except perhaps the biblical queen Jezebel, has been so decried as an example of debauched womanhood. But was Lucrezia Borgia the murdering, poisonous serpent of popular legend, or merely a woman struggling to survive and assert her identity in a male-dominated age of low intrigue and betrayal?*

Lucrezia was born in Rome in 1480, the illegitimate daughter of Cardinal Rodrigo Borgia (1431–1503) and his mistress Vannozza Cattanei (1442–1518). Rodrigo and Vannozza had three children together – Juan (1474–97), Cesare (*c.*1475–1507) and Lucrezia. Of the eight or so fathered by the cardinal these three were his favourites. He particularly adored Lucrezia, perhaps because they shared many character traits. Both were charming, sensual and clever. When his affair with Vannozza ended soon after her birth, it was Rodrigo who was primarily responsible for Lucrezia's upbringing – she had very little to do with her mother.

Lucrezia was 12 when her father was elected Pope Alexander VI (r. 1492–1503). The new pope was a man of limitless ambition who, despite his love for his daughter, had no scruples when it came to using her as a marriage pawn in his continuously shifting quest for favourable and lucrative alliances. Lucrezia was betrothed to two different men, both Spaniards, once at the age of ten and again at 11, before her father finally married his 13-year-old daughter to Giovanni Sforza, lord of Pesaro (1466–1510), in 1493.

### A POLITICAL PAWN

The 26-year-old Giovanni belonged to a minor branch of the mighty Sforza family of Milan. The pope needed an alliance with the Sforzas to shore up his position against their enemy, the Aragonese king of Naples, and the child Lucrezia was sacrificed to her father's political ambitions. Lucrezia was countess of Pesaro for four years. But by 1497 the political sands had shifted; the pope no longer needed the support of the Sforzas, as he now turned to Naples for an alliance. He demanded that Lucrezia's marriage be annulled on the grounds of non-consummation. Giovanni was apoplectic; not only would he lose his wife and her influential family connections, but his honour was also being impugned.

*The subject of this painting on wood by Bartolomeo da Venezia (fl. 1502–46), entitled* Portrait of a Woman, *is thought to be Lucrezia Borgia.*

'*And when His Excellency asked him* [Giovanni Sforza] *if this were true* [if the marriage had never been consummated], *he answered no. Rather, he had known her* [Lucrezia] *an infinite number of times. But the pope had taken her away from him only in order to have her to himself and he expressed himself at length on the subject of His Holiness.*'

ANTONIA COSTABILI, FERRARESE ENVOY TO DUKE ERCOLE I OF FERRARA

## LUCREZIA'S LOVERS

Lucrezia had two great loves in Ferrara: Pietro Bembo (1470–1547) and Francesco Gonzaga (1466–1519), marquis of Mantua. Bembo was a Venetian poet at the court of Ferrara as well as a cardinal, and Lord Byron called his letters to Lucrezia *'the prettiest love letters in the world'*. But although Bembo is often described as the love of her life, Lucrezia was captivated by the sensuous and highly sexual Gonzaga, the husband of her sister-in-law, Isabella d'Este (1474–1539). Their relationship was to last until his death from syphilis in 1519.

*A bust of Francesco Gonzaga, one of Lucrezia Borgia's lovers, by the Roman Renaissance sculptor Giovanni Cristoforo Romano (1456–1512).*

Yet he was powerless in the face of the mighty Vatican political machine. The marriage was duly dissolved.

We have no way of verifying the charge of non-consummation, but Giovanni vigorously denied it. He accused the pope of wanting Lucrezia to himself and it is from Giovanni that the famous charges of incest between Lucrezia and her father originate. Lucrezia was humiliated. The Perugian chronicler Matarazzo wrote that the non-consummation charge was ludicrous, since *'it was common knowledge that she had been and was then the greatest whore there ever was in Rome'.*

Even before the marriage was dissolved, Alexander and Lucrezia's brother Cesare had found her a new husband who would advance their political ambitions. Cesare Borgia adored his sister, but he was ambitious and determined to carve out a state for himself in northern Italy while his father lived and he had papal backing. Despite his devotion to Lucrezia (Cesare, a notorious misogynist, only ever loved Lucrezia) he had, like his father, no qualms about using her as a tool. Cesare's love was often destructive and murderous. In 1498 the body of a young Spaniard, Perotto, was found in the Tiber. This man, a servant of the pope, was rumoured to be Lucrezia's lover and his death was widely ascribed to Cesare.

### ASSASSINATION PLOTS

The bridegroom chosen for Lucrezia was Alfonso of Aragon, duke of Bisceglie (1481–1500) and the illegitimate son of Alfonso II, king of Naples (r. 1494–5). They married in the summer of 1498, but their union was doomed. Borgia ambitions were already turning from Naples towards France. Lucrezia, aware of the danger to Alfonso, was confident she could protect him. In 1499 she gave birth to a son, Rodrigo (1499–1512), but even as the boy's father, Alfonso wasn't safe. In the following year he was attacked on the steps of St Peter's, but survived the assassins' knives. Cesare was blamed but denied it, saying, *'I did not wound the duke, but if I had, it would have been no more than he deserved'.*

Although Cesare may not have been responsible for this attack, he was certainly behind the one that followed. Anxious to focus the pope's attention on their new partnership with France – and concerned that he was turning back towards Aragon – Cesare decided to dispose of the duke. Cesare's alliance with Louis XII of France (r. 1498–1515) made the family's link with Alfonso an embarrassment: Louis claimed the duchy of Naples, then controlled by Alfonso's family. Cesare's decision may also have been motivated by his jealous love for his sister. A month after the first attack, Alfonso was recovering, lovingly cared for by Lucrezia, when Michelotto, Cesare's henchman, burst into the room and strangled him. Cesare put about the story that Alfonso had tried to kill him and convinced Alexander that the assassination was necessary. But Lucrezia was overcome with grief. In

*Cesare Borgia, Lucrezia's brother, was a ruthless schemer who would stop at nothing to gain power and advantage for himself, including murder.*

September, tired of her tears, Alexander sent her to Nepi in the Lazio region of Italy.

Did Lucrezia ever forgive Cesare for the murder of her husband? He visited her several times after the assassination and stayed with her at Nepi on his way north with his army. The two were extraordinarily close – several chroniclers, including the Venetian envoy Polo Capello, ambassador to Rome from 1499–1500, accused them of incest – but Lucrezia's feelings towards him after he disposed of her husband remain a mystery.

## DUCHESS OF FERRARA

Lucrezia, now 20, took fate into her own hands. With the support of Alexander and Cesare she married Alfonso d'Este (1476–1534), heir to the illustrious dukedom of Ferrara. As its duchess, Lucrezia could remove herself from the machinations of Rome. It was inevitable that Alexander and Cesare would seek a new alliance for her, but this time she was determined it would give her autonomy from her family. Alfonso was appalled at the Borgias' unsavoury reputation and was reluctant to marry Lucrezia, but the combined might of the French king and the pope compelled him to agree.

Lucrezia and Alfonso were married in December 1501 and she quickly charmed the Ferrarese. Despite its inauspicious beginnings, the marriage was a success. Ferrarese envoys were forced to concede that Lucrezia was *'full of charm and grace'* and that *'she is full of tact, prudent, intelligent, animated, pleasing, very amiable … Her quick mind makes her eyes sparkle'*.

Alfonso d'Este fell in love with his wife. If not in love with him, Lucrezia was certainly fond of him. They had four children together including Ercole (1508–59), the future duke of Ferrara. Lucrezia created a model of a glittering Renaissance court at Ferrara, attracting numerous artists and intellectuals, and the duchy was her home for nearly 20 years. Lucrezia survived the death of her father, the fall of her brother and the election of Pope Julius II (r. 1503–13), enemy to the Borgias, because she was loved in Ferrara. She died in 1519, shortly after giving birth to a daughter, when she was only 39 years old.

## TIMELINE

**1492** Lucrezia's father, Rodrigo, is elected pope Alexander VI

**1493** Lucrezia marries Giovanni Sforza

**1497** Alexander annuls the marriage

**1498** Alexander and Cesare arrange Lucrezia's marriage to Alfonso of Aragon

**1499** Lucrezia bears a son, heir to Alfonso

**1500** Alfonso survives an assassination attempt, possibly organized by Cesare; while recovering, he is strangled; the grieving Lucrezia is sent to Nepi

**1501** Lucrezia marries Alfonso d'Este and moves to Ferrara

**1503** Alexander dies

**1504** No longer protected by his father, Cesare is exiled to Spain

**1505** The duke of Ferrara dies; Lucrezia and Alfonso inherit the dukedom; Lucrezia establishes a glittering court at Ferrara

**1507** Cesare dies at the siege of Viana in the service of King John III of Navarre

**1519** After giving birth to a daughter, Lucrezia dies; her lover Gonzaga dies the same year

# ROXELANA

## c.1500–58
## Sultana of the Ottoman Empire

*It seemed like the end of the world. The year was 1529 and cannon fire rained down on Vienna. The 'infidel' Ottoman sultan, Suleiman I, ('the Magnificent'), had encroached deep into Christian Europe and was taking his vast realm to its zenith. Suleiman created one of the most intimidating and powerful empires the world has ever known. With its capital at Constantinople on the Sea of Marmara, it stretched from the outskirts of Vienna in the west across eastern Europe, the tip of North Africa and through the Middle East to the Persian Gulf. But over time Suleiman's empire spiralled into decline, riddled with debauchery and corruption. The cause of its sickness was his slave, lover and eventual wife, the ruthless and bewitching Roxelana, a girl from the Ukraine who became the puppet-mistress of an emperor.*

*A Venetian portrait, c.1530, of the Ottoman sultan Suleiman I. He was in thrall to the bewitching Roxelana.*

Roxelana was born far from the intrigues of the Ottoman court. She was a Ukrainian peasant girl and the daughter of a priest. She was beautiful, with pale, creamy skin and long, red hair, bewitching enough to capture the attention of the Tartar raiders who streamed into the Ukraine from the Crimea. They kidnapped her and sold her into slavery at the great market at Constantinople. Before they relinquished her, they nicknamed her 'the laughing one' – for Roxelana seemed to have a gift for making the best of any situation.

She was bought by Ibrahim Pasha (c.1493–1536), grand vizier and chief advisor to the new sultan Suleiman I, 'the Magnificent' (r. 1520–66). Ibrahim knew the sultan's penchant for pale-skinned women and he presented her to Suleiman as a gift. So Roxelana was dragged from peasant obscurity to the harem of the most powerful man on earth. He fell in love with her immediately.

*Roxelana, shown here with Suleiman I, from a painting of 1780 by Anton Hickel. A Venetian envoy commented, 'There has never been in the Ottoman house a woman who enjoyed greater authority'.*

## THE WORLD OF THE CONCUBINE

The sultan's harem was a glittering, insular and conspiratorial world of eunuchs, slaves and perfumed concubines. Their purpose was to please the sultan. The Ottoman sultans never married; they had such power that there was no need for dynastic matches. This tradition was reinforced by the legend of one of Suleiman's ancestors, whose wife was captured by Ottoman enemies and forced to wait on her captors, naked, at table. The sultan swore that neither he nor his descendants would marry again; they would have children with their concubines. All Ottoman sultans would be the sons of slaves.

The sultans could own a limitless number of concubines. Those lucky enough to bear the sultan a son enjoyed a privileged status, and when Roxelana arrived there was already a first sultana, the gentle Gulbehar – 'Rose of Spring' – the mother of Suleiman's eldest son

Mustafa (1515–53). Roxelana could only hope to be second sultana. But this peasants' daughter was ruthless and cunning and defied all convention. She used Suleiman to make herself the most powerful woman in the harem. Shrewdly and stealthily she marginalized her rival and became first woman in the harem in all but name. Roxelana gave birth to a son, Selim (1524–74), within the year and she bore the sultan four other children. Within a short time Suleiman had discarded all his other concubines, even Gulbehar, and was faithful only to Roxelana.

*In this coloured engraving of 1671, the Ottoman sultan is shown visiting his harem at the Topkapi Palace in Constantinople.*

## SINGLE-MINDED AMBITION

She was now chief amongst the women. She insisted that Suleiman marry off nearly all of the virgins of the harem because she wanted no rivals. Besotted, Suleiman agreed. He began to seek her advice on affairs of state. The pair were always together – when they were separated they wrote each other love poems. But Roxelana wanted marriage.

Roxelana goaded, cajoled and beguiled her lover into ignoring the practices of his ancestors and, to the horror of his subjects, he capitulated, and put a foreign slave woman beside him at the head of the empire. It was unprecedented, and many believed their lord had been bewitched. A clerk at the Genoese Bank of St George wrote:

> *'This week, there has occurred in this city a most extraordinary event, one absolutely unprecedented in the history of the sultans. The Grand Signor Suleiman has taken unto himself a slave woman from Russia called Roxelana, as his empress, and there has been great feasting, and much rejoicing, in consequence … There is great talk all over this country about this marriage and no one can understand exactly what it means.'*

After her marriage, Roxelana began to gather power. Her first step was to use all her resources to extend her influence beyond the gilded, claustrophobic sphere of the harem.

Her immediate problem was the distance between the Old Palace, which housed the harem, and the New Palace, Suleiman's centre of government. The closer she was to government – and to her husband's apartments, she believed – the more influence she would be able to exert. But even resourceful Roxelana could think of no excuse to move the harem. But ultimately she did not have to: fate, or her own machinations, presented her with the opportunity. Constantinople's flimsy wooden buildings were prone to catching fire. And, luckily for Roxelana, one such small fire that blazed up on the waterfront of the Bosporus spread throughout the city and reduced the Old Palace to ashes.

## WHO WAS SELIM'S FATHER?

Was Selim Suleiman's son? The Italian historian Luigi Bassano, who served as a page to Suleiman, was convinced that Ibrahim had kept Roxelana as his slave before giving her to the sultan. Would Ibrahim have been able to resist a beauty who so captivated Suleiman, and could his affair with her have prompted Roxelana's later vengeance? The historian Lord Eversley wrote, *'… one is tempted to question whether the true blood of the Ottoman race flowed in the veins of these 25 degenerates* [the sultans who followed Suleiman]*'.*

*'They say she has bewitched him* [the Sultan]; *therefore they call her* Ziadi, *which means witch.'*

LUIGI BASSANO, VENETIAN PAGE TO THE OTTOMAN SULTAN, SULEIMAN THE MAGNIFICENT

## AT THE HEART OF GOVERNMENT

Roxelana and hundreds of odalisques, eunuchs, servants and slaves were now homeless. The sultana led them in a rich procession to the New Palace and formally asked her husband for shelter. He agreed. She moved into the palace and never again left it – restorations to the Old Palace, conveniently, took an age to complete. She had a private door cut between her new apartments and Suleiman's, and now had absolute access to the sultan and to the divan, or counsel of ministers. Suleiman had constructed a tower with a latticed window overlooking the divan so he could observe without being detected and it was here that Roxelana positioned herself, watching, learning and advising. The fire and Roxelana's arrival at the New Palace marked the beginning of the power of the harem. As she whispered into Suleiman's ear, she became the first woman in Ottoman history to exert influence on its government.

Roxelana was empress, but two rivals still stood between her and absolute power, and the eventual accession of her own son, Selim. They were Mustafa, Suleiman's eldest son and the people's hero, and Ibrahim, the influential grand vizier who had bought Roxelana in the slave market.

## A DOUBLE BETRAYAL

Roxelana dealt with Ibrahim first. She initiated a malicious campaign against him, and Suleiman finally yielded in the face of the rumours. The sultan dutifully gave the order to strangle Ibrahim. Some claim that Suleiman and Roxelana were sleeping in the next room while the murder took place. Roxelana, they said, covered her husband with kisses so he could not hear Ibrahim's cries. He and Suleiman had been friends all their lives.

Suleiman needed a new grand vizier and, at Roxelana's suggestion, he appointed Rustem Pasha, her daughter's husband and her own close friend. With this appointment Roxelana effectively became co-grand vizier. Together he and the sultana dealt with Roxelana's other rival, Mustafa; they convinced Suleiman that Mustafa was inciting rebellion against his father. Mustafa was a military hero, clever, able, handsome and popular. But ultimately the boy prince's gifts worked against him – Suleiman was persuaded of a conspiracy and ordered his murder. The way was cleared for Selim to inherit the Ottoman empire; after Suleiman's death in 1566, he succeeded to his father's throne.

Roxelana died in 1558. In her lifetime she set a precedent whereby favourites and mothers of sultans could influence foreign and domestic policy and act as regents for their sons. Because of Roxelana, the period from the mid-1520s to the mid-17th century is known as 'the sultanate of the women'.

## TIMELINE

**1520** Suleiman succeeds Selim I as sultan of the Ottoman empire

**1521** Suleiman invades Belgrade and Hungary

**1523** Ibrahim Pasha becomes grand vizier

c.**1523** Ibrahim Pasha buys Roxelana as a slave for Suleiman; Roxelana joins the harem

**1524** Selim is born

**1526** Ottoman forces defeat the Hungarians and take the city of Buda

**1529** Suleiman launches an attack on Austria; bombardment of Vienna

**1532** Suleiman tries again to conquer Vienna, but is forced to retreat

**1533** Peace treaty between the Ottomans and Austrians; both Austria and Hungary pay tribute to Suleiman

c.**1534** Suleiman marries Roxelana

**1535** Ibrahim Pasha and Suleiman take Baghdad

**1536** Ibrahim Pasha is executed; Roxelana has Rustem Pasha appointed grand vizier

**1553** Rumours reach Suleiman that Mustafa is planning to usurp the throne; Mustafa is killed

**1554** Suleiman signs a peace treaty, ending his expansion into Asia

**1558** Death of Roxelana

**1566** Suleiman dies; Roxelana's son takes the throne as Selim II

# MARY TUDOR
## 1516—58
## Queen of England

*Mary was England's first queen regnant. Bullied, rejected and even threatened with murder by her father, separated from her mother, unloved by her husband and spurned for her Catholic faith, Mary finally came to the throne in her late thirties. She was vilified by Protestants – they called her 'Bloody Mary' – and her five years on the throne were overshadowed by the illustrious half-century reign of her half-sister, 'Gloriana' – Elizabeth I.*

Mary was the only surviving child of Henry VIII (r. 1509–47) and his first queen, Catherine of Aragon (1485–1536). When she was born in February 1516 her parents were still in love and the young princess was greeted with the proclamation, *'God give good life and long unto the right high, right noble, and right excellent princess Mary …'.* Henry VIII, a vigorous Renaissance prince, continued to hope his 31-year-old Spanish queen would produce the vital son to justify his 'usurper' Tudor line.

As a young child Mary was adored. Henry was charmed by her pretty face and her aptitude for music; as his *'pearl of the world'*, she was his to dispose of as he saw fit in the royal game of marriage alliances. He promised her first to the *dauphin* and then to her cousin Charles V, the Holy Roman Emperor (r. 1519–56). Queen Catherine was a clever women and imparted to Mary her vast knowledge of history, philosophy and theology. She also gave her daughter the surety of her religion, learned from her parents, the devoutly Catholic Isabella (r. 1474–1504) and Ferdinand (r. 1479–1516) of Spain.

Mary received an exemplary classical education, preparing her to be an excellent queen consort. Although Salic Law (legislation disbarring women from ascending the throne, practised in France) did not operate in England, there was no precedent for an English female monarch. Moreover, as Henry continued to hope for a son, it was not anticipated that Mary would rule anyway.

### A CRUEL SEPARATION

When she was nine, Henry, furious at the emperor's rejection of his daughter in favour of an alliance with Isabella of Portugal (1503–39), separated her from Catherine for the first time. He punished his wife for her nephew's misdemeanour by banishing Mary to Ludlow, on the Welsh Marches. She returned to court two years later, while her father considered

*Queen Mary I, painted by the Dutch portraitist Antonius Mor in 1554, the year of her marriage to Philip II of Spain. Although the marriage treaty expressly forbade England from becoming involved in Spain's wars, Mary allowed herself to be drawn into conflict with France and lost England's last continental territory, the port of Calais. This loss hit her hard: she claimed that, when she died, the words 'Calais' and 'Philip' would be found engraved on her heart.*

*A painting by Michiel Sittow (1469–1525) of Catherine of Aragon, Henry's first wife and the mother of Mary Tudor.*

marrying her to the French king's second son, Henry of Orléans (1519–59). At court Mary met Anne Boleyn (?1507–36) for the first time – the woman who was to shatter her life.

Henry had become infatuated with Anne Boleyn. The daughter of a minor English nobleman, she had been educated in France. Although she was not beautiful, she was clever, capricious and witty; the king was smitten. Later, Mary would learn that Anne could also be cruel. The king was tiring of Queen Catherine, now aged 40 and unlikely to produce the desired male heir, and wanted to annul his marriage. The young Anne, he hoped, would provide him with the sons he craved.

The annulment of the marriage of Henry VIII and Catherine of Aragon was one of the most sensational events of the 16th century. Henry's Reformation plunged England into the darkness of excommunication from the Church of Rome, whose head, Pope Clement VII, had refused to sanction a divorce. Henry defiantly repudiated Catherine, married his mistress and proclaimed himself head of the Church of England. The result was a disaster for Mary. The princess her father had once fêted turned, in the king's mind, into a stubborn, arrogant woman, firmly associated with the mother who refused to set him free.

### A RIVAL CLAIMANT TO THE THRONE

In September 1533 Queen Anne gave birth to a daughter, Elizabeth. She used her moment of triumph to demand Catherine's christening robe for her daughter. Now Elizabeth replaced Mary as princess of England and in her father's affections. The following year Mary was formally cut out of the succession in favour of her half-sister and was forced to act as Elizabeth's lady-in-waiting. Mary feared for her life as she refused to renounce her claim to the throne. She longed to escape and she worried incessantly about her mother. Furthermore, Henry demanded Mary's allegiance to him as head of the church, but Mary believed her soul would be imperilled if she broke from Rome.

In 1536 Catherine died. Mary had not seen her mother for five years, nor was she allowed to attend her funeral. Her hated stepmother was executed during the same year on trumped-up charges because the king had tired of her failure to produce a son. Mary's situation did not improve, however, despite the efforts of Henry's new wife, the mild Jane Seymour (1507/8–37). Henry would accept nothing less than her admission that she was a bastard and her acknowledgment of him as head of the English church. Eventually Mary – psychologically scarred and physically frail – submitted to Henry's will. She signed a document

## HENRY'S ARGUMENTS FOR ANNULMENT

Henry based his case for divorce from Catherine on the possibility that her marriage with his elder brother Arthur had been consummated. His marriage to the princess of Aragon was therefore incestuous. After Catherine and Arthur's wedding night the bridegroom is reputed to have said, 'Tis hot work in Spain … .' But this was probably nothing more than a boyish boast – Arthur was only 15 years old. Catherine denied the allegations and, in the light of her fervent religious beliefs, she was probably telling the truth. Catherine, the daughter of the zealous 'athletes of Christ', Ferdinand and Isabella of Spain, would have feared eternal damnation of her soul if she lied.

admitting the illegitimacy of her parents' marriage and recognized Henry as supreme head of the Church of England. Had she not signed, Henry may have killed her. But she never forgave herself for what she saw as her betrayal of her mother.

## A MALE HEIR AT LAST

With her submission, Mary was invited back to court. She was 20 and she had not spoken to her father for five years. She was thankful when Jane Seymour bore a son – the succession was no longer an issue – and for the rest of Henry's life Mary acted the dutiful daughter. She happily recognized her half-brother Edward (r. 1547–53) as the future king. Mary continued to hope for a marriage – but she knew that while Henry lived he would continue to use her as a diplomatic pawn. She would remain, '… *only Lady Mary, the unhappiest lady in Christendom'.*

In 1547, when Mary was 31, Henry died. He provided generously for both of his daughters and now Mary found herself the wealthy mistress of extensive estates in East Anglia. For the six years of her brother Edward's reign she kept away from his fiercely Protestant court. When Edward became mortally ill at the age of 15, the ambitious regent, John Dudley, duke of Northumberland (1501–53), persuaded him to overturn Henry's Act of Succession. Mary and Elizabeth were cut out in favour of their Protestant cousin – and Northumberland's daughter-in-law – Lady Jane Grey (1537–54). (Although Elizabeth was Protestant, Northumberland persuaded the impressionable Edward that he could not remove one sister from the succession without the other.)

## MARY'S RALLYING CRY

When Edward died in 1553, Northumberland bullied the council into declaring Jane queen. Mary was expected to do nothing, but instead she roared out of the shadows to stake her claim. Now, as queen, she could overturn her father's repudiation of her mother and return England to the one true – Catholic – faith. The very troops sent to capture Mary rallied to her cause and the daughter of old King Henry, and England's rightful heir, was universally acclaimed. Her extreme Catholicism was overlooked, and the English acclaimed her. An Italian traveller to London at the time recorded how:

> '*Men ran hither and thither, bonnets flew into the air, shouts rose higher than the stars, fires were lit on all sides, and all the bells were set a-pealing … The people went mad with joy, feasting and singing, and the streets were crowded all night long.'*

Mary was crowned queen of England on 30 September, 1553 at the age of 37.

Mary was merciful to those who had supported Lady Jane and did not seek vengeance on her young cousin, who was only 15. She rightly supposed her to have been a mere pawn in machinations by Northumberland and his faction. Jane's life was spared and she was imprisoned in the Tower of London. Meanwhile, Jane's mother, Lady Frances Brandon, duchess of Suffolk (1517–59), remained one of Mary's closest friends. (The duchess, who preferred favour to family loyalty, did not intercede on behalf of her daughter.) Only Northumberland was condemned to death.

## TIMELINE

**1516** Mary is born to Henry VIII and his first wife, Catherine of Aragon

**1525** Henry sends Mary to Ludlow, punishing Catherine for her nephew's rejection of Mary

**1527** Mary returns to court, where Anne Boleyn had infatuated Henry

**1533** Henry annuls his marriage to Catherine and weds Anne Boleyn; Elizabeth is born later that year

**1536** Catherine dies; Mary is forbidden to attend the funeral; Anne Boleyn is beheaded; Henry marries Jane Seymour; Mary recognizes her father as head of the Church of England and returns to court

**1537** Edward, a male heir, is born to Jane Seymour, settling the question of the succession

**1538** Henry VIII is excommunicated from the Catholic Church

**1547** Henry dies

**1552** Edward falls ill; persuaded by Dudley, he revokes the Act of Succession in favour of Lady Jane Grey

**1553** Edward dies; Mary claims the throne and is crowned queen; Dudley is executed for his role in the plot to install Jane as queen

**1554** Thomas Wyatt Rebellion; Mary orders the execution of Lady Jane Grey; Philip of Spain arrives in England; Mary and Philip marry

**1558** Death of Mary

*Philip II of Spain (in a contemporary portrait by the Spanish Renaissance painter Alonso Sánchez Coello) married Mary in 1554. The nation was appalled at the thought of a Catholic foreigner sharing the English throne. An uprising ensued, but it was defeated. Philip spent little time in England with Mary and the four-year marriage produced no children.*

By this stage, Queen Mary I was no longer a pretty woman. She had lost most of her teeth and the bloom of youth was long gone. A member of Philip of Spain's household wrote, '*the queen … is … small, and rather flabby than fat, she is of white complexion and fair, and has no eyebrows. She is a perfect saint, and dresses badly*'. But as queen she swathed herself in luxurious jewels and crimson, purple and black robes. She adopted the motto, 'Truth, the Daughter of Time', and set about returning England to the bosom of Rome. But Mary failed to realize how deeply entrenched Protestantism had become. She was popular as Henry's daughter and the legitimate heir, but the English had not given her a mandate to undo the old king's Reformation. The majority had no wish to see the return of the masses and painted idols of Catholicism. But Mary believed God was on her side and repeated frequently and publicly, '*If God be with us, who can be against us?*'

Although her cousin Emperor Charles V and her advisors warned her to tread carefully, Mary believed England's return to Catholicism was inevitable. Now she turned to the question of her marriage. Mary could not rule alone – she must produce an heir to ensure her heretic half-sister did not succeed her. Manipulated by the emperor, her choice fell upon his son – Prince Philip of Spain (1527–98). He was 11 years her junior and one of the most loathsome characters on the 16th-century stage – but he was an ardent Catholic. Despite fierce opposition from most of her council and her subjects, who detested the proposed 'Spanish marriage', she fell in love first with his portrait and then with the man.

## AN UNPOPULAR ENGAGEMENT

Parliament beseeched her not to marry Philip. Knowing her due as monarch, she replied that '*Parliament was not accustomed to use such language to the kings of England*'. Then, in protest, the Protestant Thomas Wyatt (1521–54) took up arms against the queen. It was the greatest threat of Mary's reign – Wyatt and 3000 supporters marched on London – yet she handled it brilliantly. In a speech redolent of her sister Elizabeth's marvellous oratory skills, she declared to Londoners that she was their '*Queen and mother … not for having borne you as my children, but full of more than motherly love towards you since the day in which you chose me as your queen and mistress*'. She assured them that she would do nothing against their interests and that her marriage was only for their good. '*That being my mind and firm determination, I earnestly beg you, my beloved subjects, to openly state if I may expect from you loyalty and obedience, or if you will join the party of the nefarious traitor against me, your queen.*'

Wyatt was defeated, and although Mary was reluctant to spill royal blood, she could no longer risk the survival of a Protestant threat to her throne. And so Lady Jane Grey, innocent of complicity in Wyatt's revolt, was executed at the Tower on 12 February, 1554.

The queen's bridegroom arrived in the summer of 1554 and they were married at Winchester Cathedral on 25 July. Power remained vested in Mary, and she attempted to placate the English with the marriage treaty – Philip would hold no power should Mary predecease him. Now the queen spent her remaining years with her reluctant bridegroom. Despite her adoration, Philip thought her old and ugly, yet they desperately tried to conceive a Catholic heir.

A member of Philip's party wrote to Charles V's Spanish secretary:

> *'To speak frankly with you, it will take a great God to drink this cup … the best of it is that the king fully realized that the marriage was concluded for no fleshly consideration, but in order to remedy the disorders of the kingdom.'*

But Mary was unable to conceive. She suffered from irregular menstruation cycles all her life and this may have been the cause of the problem. But so urgent was her need for a child that she was blighted with phantom pregnancies, or pseudocyesis, in which all the physical symptoms were present but there was no pregnancy. Her due date came and went and Philip, disgusted, abandoned her and returned to Spain. Mary was distraught. Her devastation was compounded by her loss of England's last possessions in France, Calais and Guisnes.

## MASS BURNINGS

Mary has been vilified for her mass burnings of Protestant 'heretics'. Her biographer, Maureen Waller, argues that once Mary began the burnings, depressed by her phantom pregnancies and the loss of Philip's affection, she was too apathetic to stop them. During her reign, a total of 283 Protestants were burned alive at the stake.

Mary died of influenza on 17 November, 1558. Childless, she was powerless to stop Elizabeth succeeding her. Philip's response was typical: '… *I felt a reasonable regret for her death'*, he said.

*The burning of the Sussex martyr Thomas Iveson at Chichester in 1555, during the Marian persecutions of Protestants. Illustration from* Foxe's Book of Martyrs, *published in 1563.*

*'Now, loving subjects, what I am, ye right well know. I am your queen, to whom at my coronation, when I was wedded to the realm and the laws of the same, you promised your allegiance and obedience unto me.'*

MARY TUDOR

# CATHERINE DE MÉDICIS

## 1519—89
## Queen of France

*Catherine de Médicis has a fearsome reputation for murder by poisoning, dabbling in the occult, promoting incest among her children and the manipulative use of beautiful women – the so-called 'flying squadron' – as her spies. Her name has become irrevocably linked with the infamous St Bartholomew's Day Massacre of 1572. For the priggish Scottish Protestant reformer John Knox, she was perhaps the most hideous of his 'monstrous regiment of women'. Catherine became queen of France through her marriage to Henry, duke of Orléans (the future Henry II) and bore him ten children. After Henry's death, she was* de facto *ruler of France for nearly 30 years. But how far is her reputation based on sensationalism?*

*Catherine de Médicis, from an illustration by the Italian painter Santi di Tito (1536–1603). Excluded from political influence when her husband was on the throne, Catherine came to wield considerable power during the reigns of her sons.*

Catherine, the niece of Pope Clement VII (r. 1523–34), was the daughter of the duke of Urbino, Lorenzo de' Medici (1492–1519), and a French princess, Madeleine de la Tour d'Auvergne (1495–1519). But just a few weeks after her birth in the spring of 1519, plague carried off both her parents in quick succession and the infant Catherine suddenly found herself a fabulously wealthy orphan and a rich prize for any future suitor.

Francis I of France (r. 1515–47) coveted her wealth and the Italian territories that an alliance with the pope would bring France. In 1533 she was betrothed to his second son, Henry, duke of Orléans (1519–59) – she had no reason to suppose she would become queen of France. That same year the 14-year-old girl arrived at the French court – the most splendid and glittering in Europe.

Catherine was not beautiful, but she was graceful and witty and knew how to present herself to the best advantage. She had exquisite hands and ankles and she wore sumptuous, beautifully cut fabrics that enhanced her figure. She was the model of an

'What could the poor woman do, with five children in her arms, after the death of
her husband, and with two families in France – ours and the Guise – attempting
to encroach on the Crown? Was she not forced to play strange parts and to
deceive the one and other and yet, as she did, to protect her children, who
reigned in succession by the wisdom of a woman so able? I wonder that
she did not do worse!'

HENRY IV OF FRANCE

educated Renaissance woman, fluent in Latin, French, Italian and Greek, with a passion for mathematics, astrology and physics. Catherine believed in the power of soothsayers and her dreams. Some, including her daughter Margot (1553–1615), believed that she had second sight – years later her rival Diane de Poitiers (1499–1566) found drawings of pentacles and other examples of the 'black arts' at Catherine's Château de Chaumont.

Catherine loved only one man – her husband. But Henry was besotted with his mistress, the greedy, chilly and manipulative Diane de Poitiers. Diane was 19 years Henry's senior and her hold over her lover was to last until his death. In the meantime, Catherine was powerless; she could only wait.

## UNEXPECTED HEIRS

In 1536 Henry's elder brother, the *dauphin*, died and the 17-year-old Henry and Catherine became the putative king and queen of France. But Catherine's position was precarious. The pope had died when she was 15, leaving her in France without a protector. Furthermore, Catherine had no children, however often Diane chided a reluctant Henry to visit his wife's bed. She was a princess without a purpose, but she quickly identified the key to her survival – the king. She set out to charm him and, from wanting to repudiate her, Francis I became her champion. Charm was one of Catherine's greatest assets, a talent she would use throughout her political career.

Catherine realized the king's support was only temporary and so she used every remedy to become pregnant. She remained barren for ten years until a doctor, Jean Fernel (1497–1558), recommended a 'cure'. (Its precise nature is unknown.) In 1544 she gave birth to a son, Francis, and over the next 12 years she produced nine more children, most of whom survived. Her position was assured. However, Catherine's children were constantly sick. The nursery saw a steady stream of doctors as the children contracted infections and asthma. Later some of them would develop dementia, which may have been a genetic legacy passed down from their grandfather, the syphilitic Lorenzo de' Medici. Alone among her children Margot was physically robust all her life.

In 1547 Francis I died. Catherine genuinely mourned the loss of her protector, friend and tutor. Later, when she was forced to govern, it was his example she followed. His death meant that, at the age of 28, the merchant's daughter was queen of France; her husband was Henry II (r. 1547–59).

*A portrait of Henry, duke of Orléans by the miniaturist François Clouet (1510–72). Henry became Catherine's husband when she was just 14 years old, but reserved his affections for his mistress, Diane de Poitiers.*

## HENRY'S SENSATIONAL DEATH

While Henry lived, Catherine's concerns were domestic and her household was modest. She had little power and suffered Diane's constant interference in the royal nursery. But in June 1559 Henry was fatally wounded during a joust. Catherine watched as his opponent's lance smashed into the king's eye and splintered. Henry died in agony ten days later.

With Henry's death, Catherine was thrust into the political limelight. His legacy to his widow was a powerful, split nobility and four young, sickly sons. The new king, Francis II (r. 1559–60), was only 15 and physically weak. Before Henry had breathed his last, the kingdom faced a threat from his powerful favourites, the Guise brothers – Duke François and Charles, cardinal of Lorraine – and the Duke de Montmorency, constable of France, all of whom sought to control the young heir. Catherine forced aside her intense grief and for the next 30 years dedicated herself to protecting her children's inheritance. As an outward sign of her grief, she wore black for the rest of her life.

*Henry's mistress, the meddling and manipulative Diane de Poitiers; this portrait, from about 1571, is also attributed to François Clouet.*

The last three Valois kings were a lazy, malign brood. Not one appreciated the hard work it took to govern France, particularly a France divided between Catholics and Huguenots and on the brink of the bloody wars of religion. All were happy to leave government to their mother. The children died one by one. Francis, puny and weak, died after only 16 months on the throne. Catherine, once again forcing aside grief for the sake of her children's inheritance, declared his ten-year-old brother, Charles IX, king of France (r. 1560–74), retaining for herself the title of 'governor of the kingdom'.

## RELIGIOUS FACTIONS AND A GLORIOUS COURT

Despite her murderous reputation, Catherine's policy towards her fractious Catholic and Protestant subjects, like that of her contemporary Elizabeth I (r. 1558–1603) in England, was religious tolerance. As long as the crown was safe she was a moderate; she believed accommodation was more beneficial to the kingdom than civil war.

As a diversion to those Catholic and Huguenot nobles who fought one another and jostled to control the young king, Catherine filled her court with marvellous entertainments and distractions. A key feature of this policy was Catherine's 'flying squadron' – beautiful young noblewomen who acted as her spies. Up to 300 of these stunningly attired *'goddesses'* were in her service. It was rumoured that the queen demanded that their waists measure no more than 33 centimetres (13 in) – an impossibly small measurement, achieved by the use of torturous wooden corsets. To Catherine, show was everything. However bankrupt she was, the royal household was always magnificent.

In an attempt to reconcile her Catholic and Huguenot subjects, Catherine arranged the marriage of her daughter Margot to her Protestant cousin Henry, heir to the kingdom of Navarre and later Henry IV of France (r. 1589–1610). Margot was beautiful, charming, vivacious and the court's trendsetter. A contemporary described her as:

> 'so beautiful … that one had never seen anyone lovelier in the world. Besides the beauty of her face and her well-turned body, she was superbly dressed and fantastically valuable jewelry adorned her attire.'

But the princess was dominated by her mother and brothers. Margot was in love with Henry, duke of Guise (1550–88), and the pair wrote one another love letters. Unfortunately these were discovered by Margot's brother Henry of Anjou, who was unhealthily attached to his sister – in her memoirs Margot accuses him of rape. Anjou informed his brother the king and Catherine; the queen mother and Charles beat up the young girl, tearing out handfuls of her hair. Margot was forced to agree to the marriage with Henry of Navarre. A magnificent pageant was arranged in Paris and Huguenots flocked from all over the kingdom to witness the event. The wedding, in August 1572, was the catalyst for the St Bartholomew's Day Massacre, a crime that has sullied Catherine's name for four centuries.

## THE ST BARTHOLOMEW'S DAY MASSACRE

To protect the peace and the throne, Catherine sanctioned the assassination of a number of leading Huguenots. The Protestant Gaspard de Coligny (1519–72), admiral of France, was number one on the list. Charles was under his influence and the powerful advisor encouraged a policy Catherine thought would be disastrous: war with Spain, the most powerful nation in Europe. His assassination, she believed, would avert tragedy for France.

### THE SMOKING QUEEN

The French owe their love of tobacco to Catherine. She eagerly took up the habit when an envoy presented the substance at court in 1560. Its use spread throughout the court and the country, where it popularly became known as the *herbe de la reine* or *nicotiane*. Catherine introduced a number of other innovations to her adopted homeland – among them the side-saddle method of riding a horse for women and the fork. She also championed the wearing of knickers by women (before Catherine's era, female courtiers wore no underwear).

Paris, however, was a tinderbox at this time. The residents of that most Catholic of cities sought revenge on the Huguenots who surrounded their king. When Coligny was murdered, Parisians took this as a signal to hack down the thousands of Protestants gathered for the wedding. The Catholic Spanish ambassador reported gleefully:

> '… they are killing them all, they are stripping them naked, dragging them through the streets, plundering the houses and sparing not even the children. Blessed be God who has converted the French princes to His cause.'

Gruesome piles of corpses littered the city. Nor were the killings confined to Paris – they spread throughout France.

Once the slaughter began. Catherine and the king were powerless to stop them. For their part, the Huguenots believed that Catherine had deliberately used the wedding as a ruse to lure them to Paris.

When Charles IX died in 1574, Catherine's son Henry of Anjou took the throne as Henry III (r. 1574–89). He was lazy, vain and vindictive, but he was Catherine's favourite child, and she hoped his reign would rejuvenate the monarchy. But her hopes were ill-founded, and until her death she strove to correct his disastrous mistakes.

Catherine de Médicis died at Blois in the Loire valley on 5 January, 1589, only eight months before the assassination of Henry III, her last surviving son. Henry's death saw the end of the Valois dynasty. As predicted by Nostradamus, the throne passed to his cousin and brother-in-law, the Huguenot Henry of Navarre, the first Bourbon king. Catherine was 69 when she died and, although the cause of death was pleurisy, the dowager queen was exhausted after 30 years of shielding France from her sons' inadequacies. But her efforts were at the cost of her reputation – she was so unpopular when she died that Parisians threatened to throw her body into the Seine if her corpse was brought into the city.

*This hand-coloured illustration shows Roman Catholics butchering Huguenots in Paris during the St Bartholomew's Day massacre on 24 August, 1572. The Huguenots never forgave Catherine for the crime, calling her* La Nouvelle Jezebel.

# ELIZABETH I

## *1533 – 1603*
## Queen of England

*Elizabeth I presided over England's golden age, yet was born out of the greatest scandal of the 16th century. Her father, King Henry VIII, divorced his first wife, the Spanish princess Catherine of Aragon, to marry his alluring mistress Anne Boleyn. The result was the Reformation of the English church and its break with the church of Rome, the disgrace and murder of Anne Boleyn and the birth of Elizabeth.*

By the early 1530s Henry VIII (r. 1509–47) had waited 20 years for a legitimate son. The ageing Queen Catherine of Aragon (1485–1536) had produced only the princess Mary (1516–58) and stillborn children. When Henry met Anne Boleyn (?1507–36), he was enchanted by her wit, her sex appeal and her unyielding refusal to be his mistress; he repudiated Catherine after 22 years of marriage and wed Anne.

Elizabeth was born on 7 September, 1533 at Greenwich Palace. Anne had not produced the longed-for son but a red-haired daughter. Henry initially hid his disappointment and for the first two years of her life Elizabeth was spoilt and petted, the darling of the Tudor court. But Henry was tiring of Anne's capriciousness and in January 1536, when she miscarried his longed-for son, he disposed of her. She was indicted on false charges of treason, witchcraft and adultery and executed at the Tower of London. Elizabeth was still only two years old. Henry distanced himself from his daughter but did not abandon her. Although he declared her illegitimate, she attended the christening of her half-brother (the future Edward VI; r. 1547–53) in 1537 and had a respectful relationship with Henry; in 1544 he rewarded her deference by restoring her to her place in the succession.

### ELIZABETH'S EARLY LIFE

Elizabeth received a superb education. She was brought up in the reformed Protestant faith and was skilled in rhetoric, Latin, Greek, French and Spanish. *'Her mind has no womanly weakness,'* wrote her tutor, the humanist Roger Ascham (1515–68). *'Her perseverance is equal to that of a man'*. When Henry died in 1547, Elizabeth went to live with her stepmother, Catherine Parr (1512–48).

But Catherine's new husband, Lord Admiral Thomas Seymour (1508–49), entered Elizabeth's bedchamber and seriously compromised her. Advisors to Edward VI assumed Seymour was plotting a coup around Elizabeth; Seymour was executed, and Elizabeth pleaded her innocence. She was believed, but for the rest of her adolescence she dressed

*The full majesty of the 'Virgin Queen' Elizabeth I in her prime shines through in this portrait (c.1585–90), attributed to John Bettes the Younger. Like her father, Henry VIII, Elizabeth exploited the power of regal pomp and circumstance: 'She prides herself on her father and glories in him,' the Venetian ambassador once reported.*

'... I know I have the body but of a weak and feeble woman, but I have the heart
and stomach of a king and of a king of England too – and take foul scorn that ...
any prince of Europe should dare to invade the borders of my realm. To which
rather than any dishonour shall grow by me, I myself will venter my royal blood;
I myself will be your general, judge and rewarder of your virtue.'

ELIZABETH I, ADDRESS TO HER TROOPS AT TILBURY BEFORE THE SPANISH ARMADA

demurely and behaved studiously. As the daughter of the 'adulterous' Anne Boleyn, she realized that she had to be above suspicion. She was learning the power of the public image, which in her reign would find its glorious apogee in the cult of the Virgin Queen.

## RELIGIOUS DISSENT

Edward died childless in 1553 and was succeeded by Mary, who became Queen Mary I of England (r. 1553–8). These were the most perilous years of Elizabeth's life as Mary married the Catholic zealot Philip II of Spain (r. 1556–98) in 1554 and began to reinstate Roman Catholicism in England. Protestant Elizabeth was the natural focus of dissent but she wisely maintained the pretence of Catholicism. When implicated in the 1554 Wyatt Rebellion to overthrow Mary she protested her innocence, although she was imprisoned in the Tower of London, in the same apartments that had housed her mother before her execution. She also managed to avoid marriage to the pro-Spanish duke of Savoy; she knew that if she left England, she would never inherit the throne. Mary duly failed to have a child and slipped into ill health and depression; Philip left for Spain.

In November 1558 Mary died; her betrothal ring was taken to Elizabeth at Hatfield House, in Hertfordshire. *'The law of nature moveth me to sorrow for my sister,'* Elizabeth told the assembled nobles. *'The burden that is fallen upon me maketh me amazed.'*

## THE POPULAR TOUCH

The new queen of England had more in common with her father than any of his other children. Like him, she had an instinctive popular touch from the day of her brilliantly stage-managed coronation onwards. *If ever any person had either the gift or the style to win the hearts of people, it was this queen,'* wrote a contemporary observer. For Elizabeth it was never *'my people'*; it was always *'my loving people'*.

Historians have pondered why Elizabeth never married: was it the scar left by her father's treatment of her mother, or perhaps the terror she felt after the Seymour crisis? It seems more likely that Elizabeth did not want to share her throne. *'She was both king and queen,'* commented the Scottish ambassador. Although the Privy Council pleaded with her to wed, her unmarried state kept England free from the foreign interference that a princely marriage would bring and the court factionalism that an English marriage would cause. Instead, she used the promise of marriage as a diplomatic tool to protect her Protestant country from invasion or isolation. She dallied with the hand of Philip II of Spain, her former brother-in-law, then Archduke Charles of Austria (1540–90), then Henry, duke of Anjou (the future Henry III of France, r. 1574–89), then his brother, François, duke of Alençon (1554–84), whom, with characteristic caprice, she nicknamed *'the frog'*.

All her life she refused to discuss the succession. Although she declined to marry, when her cousin Mary, queen of Scots (r. 1542–67), her likely heir, had a son, the future James I of England (r. 1603–25), the Scottish ambassador reported, *'she* [Elizabeth] *did sit down … bursting out to some of her ladies that the Queen of Scots was lighter of a fair son, while she was but a barren stock'*.

The forces of the Counter-Reformation despised Elizabeth and considered her a bastard heretic; in 1570 the pope excommunicated her and called her *'the pretended queen of England'*. Between 1571 and 1586 the Catholic queen of Scots, who had been deposed and was living in England as Elizabeth's prisoner, was implicated in a number of plots to overthrow her.

Elizabeth's response was typical – and effective. She authorized Mary's execution and then denied knowledge of it. She had been duped, she insisted, by her councillors; she wrote a long, tortuous letter of sympathy to Mary's son, James, and refused to see her principal advisor Robert Cecil, later Lord Burghley (1520–98), for four months.

## THE DEFEAT OF THE SPANISH ARMADA

In 1588 the crisis came. Philip of Spain sent his Armada to conquer England and return it to the true faith. The skill and superior knowledge of Elizabeth's navy prevented his fleet from anchoring off the south coast, while the stormy weather was also in England's favour; the Armada was scattered. Elizabeth visited her troops at Tilbury and made the most famous speech of her reign.

Now she was enshrined as one of the most successful monarchs in English history – Good Queen Bess, the Fairie Queen, the Virgin Queen – Gloriana. She lived sumptuously, dividing her time between her many palaces; she owned over 2000 dresses and, as she aged, wore extraordinary bright red wigs.

*Elizabeth filled the romantic gap in her life with intense flirtations with her most handsome courtiers. The most enduring was with Robert Dudley, 1st earl of Leicester (1533–88), shown above.*

In the final years of Elizabeth's reign her court lost its lustre. The country that had enjoyed the Elizabethan golden age was now damaged by inflation and poor harvests. The disaffected nobility began to look towards a new age, presided over by a fresh monarch. Her last great flirtation, with the young Robert Devereux, earl of Essex (1566–1601), ended with his treason and execution. *'Men do more adore the rising than the setting sun,'* Elizabeth said ruefully. She died at the palace of her grandfather Henry VII (r. 1485–1509) at Richmond on 24 March, 1603, aged 69. She trusted Burghley's son and successor Sir Robert Cecil (1563–1612) to ensure a smooth succession, and so he did: as Elizabeth died, messengers were riding north to the first of the Stuart kings, James I.

## ROBERT DUDLEY

Robert Dudley, son of the duke of Northumberland, was Elizabeth's childhood friend. Elizabeth loved 'the gypsy' and made him her Master of the Horse. It was widely thought that Dudley wanted to marry the queen. When his wife Amy Robsart (1532–60) died in mysterious circumstances – she fell down the stairs at Cumnor Place, a house near Oxford, in 1560, having dismissed her servants – the scandal damaged Elizabeth. She refused to marry Dudley and he later secretly married her cousin Lettice Knollys (1540–1634).

# LADY JANE GREY
## *1537–54*
## Titular Queen of England

*On the morning of 12 February, 1554 the 17-year-old Jane Grey, great-niece of Henry VIII and briefly queen of England, made her last journey, dressed in the same black, velvet-trimmed gown she had worn for her trial. Servants accompanied her; her family, including her mother, had deserted her. She mounted the scaffold at the Tower of London and begged the small audience to pray for her soul. She allowed herself to be blindfolded and whispered to the executioner to 'dispatch me quickly'. She cried, 'Lord, into thy hands I commend my spirit!' and, with a swing of the axe, Lady Jane's head was severed from her body. It was the shortest reign in English history – she had been queen for nine days.*

*Lady Jane Grey, from a 19th-century painting based on contemporary portraits.*

Jane Grey was the daughter of the duke and duchess of Suffolk, Henry Grey (1515–54) and Frances Brandon (1517–59). Frances was the granddaughter of Henry VII (r. 1485–1509) through her mother Mary Tudor (1496–1533), the favourite sister of Henry VIII (r. 1509–47). The Grey family were zealous supporters of Henry VIII's Reformation and Jane was brought up as a religious Protestant. Although firmly entrenched in the Tudor aristocracy, Jane had no thought of becoming queen and was far down the line of succession – her cousin Edward, his elder sisters Mary (1516–68) and Elizabeth (1533–1601), and her own mother all came before her. But Jane's short life was spent at the mercy of her ambitious parents and their cohorts; she became their victim.

### IN THE SHADOW OF THE KING'S SON
Jane was born at Bradgate Park in Leicestershire in October 1537. (Edward, Henry VIII's son was born the same month. The prince's birth eclipsed any celebration that may have been held for Jane.) Jane's childhood was an unhappy one. The serious and scholarly girl was bullied and whipped by her parents. Roger Ascham, Princess Elizabeth's tutor, described meeting the 13-year-old Jane for the first time. She complained that:

> *'... when I am in the presence of either Father or Mother, whether I speak, keep silence, sit, stand or go, eat, drink, be merry or sad, be sewing, playing, dancing, or*

*doing anything else, I must do it as it were in such weight, measure and number, even so perfectly as God made the world; or else I am so sharply taunted, so cruelly threatened, yea presently sometimes with pinches, nips and bobs and other ways ... that I think myself in hell.'*

Meanwhile events beyond her immediate family circle were to profoundly affect her life. When her great-uncle Henry VIII died, his young son became King Edward VI (r. 1547–53). Edward, still a minor, was controlled by his uncle Somerset (c.1506–52), the Lord Protector. But Somerset's younger brother, Lord Admiral Thomas Seymour (c.1508–49), also sought to influence the king. Thomas persuaded the Suffolks that he would arrange Jane's marriage to the king. The duke and duchess sold her marriage and wardship to Seymour for £2000 and Jane was sent to live in his household.

## HAPPY DAYS SPENT WITH CATHERINE PARR

In the end, Seymour lacked the power to facilitate the match, but Jane's stay in his household was the happiest time in her short life. Thomas was married to the queen dowager, Catherine Parr (1512–48) – Henry VIII's sixth and last wife – and Catherine took Jane under her wing. The pair shared similar intellectual interests, both had a love of learning, were passionate in their pursuit of Protestantism – the 'new' religion – and Catherine nurtured Jane's education. Jane was a willing pupil; amongst her Tudor cousins she was one of the best educated. She was tutored by the brightest reformist scholars, followed a rigorous curriculum and was proficient in French, Italian, Latin, Hebrew and Greek.

*Edward VI was only nine when he ascended the throne in 1547. Because he was so young, his six-year reign was overseen by two protectors. He died of tuberculosis.*

Yet Jane's happiness at the home of Thomas Seymour was short-lived. When the unstable Seymour attempted to wrest control of the young king from his brother he was executed, and Jane was sent back to live with her parents. The king had determined that when he married, it would be to a wealthy foreign princess, *'well stuffed'*, and not to an English noblewoman. To the disappointment of her parents, Jane would not be queen by marriage.

Machinations at the Tudor court were to make Jane's fate inevitable. The Lord Protector Somerset fell in 1552, with no word of regret from his nephew the king. Edward noted his uncle's death in his journal: *'The duke of Somerset had his head cut off upon Tower Hill between eight and nine o'clock in the morning.'* Edward VI, still a minor, was now in thrall to the ambitious John Dudley (1501–53), whom he created duke of Northumberland. Unlike the Seymours, Northumberland was always careful to treat the king as an adult and he gained Edward's loyalty and respect. Northumberland attached his star to the king's, but he was to be thwarted. In 1552 Edward suffered an attack of measles. He was fatally weakened and the 15-year-old king probably succumbed to tuberculosis. Girolamo Cardano (1501–76), the Italian mathematician and physician, wrote that he could see *'the mark in his face of death that was to come too soon'*.

It was obvious to Northumberland that the king was dying. According to the terms of Henry VIII's will Edward's sister Mary was to succeed him. Northumberland would certainly be ostracized and possibly executed if the zealously Catholic Mary were to become queen. He conceived a plan to save himself. Lady Jane was key to that plan.

## A FORCED MARRIAGE

Northumberland colluded with Jane's parents and on 21 May, 1553 she was forcibly married to Northumberland's fifth son, Guildford Dudley (*c.*1534–54). Jane was appalled. She loathed the Dudleys and found Guildford spoiled. She objected on the grounds that she was already contracted to Edward Seymour, earl of Hertford (*c.*1506–52). (He had become a less enticing prospect for her parents with the death of his father the Lord Protector.) Her parents ignored her objections and whipped her until she agreed to marriage. Two Italian contemporaries, Raviglio Rosso, an emissary of the duke of Ferrara and Federigo Baoardo, the Venetian ambassador to Emperor Charles V (r. 1519–56), recorded that Jane was coerced *'by the urgency of her mother and the violence of her father, who compelled her to accede to his commands by blows'*.

The marriage took place at Northumberland's London riverside mansion, Durham House. Edward was too ill to attend, but sent gifts. The unhappy bride wore gold and silver and her hair was braided with pearls. To her relief she returned home with her parents.

With Jane safely married to his son, Northumberland determined to overturn Henry VIII's will. Henry had nominated the descendants of his younger sister Mary, rather than those

*Catherine Parr, in an undated painting from the workshop of Tudor court portraitist Hans Holbein the Younger (c.1497–1543).*

*'If my faults deserve punishment, my youth at least and my imprudence were worthy of excuse. God and posterity will show me favour.'*

of his older sister Margaret – whose granddaughter was Mary, queen of Scots (r. 1542–67) – to succeed after his own three children. Northumberland convinced the dying Edward to cut his own sisters out of the line of succession and to name Jane Grey and her heirs as his successors. He cruelly kept the king alive for as long as possible, dismissing Edward's doctors and employing a woman who probably used arsenic to prolong his life, with agonizing consequences. Meanwhile the imperial ambassadors were lobbying to secure the crown for the princess Mary, cousin of the Holy Roman Emperor, while the French king was determined to see his daughter-in-law, Mary, queen of Scots, on the throne of England.

For Northumberland it was a race to gain the king's signature before he died; he drew up the 'Device for the Succession'. He persuaded Edward that should Mary succeed, Catholicism would be restored in England. How could the king exclude one bastard sister from the succession and not the other? Although she was a Protestant, Elizabeth was also eliminated. Northumberland had persuaded Jane's mother, the duchess of Suffolk, to relinquish her claim to the throne in favour of her daughter. The king, on the verge of death, nominated Jane Grey as his successor. Both her parents and Northumberland were convinced they could control her.

### THE RELUCTANT QUEEN

Edward VI died on 6 July, but Northumberland concealed his death for as long as possible. On 9 July, Jane was summoned to Syon House where she was proclaimed queen. Jane was horrified and had a hysterical fit. This clever, articulate and outspoken young woman did not want the crown. She was astute enough to realize she only had a tenuous chance of holding on to it. Later she told Mary how distressed she was: *'For whereas I might take upon me that of which I was not worthy, yet no one can ever say that I sought it as my own, or that I was pleased with it or ever accepted it.'*

*John Dudley, created duke of Northumberland by Edward VI.*

The following day Jane took up residence at the Tower of London. A Genoese merchant by the name of Baptista Spinola was present as the young queen passed by, and reported:

> *'Today I saw Lady Jane Grey walking in great procession to the Tower. She is now called queen, but is not popular, for the hearts of the people are with Mary, the Spanish queen's daughter. This Jane is very short and thin, but prettily shaped and graceful … She walked under a canopy, her mother carrying her long train, and her husband Guildford walking by her, dressed all in white and gold, a very tall strong boy with light hair, who paid her much attention. The new queen was mounted on very high chopines [platform shoes] to make her look much taller, which were concealed beneath her robes, as she is very small and short. Many ladies followed,*

## TIMELINE

**1537** Jane Grey and Henry VIII's son, Edward, are both born in October

**1546** Thomas Seymour pledges to arrange Jane's marriage to Edward VI; she is sent to live as the ward of Catherine Parr

**1549** Thomas Seymour is executed after a plot to gain control over the young Edward VI; Jane returns to live with her parents

**1552** Somerset, the Lord Protector, is beheaded; ascendancy of John Dudley, duke of Northumberland; Edward VI falls ill with measles

**1553** Jane is married against her will to the only unmarried son of the duke of Northumberland, Guildford Dudley; Northumberland prolongs the king's life while plotting for Jane to succeed him; Edward dies and Jane is declared queen; within nine days Mary's supporters proclaim her queen and arrest Jane; Northumberland is executed

**1554** Following the Wyatt rebellion, Mary resolves to have Jane executed; Jane is beheaded and left on the scaffold before being buried beneath the chapel of St Peter ad Vincula

*with noblemen, but this lady is very heretical and has never heard Mass,*
*and some great people did not come into the procession for that reason.'*

But 'Queen' Jane was greeted with little enthusiasm. The imperial ambassador noted gleefully that few in the crowd cried *'Long live Queen Jane!'* and that Mary, as Henry VIII's eldest daughter, remained popular despite her Catholicism. Meanwhile Mary gathered her household and declared herself queen. She wrote to Northumberland and the Council, ordering them *'to cause our right and title to the crown and government of this realm to be proclaimed in our city of London and throughout the kingdom'*. No one had expected Mary to fight back but, bolstered by her cousin the emperor's declaration of support, she took the initiative. She went to East Anglia. Northumberland mustered an army against her, intending that Suffolk should command it, but Jane begged her father to stay with her. The deeply unpopular Northumberland, despised by the country and by the Council he had coerced into supporting him, was forced to abandon London and lead the army himself.

## SUPPORT FOR MARY GROWS

So detested was the great warrior that he had difficulty holding on to his troops; many of his forces defected to Mary, whose own ranks swelled to 150,000 men. Northumberland was forced to retreat to Cambridge. Away from London, he was unable to bully the Council who now declared for Mary. Jane had not yet been crowned queen of England.

Mary was proclaimed queen in London and an Italian contemporary recorded that:
*'men ran hither and thither, bonnets flew into the air, shouts rose higher than*
*the stars, fires were lit on all sides, and all the bells were set a-pealing … The*
*people went mad with joy, feasting and singing, and the streets were crowded*
*all night long.'*

Jane was deserted. Typically, her parents abandoned her. The duke of Suffolk declared for Mary, and then he and the duchess left Jane in London. Northumberland was executed and Jane was tried and condemned for treason, but Mary spared her life. She realized her young cousin had been Northumberland's pawn and chose to overlook the Suffolks' role (she was extremely fond of Frances). Meanwhile Jane was to be held in the Tower, where she was given the freedom of the grounds.

## UNFORTUNATE WOMEN

Jane did not lie alone in death. Her headless corpse was buried between the decapitated remains of two other Tudor victims – Anne Boleyn and Catherine Howard, two of the unfortunate wives of Henry VIII.

This all changed after Thomas Wyatt's rebellion of 1554. Wyatt (1521–54), son of the poet of the same name, and a fervent Protestant who opposed Mary's marriage to her Catholic cousin Philip of Spain (r. 1556–98), took up arms against the queen. Although Jane – captive in the Tower – played no part, she was a symbol of Protestant resistance. With Wyatt's defeat Mary reluctantly agreed to her death. Jane's mother, a favourite at Mary's court, made no attempt to intercede on her daughter's behalf.

Mary, determined to save her young cousin's soul before her death, despatched the new dean of St Paul's, Dr Feckenham, to persuade Jane to abandon her heresy. But Jane clung to her religion. She took her prayer book to the scaffold; the last inscription in it read:

> 'Live still to die, that by death you may purchase eternal life … for, as the preacher sayeth, there is a time to be born and a time to die; and the day of death is better than the day of our birth. Yours, as the Lord knoweth as a friend, Jane Duddeley.'

Jane's decapitated corpse was left to lie on the scaffold for the rest of the day before she was buried at the Tower beneath the chapel of St Peter ad Vincula.

The Execution of Lady Jane Grey *(1833), a romanticized depiction by 19th-century French artist Paul Delaroche.*

'… *the girl* [Jane Grey], *born to a misery beyond tears, had faced death with far greater gallantry than it might be expected from her sex and the natural weakness of her age.'*

MONSIGNOR GIOVANNI FRANCESCO COMMENDONE, PAPAL ENVOY IN ENGLAND

# MARY

## 1542–87
## Queen of Scots

*Sixteenth-century Europe was the era of queens – yet Mary must go down in history as its greatest failure. She inherited her father's Scottish throne when she was only six days old, became queen of France through marriage and had an excellent claim to rule in England. Ultimately, however, as a result of her naivety, Mary died without a kingdom. She ended her days in isolation at Fotheringay Castle, where her cousin, Elizabeth I, ordered her execution.*

Mary was born in midwinter on 8 December, 1542 at the palace of Linlithgow in West Lothian. She was the daughter of James V of Scotland (r. 1513–42) and the French noblewoman Mary of Guise (1515–60). When her father died on 14 December the infant Mary became queen of Scotland.

Mary's mother was regent. The dowager queen was a daughter of the most powerful family in France and, encouraged by her relatives, she pursued an alliance with the French against the aggression of Scotland's ancient enemy – England. She refused the demands of Mary's great-uncle, Henry VIII (r. 1509–47), who insisted Mary be brought up at the English court as a bride for his son Edward (the future Edward VI; r. 1547–53). When she was five years old Mary left for the French court; there, she was to be raised by King Henry II (r. 1547–59) and Catherine de Médicis (1519–89) as the future dauphine and wife of their eldest son, Francis (the future Francis II; r. 1559–60). Mary, already queen of Scotland, would one day also be queen of France.

### BEAUTY AND SOPHISTICATION

The young queen's new home was the most lavish and sophisticated court in Europe and Mary, rapidly becoming a great beauty, was adored. Henry II was delighted with her and pronounced her *'the most perfect child I have ever seen'*. She was welcomed into the royal nursery, and the French princes and princesses – her future husband Francis and his sisters Elisabeth and Claude – were her companions. Mary's grandmother, Antoinette (1493–1583), supervised her education and she became fluent in French and proficient in Latin, Spanish and Italian. She was high-spirited and loved to dance and to hunt.

*A contemporary portrait of Mary Stuart, better known as Mary, queen of Scots. In the religious turmoil that engulfed 16th-century Europe, she became the source of hope for all those who sought to restore papal power in England.*

The dauphine had luminous skin, auburn hair and stood nearly 1.8 metres (6 ft) tall. In contrast, her fiancé the dauphin was puny and sickly. They married in April 1558 when Mary was 15, and Francis 16. When Henry II was wounded in a fatal accident just 15 months later, Mary became queen of France.

TIMELINE

1542 Mary is born on 8 December and becomes queen of Scotland a week later on the death of her father; Mary's mother acts as regent

1548 Mary is sent to the French court

1558 Mary marries the dauphin, Francis; Elizabeth I accedes to the throne of England

1559 After Henry II's death, Mary and Francis become titular king and queen of France

1560 Francis dies

1561 Mary leaves France and returns to Scotland

1565 Mary marries Henry Darnley

1566 Murder of David Riccio, in which Darnley is implicated; Mary's son, James, is born

1567 Darnley dies amid rumours of Mary's involvement in his murder; Bothwell coerces her into marriage; a month later they are deposed; Mary is imprisoned on the island of Loch Leven

1568 Mary seeks sanctuary in England; she is imprisoned by Elizabeth for the next 18 years

1586 Discovery of the Babington plot to assassinate Elizabeth

1587 Mary is tried and executed

At her coronation she proclaimed her right to the English throne, now occupied by her cousin Elizabeth (r. 1558–1601), who had become queen in 1558 following the death of her sister 'Bloody' Mary (r. 1553–8). At Francis' coronation ceremony in September 1559 the young king and queen displayed the English coat of arms alongside those of Scotland and France. Mary claimed the English throne as the Catholic granddaughter of Henry VIII's older sister, Margaret (1489–1541); and in the eyes of Catholic Europe the Protestant Elizabeth, Henry's VIII's daughter from his marriage to Anne Boleyn (?1507–36), was a heretic – and a bastard. It would prove to be the seed of her ruin.

Mary was a cosseted queen, enjoying all the privileges of her position with none of the burdens. Francis and Mary were king and queen in name only, however: Mary's powerful Guise relatives and her mother-in-law, Catherine de Médicis, effectively ruled France. And when Francis died just 16 months after his coronation, Mary found herself alone – a childless foreign queen in an alien court. Catherine de Médicis demanded that Mary hand back the crown jewels.

## RETURN TO SCOTLAND

Although her marriage contract allowed her to remain in France, Mary chose to return to Scotland. On 14 August, 1561 the 18-year-old princess, who was now more French than Scottish, left France with the words, *'Adieu France, adieu France adieu donc, ma chère France … Je pense ne vous revoir jamais plus.'* ('Goodbye France, goodbye my dear France … I think I will never see you again.'). She was right.

Mary had no experience of queenship. She had learned nothing from the brilliant political minds that had surrounded her from birth – her mother, now dead, Henry II, Catherine de Médicis and her Guise relatives. Mary cared more for music and poetry than the tedium of governing and was an ill-prepared queen of Scotland. The land's official religion was now Protestantism and its nobles, having lacked strong government for so long, were involved in bitter, petty feuds. But Mary initially charmed the Scots. She was pretty, was content to pursue her Catholic faith in private and relied on the advice of her able and powerful bastard half-brother, James, earl of Moray (c.1531–70). Mary's undoing was her second marriage, to the venomous Lord Henry Stuart Darnley (1545–67).

## A DISASTROUS SECOND MARRIAGE

The question of Mary's next marriage had concerned her ambitious Guise relatives and her cousin Elizabeth since Francis's death. Possible bridegrooms included Don Carlos (1545–68) – the lunatic son of Philip II of Spain (r. 1556–98) – the king of Sweden and the king of Denmark. The shrewd English queen, concerned that Mary should not forge an alliance with one of her Catholic enemies, even hinted that if Mary would marry as she directed, she would name her heir; to Mary's annoyance, Elizabeth suggested her own favourite, Robert Dudley, earl of Leicester (1532–88).

But Mary chose Henry Darnley, a first cousin and a Tudor through his mother, Margaret Lennox (1515–78). For Mary, it was love at first sight. She declared him *'the lustiest and best proportioned long man that ever she had seen'.* She did not know or care that marriage to Darnley – another candidate for the English throne – would enrage Elizabeth as much as the Leicester marriage proposal enraged Mary.

James Melville, Elizabeth's Scottish envoy, could not understand the attraction: *'No woman of spirit would make choice of such a man, who more resembled a woman than a man,'* he wrote. *'For he was handsome, beardless and lady-faced.'* But Mary was besotted by his androgynous beauty, and Darnley may have been her first lover. Contemporaries believed Francis incapable of fathering a child and, although Mary had briefly thought herself pregnant in France (she had adopted the flowing tunic favoured by pregnant women), she was probably still a virgin when Francis died. Despite the fact that Darnley was an English subject they married, without Elizabeth's consent, on 29 July, 1565 in the Chapel Royal at Holyroodhouse in Edinburgh. Darnley was now titular king of Scots. On her wedding night the naïve, headstrong Mary could celebrate: she had alienated the tricky Scots nobility, her powerful cousin and her best hope of stability in Scotland – her half-brother the earl of Moray.

Henry Stuart, Lord Darnley, was Mary's second husband. Cruel and ambitious, he was murdered in 1567.

The marriage was a disaster. Darnley saw Mary merely as a stepping stone to the throne of Scotland and he abused her mentally and physically. He humiliated her by openly visiting Edinburgh's prostitutes. But his greatest crime was his murder of Mary's beloved secretary and confidant, the Pietmontese David Riccio (1533–66). Darnley, jealous of their friendship, burst into Mary's rooms and held his now heavily pregnant wife's hands behind her back while one of his cohorts held a pistol to her belly. Riccio, clinging to Mary's skirts, was stabbed to death. Mary believed that Darnley hoped she would miscarry and die, clearing his path to the throne. She never forgave him.

## REVENGE ON DARNLEY

Mary did not miscarry and their son James was born in June 1566. Now safely delivered, Mary could take her revenge. She instructed her counsellors, including Moray, to find her a way out of her marriage. But she commanded them to do nothing illegal: *'I will that you do nothing whereunto any spot may be laid to my honour or conscience'.* She convinced Darnley that she had forgiven him and lured him away from Glasgow where he had taken

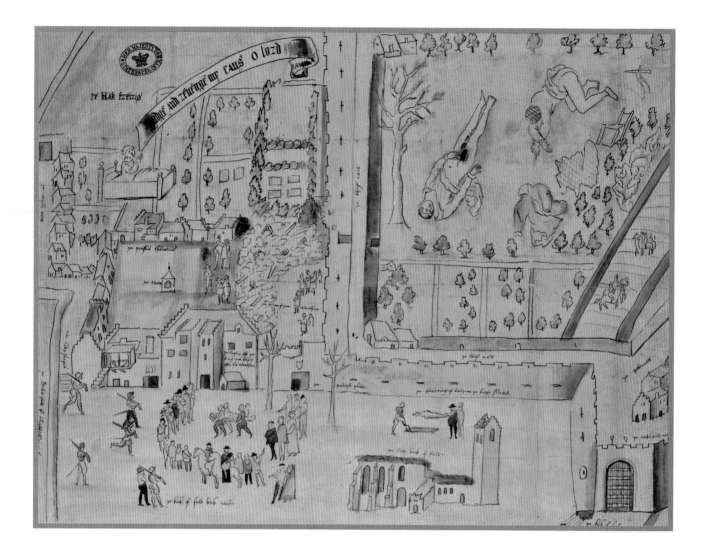

*An illustration depicting the mysterious events surrounding the murder of Lord Darnley at Kirk o'Field, near Edinburgh.*

refuge, to Edinburgh, knowing the city was filled with his enemies. Darnley was now extremely ill, possibly with syphilis. Mary took him to Kirk o'Field, a house on the outskirts of town and stayed with him for two nights, nursing him. But on the third night she left him to attend a wedding. At two o'clock in the morning an explosion blew the house to dust. Darnley escaped, but his body was found in the garden, strangled to death. The courts of Europe were stunned – did the queen of Scotland, they whispered, order the murder of her husband?

The architect of Darnley's assassination was probably James Hepburn, earl of Bothwell (*c.*1534–78) and one of Mary's most powerful nobles. Contemporaries believed him at least partly responsible. Later, Mary's detractors accused them of being lovers and of plotting to kill Darnley together, but although the queen had come to rely on the border lord there was almost certainly no truth in the charge. Elizabeth, exhibiting the ambivalence she always felt for her naïve cousin, wrote to Mary, begging her as a fellow queen to hunt down the murderers:

'[Mary is] *the daughter of debate that eke* [also] *discord doth sow.'*

QUEEN ELIZABETH I

*'… I exhort you, I counsel you, and I beseech you to take this thing so much to heart that you will not fear to touch even him whom you have nearest to you* [Bothwell] *if the thing touches him, and that no persuasion will prevent you from making an example out of this to the world: that you are both a noble princess and a loyal wife …'*

## A PATHETIC END

But Mary did nothing; in her own mind still the beloved dauphine of France, she never took good advice. She probably had a nervous breakdown and retreated to Seton. Meanwhile, in Edinburgh, protesters screamed for Bothwell's head and Mary was vilified as a prostitute. When Mary went to visit her son at Stirling in April, Bothwell kidnapped her, raped her and demanded marriage; Mary, listless and unwell, agreed. Her sworn enemy, the Calvinist preacher John Knox (c.1510–72), wrote: *'It was true she was taken against her will, but since her taking, she had no occasion to complain; yea, the courteous entertainment she had, made her forget all former offences.'*

*This illustration of 1567 depicts Mary as a mermaid – a symbol of prostitution. Mary lost public support when she married Bothwell, widely believed to be the murderer of her second husband, Lord Darnley.*

For Mary's Scottish nobles her third marriage was as unpopular as her second; for the queen it was another disaster. They loathed the fact that one among them had been raised so high, and joined forces against the queen and her new husband. One month after the marriage, on 15 June, 1567, Mary and Bothwell were forced to relinquish their freedom at Carberry Hill. Bothwell was exiled and imprisoned. Mary was dragged through the streets of Edinburgh, a pathetic spectacle with her hair hanging loose and her dirty, torn dress exposing her breasts. Her subjects had lost all sympathy for their queen and the crowd cried, *'Burn the whore! Kill her, drown her!'*

The queen was deposed in favour of her one-year-old son James (r. 1567–1625), with her brother Moray as regent. Mary was imprisoned on the island of Loch Leven, where she miscarried twins. A year later she fled to England, believing her cousin would offer her sanctuary. But while she lived, the Catholic Mary was a constant threat to the stability of Elizabeth's throne and when Moray produced the Casket letters – correspondence (probably fabricated) between Mary and Bothwell that implicated Mary in Darnley's death – Elizabeth had the excuse she needed to incarcerate her.

During the lonely and frustrating years of captivity Mary foolishly involved herself in plots to place herself on the English throne. Finally, Elizabeth's spymaster Sir Francis Walsingham (c.1530–90), proved she was guilty of involvement in the Babington plot of 1586 (in which Elizabeth was to be murdered by Spanish and papal agents and Mary freed). She was tried and condemned to death. Her son James did not speak in her defence. Mary was executed at Fotheringay Castle in Northamptonshire on 18 February, 1587.

## THE 'MONSTROUS' QUEEN

The fiery Scottish Calvinist preacher John Knox raged against the profusion of 16th-century European queens in his treatise *The First Blast of the Trumpet against the Monstrous Regiment of Women*. Mary was the principal target of his venom. When he was asked if he thought the Scottish queen should be allowed to celebrate mass in private, he replied advocating her death: *'Idolatry ought not* [only] *to be suppressed, but the idolator ought to die the death.'*

# Nur Jahan
## c.1577 — 1645
## Empress of India

*Nur Jahan, wife of the Mughal emperor Jahangir, exercised unprecedented power. Together with her family clique, she controlled government, embarked on ambitious building projects and fostered trade with European powers, as the emperor retreated into an opium- and alcohol-induced stupor. Nur effectively ruled India in all but name for 16 years.*

Nur Jahan was the daughter of Itimaduddaula (d.1622) and Asmat Begam, impoverished Persian aristocrats. In 1577 they left Persia for the court of the Mughal emperor Akbar (r. 1556–1605) at Agra, where Persian culture was prized. Nur Jahan's father hoped to advance himself, but they were attacked by robbers en route, and left destitute. When they finally reached Kandahar, Asmat Begam gave birth to her fourth child, whom she named Mihrunnisa.

### EARLY LIFE AND MARRIAGE

Akbar's court was a vibrant trading centre attracting Hindus, Muslims, Jews and Christians from all over the empire. Mihrunnisa's father found employment as the treasurer of Kabul, and her early life was spent studying Persian art, history and literature. When she was 17 she married a Turkish soldier, Sher Afgan. As both her husband and father were in Akbar's service, the emperor himself approved the marriage.

*A gold coin, from 1611, shows the head of Emperor Jahangir, surrounded by a halo with radiating points. The Arabic inscription reads:* 'A likeness of Jahangir Shah, in the year six of his reign.'

In 1607 Sher Afgan died. The new emperor, Jahangir, summoned Mihrunnisa to court as lady-in-waiting to his stepmother. But she did not encounter Jahangir for six years, and Mihrunnisa whiled away her time in the harem. The meeting eventually took place in 1611 at the New Year celebrations. The festival was held at Jahangir's palace in Agra, and women were encouraged to participate. A separate bazaar was set up in the harem and the emperor wandered among the stalls, the only man among the unveiled women. It was here that Jahangir saw Mihrunnisa's face and fell in love with her. The couple were married two months later, despite the scandal that stained her family: her father had been accused of embezzlement and one of her brothers had been executed for participating in a plot to assassinate the emperor. She was Jahangir's 20th and last legal wife.

*A Mughal miniature of c.1700–40, showing Emperor Jahangir with his consort and female attendants.*

## A BENEFICIAL UNION

Their marriage saw the astounding advancement of her family. Her father was pardoned and promoted and her brother, Asaf Khan (d.1641), received riches and honours. But the person to benefit most was Mihrunnisa herself. Jahangir honoured her with the name Nur Jahan, ('Light of the World'), and allowed her to control the government as he succumbed to alcohol and opium. But she did not rule alone. Her ruling junta included

*'Fate had decreed that she should be the Queen of the World and the Princess of the Time ...'*

CONTEMPORARY CHRONICLER MUTAMID KHAN, *IQBAL–NAMA–I JAHANGIRI*

her father, her brother Asaf Khan and her stepson Khurram, the future Shah Jahan (r. 1628–58). Jahangir had inherited an empire at its zenith and his wife's able administration ensured that, if the borders were not advanced, they were at least maintained.

Nur Jahan cunningly bound their two families together. Her niece, Mumtaz Mahal (1593–1631), was already married to Shah Jahan. Now she married her daughter by her first marriage, Ladli Begum (b.1594), to Jahangir's fourth son, the malleable Shahryar. This marriage provided her with insurance: should the political situation change, she would still exercise power under a new regime. Jahangir was delighted with his wife; he enjoyed the trappings of majesty with none of the responsibility. Nur Jahan's machinations left him free to drink, smoke opium and admire beautiful objects. But Nur Jahan's carefully crafted alliances began to unravel as early as 1617. The reasons were jealousy, money and death.

## THE TAJ MAHAL

The Taj Mahal is the most superb example of Mughal architecture. It was built by Shah Jahan for his favourite wife – and Nur Jahan's niece – Mumtaz Mahal. Shah Jahan was grief-stricken at her death in 1631; he commissioned the Taj as her mausoleum. Some historians claim that he intended to build the mirror-image of the Taj Mahal in black stone on the opposite bank of the river, to house his own mortal remains. However, he died before the project could be completed.

## ALLIANCES COLLAPSE AND RIFTS WIDEN

Shah Jahan, the third and most able of Jahangir's sons, slowly pulled away from his stepmother as he attempted to establish his own power base. Since he was the son most likely to succeed Jahangir as emperor, Nur Jahan had taken care to cultivate him. Asaf Khan grew resentful of his sister's power and, when Itimaduddaula died in 1622, the junta fell apart. In a shocking move, Jahangir gave

Intimaduddaula's entire estate to Nur Jahan, bypassing both Asaf Khan (Itimaduddaula's son), and Shah Jahan (his son-in-law). They were furious.

Family rifts widened when problems flared up in the Deccan in west-central India. Jahangir, although increasingly suspicious of Shah Jahan, appointed him to defeat the rebels there. He agreed, but only if his brother Khusrau (1587–1622) accompany him. (Shah Jahan was concerned that if he left Khusrau in Agra, he would lobby their father to succeed him as emperor.) Nur Jahan encouraged their departure – maybe she hoped for their death, leaving the way clear for her puppet Shahryar. Perhaps inevitably, Khusrau died. Jahangir was devastated by the death of his eldest and favourite son. The cause of death was officially colic, but when European commentators accused Shah Jahan of murdering his brother, Jahangir ordered him to Agra to answer the charges.

Shah Jahan refused. He raised an army and revolted against his father and stepmother. But by 1626 he was forced to ask for forgiveness. He wrote to Jahangir that he saw the *'error of his conduct ... and ... felt that he must beg forgiveness of his father for his offences'.* Jahangir and Nur Jahan forgave him on condition that he send his two young sons to Agra as hostages.

Jahangir's health, ruined by excess, was failing and the succession was uncertain. After the emperor's second son, Parviz, died, only Shahryar and Shah Jahan were left in the field. Nur Jahan tried all she could to bolster Shahryar's chances but, when Jahangir finally died in 1627 en route to Lahore he had still not named a successor. Shah Jahan was three months' march away in the Deccan and Nur Jahan confidently expected Shahryar to succeed; her position was assured. Then her brother betrayed her.

## SHAH JAHAN'S OPPORTUNITY

Asaf Khan, anxious to maintain his own position and reluctant to share power with his sister, took a gamble. He sent news to Shah Jahan of Jahangir's death and arrested Nur Jahan. At Nur Jahan's behest, Shahryar declared himself emperor, but with his most powerful supporter under guard he was largely ignored. Nur Jahan commanded him to raise an army, but he was routed by his brother. Shah Jahan gave the order for his execution and proclaimed himself emperor at Lahore in 1628. Nur Jahan, now powerless, spent the last 18 years of her life in enforced retirement in Lahore with her daughter and only child, Ladli Begum. The woman who had ruled India was now her stepson's prisoner.

She is buried in Lahore. The epitaph on her tomb reads: *'On the grave of this poor stranger, let there be neither lamp nor rose. Let neither butterfly's wing burn nor nightingale sing.'*

*Sunrise at the Taj Mahal. Built by Nur Jahan's stepson in memory of his wife, the main structure consists of a dome-topped tomb of white marble surrounded by four minarets.*

## TIMELINE

**1577** Itimaduddaula and his wife travel to Agra; Mihrunnisa is born en route

**1594** Mihrunnisa marries Sher Afgan, with the approval of the emperor

**1607** Sher Afgan dies; Mihrunnisa is recalled to court

**1611** Mihrunnisa meets Jahangir; she becomes his 20th wife, with the name Nur Jahan

**1617** Nur Jahan's 'junta' begins to fall apart

**1622** Itimaduddaula dies; Jahangir makes Nur Jahan the sole beneficiary of Itimaduddaula's estate; uprising in the Deccan; Shah Jahan leads an army, taking with him his brother Khusrau, who dies

**1626** Shah Jahan asks the emperor for forgiveness and sends two of his sons to Agra as hostages

**1627** Jahangir dies without naming a successor; Asaf Khan orders the arrest of Nur Jahan; Shahryar declares himself emperor; Shah Jahan has him executed

**1628** Shah Jahan is declared emperor

**1645** Nur Jahan dies and is buried at Lahore

# ANNE OF AUSTRIA

## *1601–66*

## Queen consort of Louis XIII of France and regent during the minority of Louis XIV

*Anne of Austria, Spanish princess and neglected queen of Louis XIII of France (r. 1610 –43), was the inspiration for the sub-plot of Alexandre Dumas' famous novel* The Three Musketeers. *The four heroes, Porthos, Athos, Aramis and d'Artagnan, protect Anne's honour against the scheming Cardinal Richelieu and the rumours that surrounded her relationship with the duke of Buckingham,* 'the handsomest and most elegant man of France and England'.

Born in September 1601, Anne was the eldest daughter of King Philip III of Spain (r. 1598–1621) and Margaret of Austria. At the age of 14 she was married by proxy to King Louis XIII of France – on the same chilly November day, Louis' sister Elizabeth was married to Anne's brother Philip. The marriages cemented a treaty between two of the greatest Catholic powers in Europe.

*Louis XIII, husband of Anne of Austria. Goaded and dominated by his mother, he was neglectful of his wife for much of their marriage – a situation made worse by Anne's suspected relationship with the duke of Buckingham.*

### A CHILD BRIDE AND GROOM

Anne met her future husband for the first time in November 1615, and the marriage was formalized on 25 November at Bordeaux cathedral. That night Louis' mother Marie de Médicis (1573–1642), fearing opposition from a powerful nobility who resented the Spanish match, forced the young couple to consummate the marriage. But Louis, perhaps frightened by the experience, did not touch Anne again for three years.

The dowager queen Marie de Médicis had acted as her son's regent since the assassination of his father, Henry IV (1553–1610). But when the young king came of age in 1614 she refused to relinquish power. Louis, starved of affection throughout childhood yet aware of his destiny as heir to the greatest throne in Europe, lacked self-confidence. He was distrustful of everyone, especially women, and had a dreadful stammer. He did not know what to do with his young bride. So he took his mother's lead: he ignored her.

*When Anne married Louis XIII, she was described as 'more beautiful than an angel'. This portrait of her, from the 1630s, is by the celebrated Flemish painter Peter Paul Rubens.*

'... *you know why and how I see you ... I see you that I may tell you that everything separates us – the sea, the enmity of two kingdoms, the sanctity of pledges. It is sacrilege to struggle against so many things ... we must see each other no more.*'

ANNE TO BUCKINGHAM, FROM ALEXANDRE DUMAS, *THE THREE MUSKETEERS*

The couple lived at the Louvre palace, but had no married life together. While her husband pursued his power struggle with his mother, Anne was left alone. When Louis succeeded in exiling his mother from court in 1617 he put his confidence in Charles d'Albert de Luynes (1620–99), the first in the series of favourites who would dominate the king. Louis arranged for Luynes to marry the heiress Marie de Rohan (1600–79), daughter of the duke of Montbazon. Marie was placed in Anne's household and she became her greatest friend. Luynes, disturbed that the king and queen were not sleeping together, badgered Louis to share his wife's bed, but it was only when Luynes frog-marched the king to Anne's chamber that they began to enjoy a normal relationship.

## DISPLACED AND DISTRUSTED AT COURT

By 1622, Marie de Médicis had wormed her way back to court and a place on the royal council. She insisted on taking precedence over Anne, and when Luynes died of scarlet fever, her influence over her son had no buffer. Marie de Médicis coerced Louis to recommend her confidante Armand-Jean du Plessis de Richelieu (1585–1642) for the cardinalate and to admit him to the royal council. Richelieu's place at court and his distrust of the queen marked the end of any warmth between Anne and Louis. Anne turned to her household for affection, particularly to Luynes' widow. In 1622 the queen became pregnant, but after a ball Marie had persuaded the queen to run the length of the great hall in the Louvre and Anne fell against the throne, causing her to lose the baby. Furious, Louis exiled Anne from court. But Marie married the duke de Chevreuse (1578–1657), a member of the Guise family, and reassumed her dominant position over Anne.

Now she encouraged Anne in potentially treasonous activity. In 1623 two Englishmen arrived incognito at the French court looking for adventure – Charles, prince of Wales, the future Charles I of England (r. 1625–49), and George Villiers, duke of Buckingham (1592–1628). The young men watched Anne and her sister-in-law Henrietta Maria (1609–69) perform in a ballet. Charles was smitten with the French princess, and Buckingham with the queen. Buckingham confided his infatuation for Anne to Lord Holland, the English ambassador to Paris. Lord Holland was Marie's new lover and now the pair mischievously encouraged a flirtation between the queen of France and the handsome duke. Anne was flattered. But Buckingham, encouraged by Marie, went too far.

## BUCKINGHAM'S PURSUIT

When Charles approached Louis for the hand of Henrietta Maria, Buckingham was involved in the negotiations. He arrived in Paris determined in his pursuit of the queen. Although Anne's behaviour was impeccable, Louis was furious; he wanted Buckingham far from Anne at the earliest opportunity. But French custom dictated that the female relatives of a royal bride accompany her to the border. When Henrietta Maria left France to marry Charles, Anne went too. Buckingham was also among the party.

The duke made his move at Amiens. Anne and a large party went for a walk and the queen allowed Buckingham to steer her away from the group. An instant later Anne, frightened, cried out. Did Buckingham try to rape her? When her friends discovered her,

*The duke of Buckingham was the great friend of the future Charles I of England. Buckingham was charming, reckless, adventurous and bisexual (he counted James I among his numerous conquests). Anne's dalliance with Buckingham caused Louis to remain suspicious of her for the rest of his life.*

the duke was gone. But his pursuit continued; when bad weather forced him to return to Amiens he burst into the queen's chamber, declaring his love. Anne had him ejected. But for the next three years, while Buckingham tried every ruse to return to Paris, they exchanged notes. At the very least Anne was flattered. She may have loved him, but Louis ensured that they never met again. He also dismissed those he held responsible for her behaviour from her household.

Louis accused Anne of participating in plots and conspiracies (many groundless) and he hounded her for her dislike of his favourite, Cardinal Richelieu. Anne erroneously believed it was Richelieu, and not Louis, who kept her from government. Still childless, she lived in fear of repudiation as Louis' and Richelieu's policies turned against Spain and the Habsburg stranglehold on Europe. Anne was lonely and an easy target of those 'friends', particularly Marie, who used her in their intrigues against the cardinal. By 1637 Anne was in crisis. In the midst of her husband's war against her homeland she had indiscreetly written to her brother Ferdinand (1609/10–41), the cardinal-infante and the Spanish king's representative in Brussels. Her letters complained of her mistreatment by Louis and referred to the political situation. Richelieu's spies discovered the letters and the queen faced charges of treason.

## THE LONG-AWAITED HEIR

Louis, once he had extracted a full written confession, publicly forgave her. But he curtailed her freedom, and his coldness to the queen only increased. But miraculously, considering their dreadful relationship, Anne was pregnant by the end of the year. After many miscarriages she carried the baby to full term and, on 5 September, 1638, she gave birth to a son at Saint-Germain – the future Louis XIV (r. 1643–1715). His conception appears to have happened on a stormy night in autumn 1637. The king visited Louise de la Fayette, a favourite who had entered a convent. Louis, deeply pious, enjoyed tortuous, non-sexual relationships with beautiful women. Louise persuaded him to spend the night with the queen – Anne conceived that night.

The birth of a son probably saved Anne. The birth of another – Philippe of Anjou (1640–1701), later to become Philippe I, duke of Orléans – in 1640 eliminated all fear of repudiation. Anne was now careful to avoid intrigue and superficially enjoyed a cordial relationship with Richelieu – she did not want to give Louis an excuse to take her children away from her. When Louis realized his health was deteriorating he was forced to consider Anne's position. He did not trust her to uphold the interests of France and their son – he was convinced she was a Spanish agent. So although she was appointed regent and his brother Gaston of Orléans (1608–60) made lieutenant-general, she had no power.

Louis did not trust Gaston either – he had been involved in conspiracies against his brother. All matters would be referred to the regency council. Anne would be regent in name only.

The king succumbed to tuberculosis on 14 May, 1643. Surprisingly, Anne and Louis displayed real affection for one another in his last days. But during his illness Anne proved herself a wily politician. She prepared the way for the constraints on her regency to be overturned, and with Louis' death, the Paris *Parlement* granted her full regency powers. Louis was wrong to suspect Anne of treason. She wanted to preserve the kingdom for her son.

## RICHELIEU – A MAN OF PASSION?

Cardinal Richelieu spent his career discrediting Anne. Could thwarted desire have motivated him? After Anne's death Madame de Motteville, a member of her household, wrote her biography of the queen. She recorded rumours that the cardinal was in love with Anne and jealous of Buckingham, and that Richelieu had even visited her to declare his love. Anne, appalled and furious, was unable to reply as the king interrupted them. It is unlikely that the ambitious cardinal would have risked all for a passion that could never be fulfilled. Conversely, he believed the Spanish were trying to discredit him by luring him into indiscreet behaviour towards the queen.

*Cardinal Richelieu and Anne. His domination of Louis XIII would last until the end of the cardinal's life. Anne was forced to forge an uneasy working relationship with him to avoid losing her children.*

When the Spanish approached Anne, believing she would grant them diplomatic favours, they were disappointed. But the queen realized she could not rule alone. She had been queen of France for 28 years, but she had learned little of statecraft. Now she turned to Richelieu's protégé and one of the most brilliant statesmen of his age as her advisor – the naturalized Frenchman, Jules, Cardinal Mazarin (1602–61).

When Richelieu had introduced them he is rumoured to have said, *'You will like him, Madame; he looks like Buckingham'*. Mazarin was probably the love of Anne's life – contemporaries

*A 17th century portrait of Louis XIV on horseback. Anne believed her son's conception was a miracle, and the child was given the name Louis Dieudonné – 'gift of God'.*

believed they were lovers. Years later, when the cardinal was temporarily forced into exile, they wrote passionate letters to one another. Their relationship was based on affection, admiration and respect. Anne was grateful for Mazarin's assistance in keeping her children – in 1642, Louis and Richelieu wanted to take them from her. Now he was Anne's first minister in all but name and she was his grateful protégée.

Until Mazarin's death in 1661, he and Anne kept France safe for the young king. They successfully fought the Fronde (1648–53), an uprising of the aristocracy against the power of the regency. Despite the king's love for Mazarin's niece, Marie Mancini (1639–1715), it was a marriage between Louis XIV and Anne's niece, Maria Theresa of Spain (1638–83) that ended 24 years of war.

Anne's policies ensured that the French monarchy would totter on until the revolution of 1789. She died of breast cancer in 1666.

# CHRISTINA
## 1626—89
## Queen of Sweden

*Christina became queen of Sweden when she was aged just six. Her court became renowned as a centre of intellectual brilliance; many poets, artists, musicians and philosophers were drawn to Stockholm from all over Europe, earning Christina the nickname 'Minerva of the North'. Her scandalous decision to abdicate was greeted with horror throughout the courts of Europe.*

Christina Augusta was born in mid-winter in 1626, the daughter of King Gustavus II Adolphus (r. 1611–32) and Maria Eleonora of Brandenburg (1599–1655). She was their fourth child – two siblings had been stillborn and a sister had died before reaching her first birthday. At Christina's birth the midwives mistook her for a boy and rushed to her father with the news. Gustavus was desperate for a male heir; his dynasty – the Vasas – was not long established and survived on the brilliance of his personal rule. He feared if he failed to have a legitimate son, the Swedish Lutheran crown would pass to his cousin, the Catholic king Sigismund III of Poland (r. 1587–1632), and plunge the country into civil war. When he learned the truth, he hid his disappointment. According to Christina, she was placed beside him so he could see her sex for himself. The king declared:

> *'This girl will be worth as much to me as a boy. I pray God to keep her, since He has given her to me, I wish for nothing else. I am content … She will be clever, for she has deceived us all.'*

Christina's father was among the greatest monarchs of his age and was dubbed the *'lion of the north'*. In the midst of the carnage of the Thirty Years' War, however, he fell in battle against the imperial army of the Holy Roman Emperor, Ferdinand II (r. 1619–37), at Lützen in 1632. When told of Gustavus' death, the slippery Cardinal Richelieu (1585–1642), chief minister of France, said: *'He alone was worth more than both the armies together.'* Christina, now six, became *'Queen of the Swedes, Goths and Vandals, Great Princess of Finland, Duchess of Estonia and Karelia, and Lady of Ingria.'* It was a burdensome title for a little girl.

*An engraving of Queen Christina on horseback. Christina succeeded her father to the throne at the age of six.*

Until she came of age at 18, her kingdom would be governed by five nobles who held the posts of grand chancellor, grand treasurer, grand marshal, grand admiral and high steward. The grand chancellor was Gustavus' friend, the seasoned soldier and statesman Baron Axel Oxenstierna (1583–1654). In her memoirs, Christina recalled that Sweden's senators were unanimous in declaring her queen; she was, she wrote:

*The coronation of Queen Christina on 20 October, 1650. Even while this ceremony was taking place, she had already decided to abdicate.*

'*their only strength and Sweden's only hope of salvation at such a dangerous time …the people were amazed by my grand manner, playing the role of a queen already. I was only little, but on the throne I had such an air, such a grand appearance, that it inspired respect and fear in everyone …*'

## INDEPENDENT AND MASCULINE

Gustavus had laid careful plans for her education. Christina was '*to receive the education of a prince*' and as much attention was to be paid to exercise as to learning. She excelled in her studies and threw herself into sport, a welcome refuge from the company of her unstable mother. Eleonora was so distraught at her husband's death that she kept his coffin with her and forced her young daughter to share her bed.

Christina was repelled by her mother's excessive femininity and began to behave more like a boy than a girl. She preferred to dress as a man and she adopted masculine gestures. She wrote later:

'*As a young girl I had an overwhelming aversion to everything that women do and say. I couldn't bear their tight-fitting, fussy clothes. I took no care of my*

*complexion or my figure or the rest of my appearance …
I despised everything belonging to my sex … What's more,
I was so hopeless at all the womanly crafts that no one
could ever teach me anything about them.'*

It is possible she was affected by her mother's criticism of her
physical appearance. She had been dropped as a baby and one
shoulder was higher than the other. Later she remarked:
*'My mother … said I was ugly.'*

## ARROGANCE, EXTRAVAGANCE AND EXHIBITIONISM

When Christina was 18, the regency ended and she showed her
arrogance publicly for the first time – she believed she could rule
without the aid of her ministers. Against all advice she made an
unadvantageous peace with the Danes. The Treaty of Westphalia
of 1648 marked the end of the Thirty Years' War, and Sweden
emerged with significant gains. But to many Swedes it was an
unpopular peace, signed before a decisive victory was concluded
for the Protestants.

*Christina's father, the
illustrious military
commander King Gustavus
II Adolphus (above),
had hoped for a son.*

Christina was also extravagant, unable or unwilling to differentiate
between her personal property and that of the country. She plundered Sweden's empty
coffers and made extravagant gifts to favourites. To the horror of the nobility, when the
money ran out she sold titles. One disgusted courtier wrote: *'The court is overrun by the
mob they call counts.'* Furthermore, the newly ennobled included Scots, Frenchmen,
Englishmen, Germans and even Danes.

To make matters worse, the queen was an exhibitionist, who revelled in the growing
public scrutiny of her sexuality. She developed a friendship with the delicate, feminine
Ebba Sparre (1626–62), and when gossips drew their own conclusions as to why they
sometimes shared a bed – many believed she was a lesbian – Christina only contributed to
these tales with the bawdy comments she was prone to making in public; for example, she
told the English ambassador that Ebba's insides were as *'beautiful as her outside'.* The
queen also fuelled speculation with her absolute refusal to marry.

As queen, it was Christina's duty to bear children, but she feared marriage. She refused
offers from many European princes and even rebuffed her childhood sweetheart and first

*'It was Victory which announced my name on the fateful field of battle – Victory,
a herald at arms proclaiming me king.'*

QUEEN CHRISTINA

FAR RIGHT: *Christina paying homage to Pope Alexander VII on her arrival in Rome. The queen had secretly converted from Lutheranism to Catholicism in the early 1650s.*

cousin, Karl Gustav (1622–60) – although she certainly adored him as a friend, and possibly as a lover. When she was 22 she finally made her intentions clear and told her senators: *'It is impossible for me to marry. I am absolutely certain about it. I do not intend to give you reasons. My character is simply not suited to marriage. I have prayed God fervently that my inclination might change, but I simply cannot marry.'* Instead she mooted the possibility of Karl Gustav being nominated her successor. It was her first step towards abdication.

## THOUGHTS OF ABDICATION

An empty treasury had delayed Christina's coronation, but when the crown was finally placed on her head on 20 October, 1650 she had already decided to give it up. Her public excuse was that she would not marry. But her real reasons were complex. She had secretly converted from Lutheranism to Roman Catholicism, a religion banned in her country. She also suffered from severe menstrual pains and was often unwell. She may have feared that the stresses of government were making her ill and she longed to escape the boredom of her freezing kingdom as she dreamed of warmer lands.

Meanwhile, she made the Swedish court a hive of intellectual brilliance. It became *de rigueur* for European thinkers to pay homage to the Swedish queen. Christina's curiosity earned her the nickname *'the Minerva of the North'*. She was intrigued by everything, although nothing held her interest for long. The French ambassador to Sweden gave this thumbnail sketch of the queen:

> *'She speaks French as if she had been born at the Louvre, she has a quick and most noble mind, a soul wise and discreet, and she has a certain air about her. Her every pastime is the Senate or her study or her exercise. She speaks Latin very easily and she loves poetry. In short, even without the crown, she would be one of the most estimable people in the world.'*

## THE DILETTANTE QUEEN

Christina persuaded the philosopher René Descartes (1596–1650) to come to her court and he duly arrived to pay homage, despite his fear of the land of 'rocks and ice and bears'. But by the time he arrived, the fickle Christina had abandoned philosophy for the study of Greek. Nevertheless, she allowed Descartes to teach her every morning at 5 o'clock in her freezing library; he contracted influenza and died of pneumonia in February 1650. Christina, perhaps feeling responsible, planned a magnificent funeral at Stockholm's Riddarholm Church and burial among the former kings of Sweden. As with so many of the queen's schemes, however, it came to nothing. Descartes was buried in a modest graveyard in Stockholm, and his remains were later exhumed and reburied in the church of Sainte-Geneviève-du-Mont in Paris.

After three years of wrangling, the *Riksdag* – the Swedish Diet – finally agreed to Christina's abdication in 1654. The ceremony took place at Uppsala Castle on 6 June. But her subjects refused to remove her crown and she was forced to ask two favourites, Count Tott and Baron Steinberg, twice before they reluctantly took it from her. Her cousin Karl Gustav (r. 1654–60) was crowned the same day. Christina left Sweden immediately. She hacked off her hair, dressed in men's clothes – complete with sword – took the pseudonym 'Count Dohna' and left crying: *'Free at last! … Out of Sweden, and I hope I never come back!'* Her destination was Rome.

In Italy, the ex-queen of Sweden – who now styled herself simply Maria Christina Alexandra – was greeted with magnificent pomp. Pope Alexander VII (r. 1655–67)

invited her to be his guest at the Vatican and she flourished, attracting a wide circle of artists, musicians and thinkers to her 'court'. She also fell in love with the ambitious, clever Cardinal Decio Azzolino (1623–89). Gossips speculated that they had an affair – the cardinal had an unorthodox history with women. Even if they did not become lovers, they remained friends for the rest of her life.

## AN ATTEMPT TO SEIZE THE CROWN OF NAPLES

By 1656, however, Christina's restless. spirit reasserted itself once more. She entered into a scheme with Cardinal Mazarin (1602–61), the chief minister of Louis XIV of France (r. 1643–1715), to take the throne of Naples from the Spanish for the duration of her lifetime; at her death it would pass to Louis' brother, Philippe I, duke of Orléans (1640–1701). Christina visited France, where her masculine manner shocked the women. Madame de Motteville, lady-in-waiting to the dowager French queen, recorded her impressions:

> *'We saw the arrival of the queen of Sweden, of whom we had heard so many extraordinary things … once I had looked at her for a bit, and got used to her clothes and her odd hairstyle, I saw she had beautiful, lively eyes, and a sweet expression, also rather proud …'*

But in France Christina, famed for her religious tolerance and her charitable works, made a mistake: she ordered the assassination of her master of the horse, whom she believed had betrayed the plot to march on Naples. She was legally allowed to do so, but the French were horrified, and the scheme came to nothing. Back in Rome Azzolino persuaded her to pursue the vacant crown of Poland, but the Poles rejected her; they preferred to be ruled by a man.

Christina wore a crown for less than half her life, and the years following her abdication were restless ones. After the death of Karl Gustav in 1660, frustrated by her lack of funds (she had been given an annuity by the Swedish Diet, but it was frequently late or never came at all), she attempted to be reinstated as queen of Sweden, but was refused. She spent the rest of her life in Rome and died there in the spring of 1689. She is buried in the Basilica of St Peter's in the Vatican.

## TIMELINE

**1632** Gustav II dies on the battlefield; Christina inherits the throne, with five nobles as regents

**1644** Christina comes of age and dismisses her ministers

**1645** Christina negotiates the Treaty of Brömsebro with Denmark

**1648** The Thirty Years' War ends and the Treaty of Wesphalia is signed

**1650** Christina is crowned, but has already decided to abdicate; she invites Descartes to Stockholm

**1654** Christina abdicates; Karl Gustav is crowned; Christina travels to Rome

**1656** A plot by Christina and Mazarin to seize the crown of Naples fails

**1689** Christina dies in Rome

# MARY II

## *1662–94*
## Queen of England

*Mary was the first Stuart queen regnant and the first female to ascend the English throne since the death of Elizabeth I. But Mary chose not to reign. Instead, she willingly handed over the reins of power to her husband, William of Orange, in the Dual Monarchy.*

Mary was the eldest daughter of James, duke of York, the future James II (r. 1685–8) and his commoner duchess, Anne Hyde (1637–71). She was born on 30 April, 1662 at St James' Palace, two years after her uncle, Charles II (r. 1660–85), was restored to the throne. Mary was not seen as important. Her uncle was married to his Portuguese queen and her father expected to have more sons, although her older brother, Charles, duke of Cambridge had died. But although the Yorks had eight children, only Mary and her younger sister Anne (1665–1714) survived infancy. When Queen Catherine (1638–1705) failed to have children, Mary and Anne became second and third in line to the throne after their father.

Mary was clever, but her education was virtually non-existent – astonishing considering how close she was to the throne. Although there were precedents for strong female rulers – Matilda, Lady of the English (r. 1141), Mary I (r. 1553–8) and Elizabeth I (r. 1558–1603) – it was expected that if Mary and her sister Anne were to ascend the throne, their husbands would rule. When her father and mother secretly converted to Catholicism, the king was appalled, and after the duchess died of cancer, Mary and Anne were removed from the apostate James' care. They became children of the state and were brought up at Richmond Palace in the household of the Protestant Edward Villiers and his family. By this time, Mary was nine years old. Suddenly a great deal of attention was paid to their religious education and both Mary and Anne became zealous Protestants.

*Prince William of Orange (above) was a Dutch war hero. But for Mary (right) he was not an enticing marriage prospect. He was 12 years older than her, 13 centimetres (5 in) shorter, suffered from asthma and was solemn by nature.*

Mary was pretty. She was tall, with pale, translucent skin, thick auburn hair and a sweet face. She was kind, impetuous and highly strung; she loved to dance, as the diarist Samuel Pepys noted: *'I did see the young duchess, a little child in hanging sleeves, dance most finely, so as almost to ravish me ...'*

### GIRLISH INFATUATION

Even at such a young age Mary happily took the subordinate role. The passionate little girl developed a crush on the slightly older Frances Apsley (*c.*1653–1727), to the point

where Mary even assumed the role of wife to Frances' husband: *'Why dear cruel loved blest husband …'*, she wrote.

In October 1677, when Mary was 15, she was introduced to Prince William of Orange (1650–1702), stadtholder (head of state) of the Dutch Republic. The nephew of Charles II and James, duke of York, William was Mary's first cousin and stood to inherit the throne after James, Mary and Anne. Charles, anxious to appease parliament, sought a match between his Protestant nephew and niece, but James disagreed. He preferred the Catholic *dauphin* of France as a husband for his daughter. Ignoring his brother's wishes, Charles approached William as a prospective bridegroom for Mary. The Dutchman insisted on meeting Mary first, and was captivated. She was in the first bloom of her beauty – and he readily agreed to the marriage.

## MARRIAGE TO WILLIAM

Mary cried when her father informed her that the austere William was to be her husband. But within weeks they were married at St James' in an intimate ceremony on the evening of 4 November, 1677. To her surprise and delight, Mary fell in love with Holland. She loved its cleanliness, its simplicity and the forthright manner of its people. She also fell in love with her husband. During their honeymoon at William's charming palace of Honselersdijck, Mary wrote to Frances Apsley that *'she had played the whore a little'*.

Mary was determined to play the submissive role; after the instability of her childhood she was content not to rule. William governed while Mary created a charming, feminine atmosphere in their apartments. She had superb taste and decorated their palaces – Honselersdijck, Soestdijck, Direen and Het Loo. When she discovered she was pregnant, she was ecstatic. William had returned to his army at Antwerp and Mary, missing him, travelled along treacherous winter roads to join him. Sadly, as a result of her reckless journey, she lost the baby. Although she believed she was pregnant again in 1678, she had in all likelihood suffered an infection with her miscarriage, and was unable to conceive. Depressed, she became more introspective as she sought solace in prayer and study.

## MARY BECOMES HEIR

When Mary's uncle Charles II died in 1685, the naïve James assumed the throne as James II with little fuss, despite his Catholicism and inclination towards friendship with despotic France. James had married Princess Mary Beatrice d'Este of Modena (1658–1718) when Mary was 11, but none of Mary Beatrice's children with James survived. Mary was now heir to the throne. Mary slowly lost patience with her father. He refused to acknowledge her new position with financial assistance – James claimed he feared any money he sent to Mary would be used by William to fight against him – and attempted to impugn William's fidelity by telling Mary her husband was having an affair with Elizabeth Villiers. When Mary confronted William with the – probably spurious – accusation, he vehemently denied it.

*A portrait (c.1690) of Mary's father King James II, by the French painter Henri Gascars. The threat of James' Catholic son and Mary's half-brother James Francis Edward Stuart (the 'Old Pretender') succeeding him prompted William of Orange to mount an invasion of England. As a result, James fled, and the Protestant William and Mary ascended the throne in the Dual Monarchy.*

Mary was disappointed again when James refused to come to the couple's aid after the forces of Louis XIV (r. 1643–1715) occupied William's principality of Orange. She confided to her diary:

> 'The only thing I ever asked the king, my father, to do was to use his influence with the king of France to prevent the seizure of the Principality of Orange … but my father preferred to join with the king of France against my husband.'

Meanwhile, Mary was eager to assure her husband that, if she should succeed to the throne and become the queen of England, she would assume a subservient position. Nothing would change. Gilbert Burnet, a Scottish clergyman who spoke to her about it, recorded that Mary claimed:

> '… she did not think that the husband was ever to be obedient to the wife: she promised him [William] he should always bear rule; and she asked only, that he would obey the command of "husbands love your wives", as she should do that, "wives be obedient to your husbands in all things".'

*'Oft I have heard of impious sons before*

*Rebelled for crowns their royal parents wore*

*But of unnatural daughters rarely hear*

*'Till those of hapless James and old King Lear.'*

A JACOBITE POEM DECRYING MARY'S ASSUMPTION OF THE THRONE IN
PLACE OF HER FATHER, THE CATHOLIC JAMES II

## A CONSPIRING SISTER

Mary's ambitious sister Anne fuelled the discord between James and Mary. In March 1688 she convinced William and Mary that the now pregnant Mary Beatrice was not pregnant at all; it was part of a Catholic conspiracy to bypass Mary and Anne as the Protestant heirs, and to place a Catholic changeling on the throne. But the conspiracy was Anne's. She probably realized that her sister would remain childless and that when she died, Anne would inherit the throne herself. Her plan relied on discrediting any children her stepmother might have.

When the son of James II and Mary Beatrice, James Francis Edward (1688–1766), was born on 10 June, 1688, William was invited by several leading statesmen to restore the Protestant succession. In the absence of other evidence, William and Mary believed Anne's story. The English would no longer tolerate a Catholic monarchy: William would be their saviour. When James learned of his son-in-law's proposed invasion, he wrote to Mary:

*'I hope it will have been as real a surprise to you as it was to me … being sure it is not in your nature to approve of so unjust an undertaking. I have been all this day so busy, to endeavour to be in some condition to defend myself from so unjust and unexpected an attempt … and though I know you are a good wife … yet for the same reason I must believe you will be still as good a daughter to a father that has always loved you so tenderly …'*

William and his fleet set sail. James fled in the wake of the invasion and the English, kingless, debated what to do. It was mooted that Mary be offered the crown but she was horrified, and William refused to be a 'gentleman usher'. He held Mary to her promise of maintaining the status quo in their marriage. If the English wanted William's continued presence they must accept him as king in a dual monarchy, with Mary as titular queen.

## WILLIAM ASSUMES POWER

Although she suffered guilt and anxiety over her father's fate, Mary's chief concern was to preserve her marriage and to ensure a Protestant monarchy. On 13 February, 1689 William and Mary accepted power in the Banqueting House at Whitehall. She remained mute and clung to William's hand throughout the ceremony in which they were offered the crown. Mary's submission affirmed William's right to rule in her stead; all power was vested in her husband.

Mary was unhappy in England. She had come to love the Netherlands and missed her quiet life there. Anne offered her no solace – she had supported her brother-in-law's

## MARY'S INDULGENCE

Mary adored tea and saw it as an extravagance. Introduced to Europe by the Dutch East India Company at the beginning of the 17th century, it was expensive and enjoyed only by the wealthy. Meanwhile, tea had been drunk throughout China for almost 5000 years.

invasion, until she learned he had replaced her in the line of succession. As William III he would rule for the rest of his life. Anne, embittered, pointedly stayed away from court.

She also tormented her sister with her inappropriate friendship with Sarah Churchill (1660–1744). Mary and William were convinced that Sarah's husband John Churchill, the earl of Marlborough (1650–1722), was communicating with the deposed James and Louis XIV, and dismissed him. Mary ordered Anne to send away her favourite, and Anne's refusal led to an irreparable breach between the sisters. With William fighting his wars against his father-in-law and Catholic aggression in Europe, Mary was very lonely. But despite her feelings of inadequacy, she was an able regent in William's frequent absences. Although the pro-James Jacobites hated her, her kindness, religious tolerance and philanthropy made her extremely popular. She revelled in modernizing her palaces.

But Mary's health was suffering. She felt guilty about her father and miserable about the breach with her sister. She was also working too hard, conscientiously informing William of her every decision. She wrote to William: *'I must grin when my heart is ready to break, and talk when my heart is so oppressed I can scarcely breathe.'*

Mary died of smallpox on 28 December, 1694, aged just 32. To the astonishment of the English, William was devastated – they erroneously believed he was rather cool towards his wife. William himself succumbed to pneumonia in March 1702. On ascending the throne after his death, Anne did not emulate her sister. The last Stuart queen bypassed her feeble husband, Prince George of Denmark (1653–1708), and presided gloriously – and alone – over England's second golden age.

*This contemporary woodcut depicts William III disembarking his troops on the English coast at Brixham in Devon in November 1688. The Dutch fleet comprised 200 transport ships and 50 warships.*

# ANNE

## 1665 – 1714
## Queen of England

*History remembers Anne Stuart as a woman with none of Elizabeth I's fire, although, like Elizabeth, she was the last of her dynasty to rule. Anne's chroniclers write her off as drab and with no opinions of her own: a woman who lived at the whim of her grasping favourites, a powdered cipher at the centre of a second British golden age. Anne may have been slow to act, but she was shrewd and intelligent. She fought successful wars against the two superpowers of the day – France and Spain – quelled the excesses of the anti-papists, ensured the Protestant succession and united England with Scotland. She was also instrumental in the deposition and disgrace of her weak and libidinous father. 'Good Queen Anne' is a myth.*

Anne's father James, duke of York – the future James II (r. 1685–8) – was the younger son of the deposed and murdered Charles I (r. 1625–49). Her mother, Anne Hyde (1637–71), was a commoner whom James married before the Stuart dynasty was re-established after the death of Oliver Cromwell and the fall of his Commonwealth in 1660. Anne was born in February 1665. Her uncle Charles II (r. 1660–85) – libidinous, shrewd and charming – was king and it was anticipated that his queen, Catherine of Braganza (1638–1705), would perpetuate the Stuart line. As a child, Anne was deemed irrelevant. She was one of eight children, including sons, but most of them died. Only Anne and her older sister Mary (1662–94) survived infancy (see Mary II, pages 164–169).

Anne Hyde was not maternal, and when her daughter Anne was three, the little girl went to live with her grandmother, the dowager queen Henrietta Maria (1609–69), in France. When her grandmother died, she was sent to her aunt Minette, duchess of Orléans (1644–70). But Minette also died; by the age of five the princess was back in England. In her absence her parents had secretly converted to Roman Catholicism, and Charles II was furious. James was the heir apparent – it seemed unlikely that Queen Catherine would have children – and England was fiercely Protestant. Mary and Anne, now second and third in the line of succession after their father, were swiftly removed from their parents' influence and made children of state. Anne was barely six.

Portrait of Princess Anne of England *(1700) by Sir Godfrey Kneller. Although overshadowed by her glorious older sister Mary, Anne was nevertheless a beauty.*

'And what men that little rustic England could breed! A nation of five and a half millions that had Wren for its architect, Newton for its scientist, Locke for its philosopher, Bentley for its scholar, Pope for its poet, Addison for its essayist, Bolingbroke for its orator, Swift for its pamphleteer and Marlborough to win its battles, had the recipe for genius.'

THE HISTORIAN G.M. TREVELYAN ON QUEEN ANNE'S ENGLAND

## PROTESTANT INDOCTRINATION

Although princesses, their education was criminally poor. They were instructed in the Protestant faith and indoctrinated with anti-papism, but all other intellectual subjects were ignored. Anne wrote to Mary: '*... the doctrine of the Church of Rome is wicked and dangerous ... plain, downright idolatry*'. Husbands would be found for them and, even if one or both of them should come to the throne, they would not be expected to rule.

Two years after their mother died in 1671, James remarried. His second wife was the beautiful 15-year-old princess Mary Beatrice d'Este of Modena (1658–1718). '*I have brought you a new playfellow,*' James told his eldest daughter. Although Princess Mary liked Mary Beatrice, Anne loathed her. Now a zealous Protestant, she feared her stepmother's Catholicism and the riots her father's marriage inspired.

Anne had become a beauty. Her portrait by the artist Michael Dahl (1659–1743) shows a princess with translucent skin, beautiful hands and arms, and a sensuous mouth. When she was 18, a husband was presented: the dull Protestant Prince George of Denmark (1653–1708). Her uncle the king quipped, '*I have tried him drunk and I have tried him sober and there is nothing in him*'. But Anne adored him. The couple married in the summer of 1683 in Inigo Jones' Chapel Royal at St James', and the king gave them a London residence known as the Cockpit (on the site of today's Downing Street) as a wedding present. Anne became pregnant almost immediately after her wedding. But in the spring of 1684 her daughter was born dead. This was the first of Anne's 18 pregnancies, and the beginning of a catalogue of personal and public anguish. Of her children born alive, only one would survive infancy.

Charles II died in February 1685 and the duke of York, Anne's father, became King James II. Anne, now second in line to the throne, feared Mary Beatrice would give birth to a son and perpetuate the Catholic line. In 1687 the queen was pregnant again – since she married she had given birth to several children but none had survived, possibly because James suffered from venereal disease – but Anne maliciously perpetuated rumours that Mary Beatrice was not pregnant. A changeling, she gossiped, would instead be brought into her stepmother's birthing chamber to foist a Catholic heir onto the nation.

## DUTCH INVADERS

Anne wrote to her sister Mary, now married to their cousin, William of Orange (1650–1702) and living in the Netherlands, and persuaded them of the truth of her story. She then ostentatiously went to Bath so she would not have to attend the 'scandal'. When Prince James Francis Edward (1688–1766) was born on 10 June, 1688 his half-sister wrote again to Mary:

> '*It may be it is our brother, but God only knows, for she* [Mary Beatrice] *never took care to satisfy the world, or give people any demonstration of it ... for my part ... I shall ever be one of the number of unbelievers.*'

*Sarah Jennings Churchill (1660–1744), Anne's childhood friend who later became the duchess of Marlborough, was the most important person in Anne's life. Their letters to each other – written under the pseudonyms Mrs Morley (Anne) and Mrs Freeman (Sarah) – were numerous and passionate.*

William of Orange, meanwhile, invaded to save England from the papists and their prince. When his army landed in the West Country, Anne, her husband and John, Lord Churchill (1650–1722), the brilliant soldier and husband of Sarah Churchill, deserted the king. Distraught at the rumours surrounding his son's birth and Mary's defection, James lost the will to fight. Back in London, finding that Anne had left the capital with Sarah Churchill, he lamented: *'God help me! My own children have deserted me.'*

*Anne's sister, Mary, shown here with her husband, William of Orange. Following his 1688 invasion of England, they were crowned king and queen. Anne's relations with them both cooled considerably – she even called William 'the Dutch abortion'.*

After James fled, Anne returned to the capital to greet the triumphant William and Mary, jubilantly festooned with orange ribbons. Anne showed no pity for her father's plight; instead, she went to the theatre and wrote of the necessity of painting the back stairs at the Cockpit. She hitched her wagon to the new regime.

## A FAMILY RIFT

Although parliament offered William and Mary a dual monarchy, Mary was happy to let power reside with her husband. He was polite to Anne, but the princess was marginalized throughout his reign. Like everyone else, William thought Prince George was an idiot and excluded him. Anne was furious with William and treated her sister with a studied coolness that fractured their relationship. Sarah gleefully encouraged the breach. When Mary demanded that the favourite be dismissed, Anne refused and relations deteriorated still further. Anne did not return to court until her sister's death in 1694.

In 1689 Anne gave birth to a son – William, duke of Gloucester (1689–1700). Despite the fact that she would endure ten more pregnancies, William was the only child to survive infancy. His parents were devoted to him, but he was a delicate boy. He suffered from hydrocephalus ('water on the brain') and had an enlarged head. In July 1700, he died. He was only 11 years old, and Anne never recovered. After her son's death she signed her letters to Sarah, *'Your poor unfortunate faithful Morley'*. Moreover, it was not merely a personal tragedy – there was now a succession crisis.

## QUEEN ANNE AND GREEN PARK

When Anne asked the young politician (later to become prime minister) Robert Walpole: *'Were I to enclose Green Park within my garden, what would be the cost?'*, Walpole reputedly replied : *'A monarchy, Madam, a monarchy.'* She wisely elected not to pursue her scheme to turn this large public park in London into the monarch's personal property.

The English would not tolerate another Roman Catholic monarch and James II's children by Mary Beatrice were excluded. But Charles I's sister Elizabeth of Bohemia (1596–1662) had 13 children. Her 12th child, Sophia (1630–1714), had married the Protestant Elector of Hanover, and the 1701 Act of Settlement named Sophia and her heirs as Anne's successors. When William died in 1702 it seemed increasingly likely that Sophia, followed by her eldest son, 'German George' (1660–1727), would rule in England.

## A TRULY ENGLISH QUEEN

With William's death Anne became queen, to great acclaim. During her first speech to parliament she recalled the ghost of her ancestress Elizabeth I (r. 1558–1603) and shrewdly adopted her motto, *Semper Eadem* ('Always One and the Same'). Anne promised: *'As I know my heart to be entirely English, I can very sincerely assure you there is not anything you can expect or desire from me which I shall not be ready to do for the happiness and prosperity of England.'* She chose exceptional advisors, including John Churchill, Sidney, Lord Godolphin (1645–1712) and Robert Harley (1661–1724), and she wisely continued William's policies. Marlborough pursued the war with Louis XIV of France (r. 1643–1715), and union with Scotland was sought and finally achieved in 1707.

Anne showered the Churchills with honours – Marlborough was given the Order of the Garter and, after his magnificent victory at Blenheim in 1704, was made a duke. Sarah took the office of Groom of the Stole, Mistress of the Robes and Keeper of the Privy Purse and had unlimited access to the queen. Anne wrote lovingly to her: *'… if you should ever forsake me, I would have nothing more to do with the world, but make another abdication, for what is a crown when ye support of it is gone …'.*

## SARAH'S FALL FROM GRACE

Yet the duchess of Marlborough overplayed her hand, failing to treat her friend with the deference due to her as queen. Sarah nagged her constantly; she whispered of Tory plots to place her half-brother on the throne and, despite the duke's warnings to desist, relentlessly pushed the cause of the Whigs, the Marlboroughs' preferred party. John Churchill was better acquainted with the queen's personality than his wife, and warned Sarah: *'You know that I have often disputes with you concerning the queen, and by what I have always observed that when she thinks herself in the right, she needs no advice to help her to be very firm and positive.'* Although Anne favoured the Tories, in the febrile atmosphere of emerging party politics, she believed the monarch should be impartial, and Sarah's pestering strained the relationship. Sarah was bored by Anne's illnesses – her pregnancies had ruined her health, she was obese and could barely walk – and she deserted court. Into the power void stepped Sarah's cousin, the Tory Abigail Masham (c.1670–1734).

Sir Winston Churchill (1874–1965), a descendant of Sarah, said that Abigail Masham was *'probably the smallest person who ever consciously attempted to decide and in fact decided the history of Europe'*. When Sarah heard of her cousin's usurpation in 1708 she swept back to court. She brought with her a slanderous poem that accused Queen Anne of lesbianism.

Anne was appalled, but avoided a public breach with Sarah while Marlborough continued to crush the French and the Spanish armies. But the war was increasingly unpopular and Anne backed the Tories. She was determined to rid herself of the Marlboroughs and, in 1711, finally dismissed them from court. Anne and Sarah had been inseparable for 27 years and, in a frenzy, Sarah wrecked her apartments at St James' and threatened to publish Anne's letters. *'Such things are in my power … that might lose a crown,'* she spat. The letters were explosive – they contained phrases such as, *'I wish I may never see the face of Heaven if ever I consent to part with you …'* In the end Sarah did not publish, but she remained bitter for the rest of her life.

Anne's last years were lonely. George died in 1708 and after their acrimonious parting she never saw Sarah again. The historian G.M. Trevelyan (1876–1962) sums up Anne in the following terms:

> *'… for a dozen weary years the invalid daily faced her office work. She did not leave affairs to her favourites or even wholly to her ministers. In order to do what she thought right in church and state, she slaved at many details of government. And the ideas that inspired her were those of moderation, good sense and humanity … '*

The England she left to her cousin, the first of the Hanoverian Georges, was a world power. Anne died of a stroke in 1714.

*John Churchill accepts the surrender of the French at the Battle of Blenheim (1704) – scene from a tapestry at Blenheim Palace, England. A grateful Anne rewarded him by making him duke of Marlborough. Aware that Churchill's military skills were far superior to those of her husband, Anne awarded him the post of captain general, denying George the opportunity to conduct her wars.*

# MARIA THERESA

## 1717–80

## Archduchess of Austria, Queen of Hungary and Bohemia

*Maria Theresa was pious, sanctimonious and an arch-reactionary. She was a daughter of the Habsburgs, German princes who had acquired vast swathes of territory through matrimony. They were among the most powerful dynasties in Europe; at their zenith, their lands encompassed Austria, the Low Countries, Spain, Hungary, Bohemia, Silesia and much of central Europe. Since 1438 the largely symbolic, but still highly prestigious, position of Holy Roman emperor, first held by Charlemagne in 800, had been occupied by a Habsburg. Females could inherit Habsburg territory, but were disbarred from taking the imperial title. Accordingly, Maria Theresa fought hard to ensure her weak husband assumed the purple. But she remained the real power behind the throne.*

*Frederick II of Prussia (above) and Maria Theresa were lifelong enemies. On her accession, he pointedly insulted her by addressing her as 'duchess of Tuscany' (alluding to her husband Francis Stephen's official title) and took every opportunity to snub her.*

Maria Theresa was the eldest daughter of the Holy Roman Emperor Charles VI (r. 1711–40) and his wife Elisabeth of Brunswick-Wolfenbüttel (1691–1750). Four years before her birth, their son had died. Charles, anxious in the absence of sons that his daughter should succeed him, issued the Pragmatic Sanction. This piece of legislation was an insurance policy – if he failed to produce a male heir, it ensured that Maria Theresa would inherit his throne – and for ten years Charles tried to coerce the rulers of Europe into ratifying it. Most acquiesced, though France, Prussia, Bavaria and Saxony later reneged.

When she was 19 Maria Theresa married Francis Stephen of Lorraine (1708–65). He was a warm, charming sybarite and the young archduchess was instantly besotted with him. The English ambassador remarked that, *'she sighs and pines all night long for her Duke of Lorraine … '*. For Francis Stephen, however, the considerations were more practical – his wife stood to inherit an empire.

*Maria Theresa of Austria was born in Vienna, the vibrant, polyglot capital of the Habsburg empire. She was a key figure in 18th-century European power politics. This portrait was painted in c.1727–39 by Gabriel Mathei.*

Charles VI died in 1740. On his death his wife had still not borne him a son. The fault may have been the emperor's: he preferred his mistress to his obese wife and spent six years in Spain, away from the marriage bed, pursuing the Habsburg claim to the Spanish throne. Moreover, despite his efforts, Charles VI's Pragmatic Sanction was ignored as the Elector of Bavaria, Prince Charles Albert was nominated Holy Roman Emperor, instead of Maria Theresa's husband. Of her accession to the Habsburg dominions, which included present-day Austria, Hungary, the Czech Republic and much of the Balkans, she wrote, *'it would not be easy to find in history an example of a crowned head acceding to government in more unfavourable circumstances than I did myself'.*

Charles VI thus bequeathed his 23-year-old daughter an empty treasury and a contested right to the imperial title. Having neglected to give her any instruction in politics or diplomacy, she was left to teach herself the art of government, a task at which she proved highly adept. Count Otto Christian Podewils, the Prussian ambassador to Vienna, later reported back to the Prussian king Frederick II (r. 1740–86):

> *'Her mind being lively and keen, her memory excellent, and her judgment sound, she is perfectly capable of dealing with affairs of state ... ambition has instilled her with the desire to govern herself. She is more successful in that respect than most of her ancestors ...'*

*'I am only a poor queen, but have the heart of a king.'*

MARIA THERESA

## ENEMIES OF THE EMPIRE

Two months after Charles' death Frederick II invaded Silesia, Maria Theresa's richest province. Silesia became her obsession, but despite her efforts over the years it was never returned to the Habsburg fold. Frederick's invasion prompted other European powers who coveted Habsburg lands to enter the fray and Maria Theresa spent the first eight years of her reign fighting to hold her empire together. Almost exactly eight years after her father's death, in October 1748 the Treaty of Aix-la-Chapelle concluded the wars reasonably successfully for Maria Theresa. But she never recovered from the loss of Silesia, which she called *'the crown's most precious jewel'*.

## MARIA TRIUMPHS

In 1745, in the midst of the war, the Holy Roman emperor Charles VII died. Now Maria Theresa manoeuvred for Francis Stephen to be elected Holy Roman Emperor. The crown was hers to bestow, so she believed, by right of her Habsburg blood. He was crowned on 4 October – his name day – in Vienna and would rule as Francis I from 1745 to 1765. The German writer Johann Wolfgang von Goethe (1749–1832) records how, as the new emperor returned from the cathedral, Maria Theresa delightedly waved her handkerchief and shouted out to him, *'Vivat Emperor Francis!'*

Despite Francis' infidelities, the marriage was a happy one. The indolent Francis Stephen enjoyed titular power while his wife ruled, and Maria Theresa stoically resigned herself to his dalliances. He made his bid to lead his wife's armies during the War of the Austrian Succession (1740–8) but Maria Theresa, fearful for his life, refused to let him go. Although she herself had married for love, only one of her children – her favourite, Maria Christina (1742–98) – was allowed to do so. The rest were sacrificed to unhappy marriages in far-flung courts. Her most famous daughter, Marie Antoinette (1755–93), facilitated an alliance with France and lost her head in the French Revolution of 1789.

## NEW ALLIANCES

The Seven Years' War from 1756 saw Maria Theresa turn her back on her ancient ally, Britain, and forge an alliance with France and Russia against her foe Frederick II of Prussia. For the empress, it was a desperate bid to recover Silesia, but again she failed. When Francis Stephen died in 1765, Maria Theresa plunged into desperate grief. Yet her sorrow did not prevent her promoting Habsburg interests. Her eldest son, Joseph, ascended the imperial throne as Emperor Joseph II (r. 1765–90). He became her co-ruler and frequent adversary. Joseph, a keen advocate of the tenets of the Enlightenment and an admirer of all those contemporary personalities whom Maria Theresa loathed – Frederick II of Prussia, Catherine II of Russia (r. 1762–96) and her morganatic husband Grigory Potemkin (1739–91) – consistently outraged and offended his reactionary mother.

## RUTHLESS HYPOCRISY

Despite her antipathy for Frederick II, Maria Theresa had no compunction in joining him and Catherine the Great of Russia into one of history's most nefarious land appropriations: the First Partition of Poland in 1772. The empress, conveniently imagining that her actions

were for Poland's good, signed the treaty in tears. Frederick II commented *'She weeps, but she takes'*. This was perceptive of him – although Prussia and Russia participated enthusiastically in dismembering a sovereign nation, the prime mover was Maria Theresa. Throughout the 1760s she sent aid to the Polish Catholics against the threat of Russian Orthodoxy. When she marched into Poland on the pretext of preserving the peace, all Europe knew her intentions. Frederick and Catherine cared little for their reputations, but when Maria Theresa's character was decried throughout Europe for her involvement in the partition of Poland, she was mortified.

*Maria Theresa and her family, seen here in a painting by Heinrich Füger, lived at the Hofburg, a vast palace in Vienna. She bore 16 children; of the ten that survived, nearly all furthered her dynastic ambitions.*

Catherine the Great once called Maria Theresa 'Lady Prayerful,' but her piety was far from saintly. She detested Protestants and was a virulent anti-Semite – she expelled the Jewish population from Bohemia and Moravia in 1744 and from Prague in 1745. She was an able ruler, overhauling the empire's administration and laying the foundations of Habsburg hegemony until 1806. Her empire then survived in another guise – the Austro-Hungarian empire – until the end of the First World War. Maria Theresa died of dropsy on 29 November, 1780. Refusing to sleep, she greeted death with the words: *'At any moment I may be called before my Judge. I don't want to be surprised. I want to see death come.'*

## A MUSICAL GENIUS AT MARIA THERESA'S COURT

In October 1762 a six-year-old child prodigy from Salzburg, named Wolfgang Amadeus Mozart (1756–91), played the harpsichord for Maria Theresa, Francis Stephen and their children. The royal family were thrilled by his precocious skill, and one story recounts that he was so exhilarated by his performance that he threw himself into the empress' lap and pledged to marry the young archduchess Marie Antoinette.

# Jeanne-Antoinette Poisson

## 1721–64
## Marquise de Pompadour

*The first time Jeanne-Antoinette d'Étioles, the future marquise de Pompadour, met Louis XV in public he was dressed as a tree. The king was encased in a papier-mâché yew as part of the elaborate festivities to celebrate the marriage of his son, the dauphin Louis. Jeanne-Antoinette set her sights on ensnaring the king and he was duly captivated. Ruling over him, Versailles and France for the rest of her life, she became the greatest royal mistress in French history.*

Jeanne-Antoinette was born in Paris on 29 December, 1721, the eldest child of the middle-class Louise-Madeleine de la Motte and François Poisson. After a fortune teller read the girl's palm and predicted a prosperous future, her mother was convinced her pretty daughter was born to be the mistress of a great man and called her *Reinette* ('little queen'). Jeanne-Antoinette left the fortune teller, Madame Lebon, 600 livres in her will '... *for having told her at the age of nine that she would one day be the mistress of Louis XV'.*

Monsieur Poisson was a chancer, an employee of the government's bankers, the Pâris brothers. In 1726 he was involved in a wheat fraud and was forced to flee to Germany. Jeanne-Antoinette and her younger brother, Abel-François (1727–81), were left in his wife's care.

*Jeanne-Antoinette – seen here in a lithograph after a painting by the Rococo artist François Boucher – was a commoner, loathed by the aristocrats and courtiers at the court of Louis XV. However, such was her hold over the king that they were forced to ingratiate themselves into her favour.*

Jeanne-Antoinette received an exemplary convent education at Poissy. Then she was returned to her mother. According to a contemporary, Louise-Madeleine was '*one of the most beautiful women in the country, and very clever'.* Her detractors accused her of prostitution. 'Uncles' certainly featured in the young Jeanne-Antoinette's life during her father's absence. Chief among them was Charles Le Normant de Tournehem (1684–1751), a wealthy banker. (Some historians have speculated that he may have been her father.) Louise-Madeleine persuaded him to finance her daughter's 'real' tuition.

'... she is excessively common, a bourgeoise out of her place who will displace all the world if one cannot manage to displace her.'

THE COMTE DE MAUREPAS

## A COURTESAN IN TRAINING

Under de Tournehem's tutelage, Jeanne-Antoinette was educated to be the most exceptional courtesan of her generation. Her contemporary Moffle d'Angerville, author of *The Private Life of Louis XV*, tells us that she:

> '… was just a beautiful woman if she so desired, or beautiful and vivacious, together or separately, having acquired these arts from the lessons her mother had procured for her from actors, famous courtesans, preachers and lawyers. The diabolical woman had gone to all the professions that call for subtle and varied expressions for private instruction, in order to make her daughter really "a morsel fit for a king" … She could weep – like an actress. She could be at will superb, imperious, calm, roguish, a tease, judicious, curious, attentive, by altering the expression of her eyes, her lips, her fine brow. In fact, without moving her body, her mischievous face made of her a veritable Proteus … '

In 1741, when she was 19, her mother's lover, besotted with his charming 'niece', married her to his nephew and heir, Charles-Guillaume Le Normant d'Étioles. He gave them a large income, a house in Paris and a country estate, the Château d'Étioles. Jeanne-Antoinette developed a charming salon, frequented not by the aristocracy, of course, but by notable members of the Parisian bourgeoisie, including Voltaire (1694–1778). But the marriage did not stop the aspirations of her mother and her 'uncle'. The new Madame d'Étioles enthusiastically allowed them to place her in the path of the king.

*Louis XV, dubbed 'the handsomest man in France', was the great-grandson of the 'Sun King' Louis XIV (r. 1643–1715). He was lazy and easily bored – his chief interests were women and the hunt.*

## THE PROFLIGATE KING

Louis XV (r. 1715–74) was an extremely inept ruler. He came to the throne at the age of five, but let ministers govern for him all his life. René-Louis, marquis d'Argenson (1694–1757), who later became secretary of state for foreign affairs, described Louis in 1739: *'He rises at 11, and leads a useless life. He steals from his frivolous occupations one hour of work; the sessions with the ministers cannot be called work, for he lets them do everything, merely listening or repeating what they say like a parrot. He is still very much a child.'* Others were even more damning. The duc de Choiseul, a minister and a favourite of Pompadour, called Louis *'a man without heart or brains'*.

In 1725 Louis married the impoverished Polish princess Marie Leczinska (1703–68). Between 1727 and 1736 she bore the king ten children. Louis had received his religious education from Bishop André Hercule de Fleury (1653–1743), who acted as his first minister until his death in 1743. Fleury inculcated faithfulness in the king – if he strayed, the cardinal warned, God would deny him a son.

## LOUIS' PHILANDERINGS

But with the birth of a *dauphin* in 1729, Louis embarked on affairs with three of the Nesle sisters: Madame de Mailly (1710–51), the marquise de Vintimille (1712–41) and the marquise de la Tournelle (1717–44). The first two were remarkably unattractive. But

Louis was truly enchanted by the third sister, who, unlike her siblings, was pretty and shrewd. Louis cruelly abandoned the faithful de Mailly, to whom he had returned after de Vintimille died in childbirth, and banished her from Versailles. The marquise was created duchesse de Châteauroux. Tutored by her former lover, the dissolute Louis François Armand du Plessis, duc de Richelieu (1696–1788), she dominated the king.

But when the duchess died in December 1744, the post of royal mistress became vacant. Although the masked ball at Versailles on 25 February, 1745 was ostensibly a celebration of the betrothal of the *dauphin* to the Spanish *infanta*, the court believed Louis was using it to look for a mistress. He probably met Jeanne-Antoinette before the ball – the Château d'Étioles was near his hunting lodge at Sénart, and her cousin Gérard Binet was *valet de chambre* to the dauphin – and when she appeared, appropriately, as Diana, goddess of the hunt, Louis was completely smitten. But she was not an aristocrat; she was a bourgeoise.

## JEANNE-ANTOINETTE TRIUMPHS

Traditionally only a member of the aristocracy could become the king's *maîtresse déclarée*. Jeanne-Antoinette, however, would settle for nothing less. Louis ennobled her; he resurrected the marquessate of Pompadour, and the newly created marquise left her one-year-old daughter and her husband for good. She spent the following months diligently studying the unique world of Versailles. When Pompadour was formally presented in September she had armed herself with all the knowledge she needed to survive the French court.

But she was loathed. The dauphin called her 'Madame Whore', courtiers were stunned at the elevation of a bourgeoise and 'the fishes' daughter' (a play on her father's name – Poisson, meaning 'fish') inspired a series of slanderous verses: the *poissonades*. So Pompadour, having conquered the king, set out to conquer Versailles. She relentlessly courted the queen (who eventually tolerated her society, while not exactly enjoying it), the *dauphin* and the rest of the royal family. All eventually capitulated. The court quickly learned that if they wanted favour with Louis, they must flatter his mistress.

## 'MISTRESS OF THE REVELS'

Pompadour had a gruelling regime. As Prince Kaunitz (1711–94), who later became the Austrian ambassador to France, wrote, *'It requires more skill than one might think to feign being madly in love without making oneself ill'*. She was not sexually adventurous and found Louis' appetite exhausting; later she told Madame de Hausset *'He [Louis] thinks me very cold ...'* She feared if the king was bored, she would lose him; so she became his 'mistress of the revels'. Aware of the king's desperate need for a private life, she presided over elegant and intimate suppers. She created the exclusive *Théâtre des Petits Cabinets*, where the king watched his mistress perform in operas, ballets and plays. She ensured that she was the first with salacious court gossip and recruited spies as her informants. She purchased château after château, and the king of France and his mistress patronized the greatest contemporary craftsmen in their pursuit of the perfect home. She dedicated herself to the king's pleasure.

Pompadour's extravagances enraged the French, who called her a 'leech'. But her influence grew. Her friends and relatives were favoured – Voltaire was appointed Gentleman of the Bedchamber and Historiographer of France – and she was now courted at Versailles. Emmanuel, duc de Croÿ (1718–84) said:

> 'It was most agreeable to deal with such a pretty prime minister, whose laughter was enchanting and who was such a good listener … there was perhaps not a single office or favour that had not come from her.'

All the king's business was reviewed by the marquise. The Austrian diplomat Charles Joseph, prince de Ligne (1735–1814) recorded how 'After paying my respects to all the royal family, I was taken to a sort of second queen, who had the air of being the first'.

But in 1751 tragedy struck: she was forced to abandon her sexual relationship with Louis. She may have torn during childbirth, and intercourse became increasingly difficult and painful. Yet she engineered the transition from lover to trusted friend and, amazingly, Louis still loved her and she retained her influence. Even so, the effort of being the most dazzling woman at court was exhausting:

> 'The life I lead is terrible; I hardly have a minute to myself. Rehearsals and performances, and twice a week, continual journeys to the Petit-Château or La Muette, etc. Enormous load of indispensable duties, queen, dauphin, dauphiness, three daughters, two infantas; you can judge whether it is possible to breathe. Be sorry for me.'

## LES LIAISONS DANGEREUSES

The dissolute duc de Richelieu, Pompadour's adversary and the grand-nephew of the great cardinal, was probably the model for the depraved character Valmont in the play *Les Liaisons Dangereuses*, by Pierre Choderlos de Laclos (1741–1803). The vicomte de Valmont and his friend the marquise de Merteuil wantonly destroy a young girl's future and a noblewoman's virtue for a wager. The novel highlighted the debaucheries of Versailles during the closing years of the *ancien régime*.

## THE KING'S BROTHEL

Pompadour dreaded another mistress – her successor – stealing Louis' confidence. Louis was equally concerned not to offend the marquise. But there remained the problem of the king's enormous sexual appetite. The duc de Richelieu may have been the inspiration behind a solution: the notorious Parc aux Cerfs.

With Pompadour's consent, an anonymous, superficially respectable house in the Parc aux Cerfs, a suburb of Versailles, became the king's brothel. Louis' agents procured young virgins, usually from the Parisian working classes, who had not yet menstruated (Louis feared venereal disease), and they were housed for him at No. 4,

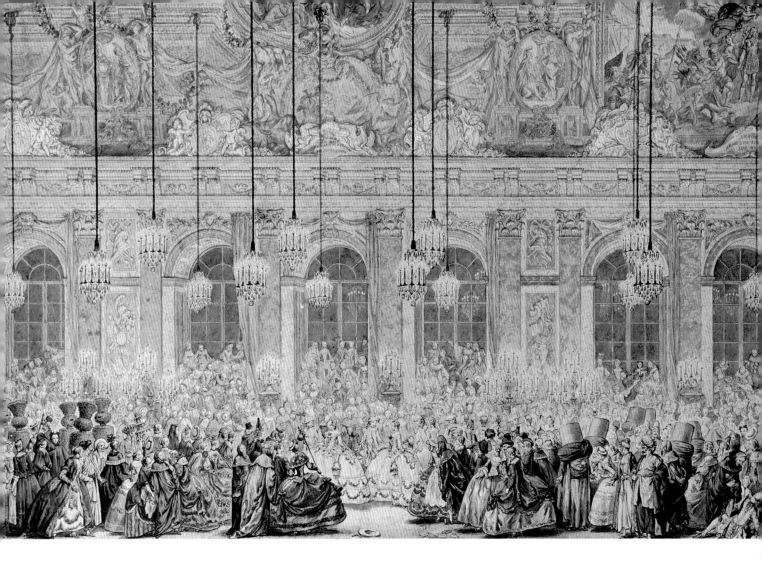

Rue Saint Médéric. The girls were looked after by a Madame Bertrand, and they had servants, teachers and a private box at the theatre. But they had to endure nightly visits from an anonymous Polish count – the king in disguise. He frequented his brothel for 15 years. Parisians saw it as Pompadour's creation, and a contemporary verse claimed:

> *Here lies one for twenty years a virgin,*
> *Eight years a whore,*
> *And ten years a pimp.*

*The magnificent masked ball in the* Galerie des glaces *(Hall of Mirrors) at Versailles in 1745, where Louis was first captivated by Jeanne-Antoinette.*

Pompadour's critics also blamed her for plunging France into the Seven Years' War when Frederick the Great of Prussia (r. 1740–86) insulted her. This war, which involved all the major European powers, was the last major conflict of the *ancien régime*. Pompadour directed operations from her bedroom at Versailles. She was clever, but was no statesman and the war was a disaster for France. The peace treaty of 1763 saw the feeble Louis cede France's vast empire in America, Canada and India. Depression over the punitive settlement may have hastened Pompadour's final illness. Her health had always been poor, and she now contracted pulmonary tuberculosis. She died at Versailles on 15 April, 1764, aged 42.

It was not the king of France who immortalized France's greatest mistress, but her enemy, Frederick the Great. He carved her in stone and placed her next to two other women he loathed: Empress Elizabeth of Russia (r. 1741–61) and Maria Theresa of Austria (r. 1740–80). Together, these three 'furies' hold aloft the dome of his magnificent palace at Potsdam.

# CATHERINE THE GREAT

## *1729 – 96*
## Empress of Russia

*Catherine was not even Russian, yet she became empress of Russia. She flirted with the prevailing fashion – the liberalism of the Enlightenment – before becoming an arch-reactionary. She was famous for her 'night emperors,' the greatest of whom, Grigory Potemkin, founded her an empire in the south. She was a fantasist, but she made her fantasies real. After her death her son tried to destroy her name.*

*Grand Duke Peter (above), who married Princess Sophie, later Catherine (right), in 1745, was a wastrel who played with toy soldiers while his wife schooled herself in statecraft. The portrait of Catherine is by Fyodor Rokotov and shows her in 1770, aged 41.*

Catherine was German by birth, the daughter of Prince Christian August von Anhalt-Zerbst (1690–1747) and his wife Johanna Elizabeth of Holstein-Gottorp (1712–60). She was born in Stettin on 21 April, 1729 and christened Sophie Friederike Auguste. When she was 14, the Russian empress Elizabeth (r. 1741–61) chose her to marry Grand Duke Peter (1728–62), the empress' nephew and heir. Peter, the grandson of Peter the Great of Russia (r. 1682–1725), was the duke of Holstein-Gottorp – and Sophie's cousin – and the empress expected the two young Germans to perpetuate the Romanov line. Princess Sophie left her home accompanied by her mother, but the fiercely religious empress refused to let Sophie's Protestant father onto Russian soil. She never saw him again.

At the empress' behest the young princess converted to Russian Orthodoxy and changed her name to Ekaterina (Catherine) Alekseyevna. She and the grand duke were married at the Church of Our Lady of Kazan in Peter the Great's splendid city of St Petersburg on 21 August, 1745. The marriage was a disaster. Peter, who had been abused as a child by his sadistic father, was probably mad. Although he boasted of his sexual conquests, Catherine claimed in her memoirs that the marriage was never consummated.

### THE LONELY DUCHESS

Peter remained stubbornly attached to Germany. Unlike the clever and adaptable Catherine, he never saw himself as Russian, loathed his adopted country and alienated the fiercely anti-Prussian court as he continued to worship his homeland. Lacking any proper married life with her husband, Catherine was in a precarious position. The empress, desperate for an heir, facilitated her first affair.

Catherine said of herself: *'I was never beautiful, but I pleased. That was my long suit.'* She was energetic, vivacious, flirtatious and very attractive to men. Her detractors have accused her of unsavoury sexual practices, even of intercourse with animals – a spurious story exists of Catherine meeting her death while having a horse lowered on top of her.

Catherine enjoyed sex and had youthful lovers into her old age, but was not a sexual degenerate. She probably had 12 lovers, the first of whom was a Russian nobleman and courtier, Serge Saltykov (c.1726–65). Catherine had a miscarriage before giving birth to a son, Paul Petrovich, on 20 September, 1754. The child was almost certainly her lover's.

On Christmas Day 1761 the empress Elizabeth died. Her unstable and unpopular nephew was proclaimed Tsar Peter III. Catherine publicly mourned Elizabeth, while Peter behaved wholly inappropriately. According to Catherine, on the day of the funeral:

> *'the emperor was very gay … and during the sad ceremony invented a game for himself; he loitered behind the hearse, on purpose, allowing it to proceed at a distance of thirty feet, then he would run to catch up with it … The elder courtiers, who were carrying his black train, found themselves unable to keep up with him … '*

At the time Catherine was already six months pregnant with the child of her lover Grigory Orlov (1734–83).

## USURPERS AND ASSASSINS

A plot to usurp the throne from Peter was probably afoot before Elizabeth's death. Catherine feared that Peter, fascinated with his mistress, would repudiate her – he had threatened to do so in public. Orlov, an army lieutenant, could deliver her the military support she needed for a successful coup. Members of the nobility pledged to back her, but Catherine wisely delayed. She wanted to be safely delivered of her baby. Meanwhile Peter continued to alienate everyone. He concluded an unpopular and unnecessary peace with his hero, Frederick II ('the Great') of Prussia (r. 1740–86) and engaged in a pointless war with Denmark. His actions consistently served German rather than Russian interests.

Catherine gave birth to a boy, Alexei Grigoryevich Bobrinsky, on 10 April, 1762. Now she was free to act. Orlov and his brother placed military forces at her disposal and she took power with mass popular support on 28 June, 1762. She was crowned in Moscow three months later. At the age of 33 this minor German princess was empress of Russia and the most powerful woman in the world.

Catherine was a friend and patron of the Enlightenment philosophers Voltaire (1694–1778) and Denis Diderot (1713–84), and her admiration of reformist principles earned her support from the aristocracy when she first took power. But after assuming power she found the reality very different. To apply Enlightenment philosophy to a mass, unruly society in which wealth was measured by the number of 'souls' – serfs or enslaved peasants – a man possessed, was, she believed, impossible. With seemingly little regret, she became one of the most reactionary rulers in Russian history.

*Portrait of Count Grigory Orlov (c.1765) by Andrei Ibvanovitch Cherny. Orlov was a lieutenant in the Izmailovsky Guards. He helped Catherine depose her unpopular husband and was implicated in his murder. It is not known whether Catherine was complicit.*

In 1772 Catherine, acting against her liberal pretensions, carved up Poland. She had installed her former lover, Count Stanislas Poniatowski (1732–98), on the Polish throne in 1764, but Poniatowski was as weak as the throne he occupied and unable to defend himself against the aggression of Maria Theresa of Austria (r. 1740–80). When the Austrians marched into Poland in 1771, Frederick the Great of Prussia negotiated a settlement – all three powers, rather than go to war, would take their share of Polish territory.

## THE PUGACHEV REBELLION

Despite her audacious behaviour she remained the heroine of the Enlightenment philosophers. But the Pugachev Rebellion of 1773 finally destroyed her liberal reputation. Since her husband's murder a rash of impostors had presented themselves as the dead tsar. Now the Cossack Emelyan Pugachev (1740/2–75) attracted a formidable following just as Catherine, distracted by the war with Turkey which she had instigated in 1768, was unable to mobilize troops to quell a rebellion.

*Catherine's lover Grigory Potemkin. She wrote to him, 'there is not a cell in my whole body that does not yearn for you, oh infidel! ... My head is like that of a cat in heat ...'*

Pugachev's manifesto promised freedom. His peasant army rampaged through eastern Russia and finally stood only 120 miles (190 km) from Moscow. In 1774, when Catherine finally had the necessary troops at her disposal, the revolt was swiftly and bloodily suppressed. Noblemen pursued their own vendettas and murdered any serf even suspected of having Pugachev sympathies; Pugachev himself was executed.

Catherine wrote to an apoplectic Voltaire: *'He [Pugachev] was an extremely bold and determined man. If he had offended only myself, I should pardon him, but this cause is the empire's and that has its own laws. No one since Tamerlane had done more harm ...'*

Diderot, too, was appalled at her brutal suppression. Catherine recorded:
> *'If I followed his advice I would have had to turn everything in my empire upside down. I would have had to do away with what existed and substitute castles in the air ... Then I told him frankly: "I have listened with great pleasure to everything you have told me, with admiration for your brilliant mind. In your plans for reform, you forget the difference in our situations. You philosophers are fortunate: you write only on paper, which is smooth, obedient to your commands and does*

*not raise any obstacles to your imagination – while I, poor empress, have to write on the ticklish and easily irritated skins of human beings.'*'

## A PASSIONATE AFFAIR

In 1774 Catherine began an affair with one of the most mercurial characters in Russian history, Grigory Potemkin (1739–91). Potemkin first saw Catherine on the night she took power, when he was 22 and an officer in the Guards. She called him her 'twin soul' and wrote excitedly to a friend that Potemkin was, *'... one of the greatest, most amusing and original personalities of this iron age'*. Senator Ivan Yelagin commented, *'She is crazy about him. They may well be in love because they are exactly the same.'* Both were visionaries, clever, warm, fun, passionate and theatrical and they had a huge appetite for life. They had a love of creating castles in the air – and then moving in.

> ## A SON'S TREACHERY
>
> Catherine and her son Paul Petrovich, the future emperor of Russia (r. 1796–1801), hated each other, and after her death Paul attempted to obliterate her name from the annals of Russian history. He buried her as a consort, not an independent empress. He exhumed Tsar Peter's bones, reassembled the skeleton, dressed it in military uniform and placed it on public display at the Winter Palace, where the nobility were ordered to pay homage to the dead tsar. Then he buried the corpses together with the epitaph, *'Divided in life, joined in death'*.

Their affair only lasted for two years before they pursued even greater dreams – of an expanded Russian empire. Potemkin delivered Catherine the Crimea, and a grateful empress made him prince of Tauris (the ancient name of the peninsula). They may even have married – Catherine addressed him as 'husband' for the rest of his life. But although Catherine, with Potemkin's blessing, moved on to her younger and more athletic favourites – the so-called 'night emperors' – and Potemkin, far away in the Crimea pursued affairs of his own with his nieces, he remained the dominant force at Catherine's court until his death.

In common with her brother and sister monarchs in Europe, Catherine watched the ravaging of the *ancien régime* in France with mounting horror. Her reaction to the French Revolution of 1789 was to conduct even greater oppression within her own empire. When Poland sought a liberal constitution, Russian troops moved in and Poland was finally obliterated in 1795 as Russia, Prussia and Austria annexed its remaining territory. It would not reappear on the map until the end of the First World War in 1918.

When Potemkin died in 1791 Catherine, prostrate with grief, wrote her own obituary. She outlived her lover by five years, dying in 1796 at the age of 67.

*'I beg you no longer to call me, nor to give me any more the sobriquet of Catherine the Great, because, primo, I do not like any sobriquet, secondo, my name is Catherine II, and tertio, I do not want anyone to say of me ... that they find me badly named; fourthly, in size I am neither great nor small.'*

CATHERINE II OF RUSSIA TO HER CORRESPONDENT, FRIEDRICH MELCHIOR GRIMM

# MARIE ANTOINETTE
## *1755 – 93*
## Queen consort of King Louis XVI of France

*Marie Antoinette, last queen of the* ancien régime, *was really quite ordinary. She was an Austrian archduchess, married at 14 to the* dauphin *of France. Bored, listless and neglected by her husband, she gambled, shopped and decorated. It was only later, as a hunted queen, that she was made extraordinary by the events of the French Revolution of 1789.*

Marie Antoinette was born on 2 November, 1755, the 15th and penultimate child of Archduchess Maria Theresa (1717–80) of Austria, and the Holy Roman Emperor Francis I (r. 1745–65). She was frivolous, vacuous and pretty (although purists condemned her 'Habsburg chin') and her education was abysmally poor. She was destined to be a pawn in her ambitious mother's game, and what education Antoine did receive subjugated her to her mother's will. Maria Theresa said of her children, *'They are born to obey ...'* and she zealously pursued the family motto to weave her descendants into all the courts of Europe: *'Others have to wage war but you, fortunate Habsburg, marry!'*

### AN UNPOPULAR ALLIANCE
Maria Theresa needed a daughter to cement an alliance with France. A match between the Austrian archduchess and the French *dauphin* was unusual: Austria and France were traditional enemies and the alliance was unpopular in France. But Maria Theresa expected her naïve daughter to influence French policy and, despite her ineptitude at espionage, Antoine would be known throughout her life in France as *l'autrichienne* ('the Austrian'). She would marry the grandson of King Louis XV (r. 1715–74), the *dauphin* Louis Auguste (1754–92) – and she would be reviled.

Antoine and Louis were betrothed in June 1769 and a proxy wedding took place in Vienna the following year. Her brother the archduke Ferdinand (1754–1806) stood in for the bridegroom in a magnificent evening ceremony. Although she had not yet met her husband, the 14-year-old archduchess was styled Madame la Dauphine. She set off, obedient but sobbing, for the French border. From her relatively simple upbringing Marie Antoinette (she adopted the French version of her name) entered the social labyrinth of Versailles. She had only Count Mercy d'Argenteau (1734–1819), the elderly Austrian ambassador, to help traverse the maze. From the first she was the most important woman

*Marie Antoinette was christened Maria Antonia Josepha Joanna, but her family called her Antoine. When two of her older sisters died, she became the focus for her mother's political ambitions. This 1783 portrait is by the French painter Elisabeth Vigée-Le Brun.*

'*If one is to consider only the greatness of your position, you are the happiest of your sisters and of all princesses.*'

THE EMPRESS MARIA THERESA TO HER DAUGHTER MARIE ANTOINETTE ON HER MARRIAGE TO THE FRENCH DAUPHIN

at court – Louis XV's queen and the dauphin's mother were both dead – and every aspect of her life was exposed to scrutiny. The courtiers who thronged the palace of the 'Sun King' Louis XIV at Versailles were entitled to watch the *dauphine* get up (her *levée*), go to bed (her *coucher*) and eat (the *grand couvert*). She told her mother, *'I put on my rouge and wash my hands in front of the whole world'.*

Marie Antoinette and the dauphin were incompatible. But compatibility between princes and princesses was irrelevant; the only reason to marry was to produce an heir. However, the young *dauphin* and *dauphine* were unable to consummate the match. They suffered the humiliation of being put to bed together publicly – then nothing happened. Maria Theresa blamed her daughter. She sent frantic letters on how to please a husband and despaired at each monthly report of Marie Antoinette's menstruation. *'Everything depends on the wife,'* she told the dauphine, *'if she is willing, sweet and amusante.'* While the marriage remained unconsummated Marie Antoinette feared repudiation and the destruction of the fragile Franco-Austrian alliance.

*Marie Antoinette married Louis XVI (above) by proxy when she was 14 years old. They were not compatible, however; he was fat, pious, studious and liked to hunt, whereas she could barely sign her name on the marriage contract and liked diamonds and parties.*

## THE PURSUIT OF PLEASURE

Lacking any married life, she turned to her favourites for comfort. She sang, hunted and played billiards and cards. She visited Paris for the first time in the summer of 1773 where she was fêted. She wrote rapturously to her mother, *'How fortunate we are, given our rank, to have gained the love of a whole people with such ease'.* Now she frequented the Parisian opera, theatres and balls. Her happiness was complete when she believed, erroneously, that her marriage had been consummated. Again she wrote to Maria Theresa: *'I think I can confide to you, my dear Mama, and only to you, that my affaires have taken a very good turn … and that I consider my marriage to be consummated; even if not to the degree that I am pregnant …'* But she was wrong. She remained in danger.

On 10 May, 1774 Louis XV died of smallpox. The young *dauphin* and *dauphine* became king and queen of France and they were, at first, immensely popular. The dissolute and lazy Louis XV had ruled France since he was five years old. Now it was generally hoped that his grandson, now Louis XVI (r. 1774–92), would rejuvenate France's fortunes.

Louis inherited a France bankrupted by the disastrous Seven Years' War, yet plunged the country further into debt with his support of the American Revolution. The harvest failed in 1774 and the price of bread soared. Yet the royal family continued to spend money, with Marie Antoinette's expenditure the most visible. The queen was impetuously generous and she lived beyond her vast income. To satisfy Marie Antoinette's quest for a simple, rustic idyll, Louis gave her the Petit Trianon, a small but lavish palace at Versailles.

*The* Petit hameau *(right) was the rustic-style retreat built for Marie Antoinette in a section of the Petit Trianon. Inside, however, the rooms incorporated all the luxury and comfort to which the queen and her ladies were accustomed.*

Despite the hopes of Marie Antoinette's Austrian family, Louis never let the queen influence him in favour of her homeland. Her few attempts were clumsy and, although her detractors claimed she was an Austrian spy, she never achieved anything in that direction.

Prince Kaunitz (1711–94), the Austrian foreign minister, realized the queen had absolutely no political influence: '... *let us count on her for nothing, and let us just be content ... with anything we can get out of her ...*'.

## A CURE FOR LOUIS' IMPOTENCE

In the spring of 1777 her brother, Emperor Joseph II (r. 1765–90), arrived incognito at the French court, determined to save his sister's marriage. Joseph concluded that the pair were 'two complete blunderers'. He wrote to his brother, Archduke Leopold (1747–92):

> '*Imagine, in his marriage bed – this is the secret – he has strong, perfectly satisfactory erections; he introduces the member, stays there without moving for about two minutes, withdraws without ejaculating but still erect, and bids goodnight. It's incredible because he sometimes has night-time emissions; it is only when he is actually inside and going at it, that it never happens. Nevertheless, the king is satisfied with what he does ... Oh, if only I could have been there! The king of France would have been whipped so that he would have ejaculated out of sheer rage like a donkey.*'

Joseph's mission was a success – on 30 August 'the great work', as Louis called the consummation, was finally achieved. The following December Marie Antoinette gave birth to a daughter, Marie-Thérèse-Charlotte (1778–1851), or Madame Royale. She lovingly told her daughter, '*A son would have been the property of the state. You shall be mine; you shall have my undivided care; you will share all my happinesses and you will alleviate my sufferings ...*'

On 22 October, 1781 Marie Antoinette gave birth to a boy, Louis Joseph (1781–9). The king delightedly told her on her delivery bed: '*Madame, you have fulfilled our wishes and those of France, you are the mother of a* dauphin.' Marie Antoinette revelled in motherhood and appointed her closest friend,

*This 1872 painting by the Hungarian Gyula Benczur shows Marie Antoinette and Louis XVI with their children at Versailles on 6 October, 1789, as the flames of revolution engulfed France.*

Yolande de Polignac (1749–93), 'Governess to the Children of France'. Her third child, Louis Charles (1785–95), was born in March 1785.

But the popularity Marie Antoinette had enjoyed as a young dauphine and queen was fading. As the economy foundered *l'autrichienne* became the scapegoat for the ills of France. She was accused of lesbianism, of cuckolding Louis with the Swedish nobleman Count Axel Fersen (1755–1810), of incest with her brother-in-law the comte d'Artois and of extravagance. As the apathetic Louis had been unable to solve France's financial problems, his wife was vilified as a grasping, frivolous whore.

### THE REVOLUTION APPROACHES

Contrary to popular opinion, Marie Antoinette struggled to relieve France of its financial desperation. In August 1788 she suggested the capable Jacques Necker (1732–1804), whom she disliked, as controller of finance. But it was too little, too late. The cruel winter of 1788 forced the price of bread even higher and in the spring of 1789 there were riots in Paris. On 4 May the Estates General met at Versailles and once again Marie Antoinette retreated into the political shadows. She was hated all over France. Her spending, the popular press maintained, had single-handedly reduced France to penury. Tragedy struck the royal family with the death of the *dauphin* Louis Joseph in June, but there was little public sympathy. The country plummeted towards revolution. On 14 July the Bastille was stormed. The duc de Liancourt (1747–1827) brought the news to his king. *'Is it a revolt?'* asked Louis. *'No Sire'*, replied the duke, *'It is a revolution'*.

On 6 October a mob marched on Versailles and forced the royal family to Paris and the ramshackle Tuileries palace. They would never see Versailles again. Overnight Marie Antoinette morphed from a pampered, frivolous queen into a hardworking and loyal wife and mother. The king, possibly depressed, failed to grasp the danger. But Marie Antoinette understood from the beginning. She told Madame Campan, First Lady of the Bedchamber, *'Kings who become prisoners are not far from death'*.

The freedoms of the royal family were gradually curtailed, particularly after a failed escape. The queen desperately lobbied Austria to save her family. But Austria did nothing. Marie Antoinette's brother, Emperor Joseph, was dead, his successor Leopold II (r. 1790–2) was not fond of his sister and when Leopold's son took power in 1792 as Francis II (r. 1792–1806), Marie Antoinette's cause was lost – he had never even met his aunt.

## SENTENCED TO DEATH

In April 1792 Louis, now a constitutional monarch, was forced to declare war on Austria. Later that year a mob stormed the Tuileries and the royal family sought sanctuary with the National Assembly. They were imprisoned in the Tower of the Temple to await their fate. The fanatically anti-royalist Commune stripped Louis of his remaining powers and declared him a private citizen: 'Louis Capet'. In January 1793 he was sentenced to death. One of his last thoughts was for Marie Antoinette: *'Unfortunate Princess! My marriage promised her a throne; now, what prospect does it offer her?'* He had finally come to love her and to admire her courage and determination. Louis was executed on Monday 21 January.

Now, if Austria had been inclined, Marie Antoinette could have been saved. An exchange of prisoners was mooted. But Austria did not intervene in French internal affairs – the queen was after all a diplomatic failure – and her situation worsened. The eight-year-old *dauphin*, Louis Charles, was taken from her care; his jailors and tormentors forced him to accuse his mother of sexual abuse. Devastated, she hardly cared when she was moved, alone, to Paris's ancient prison, the Conciergerie.

Her trumped-up trial began on 14 October; the verdict was decided before the trial even began. Marie Antoinette, the foreigner, paid the price for France's economic devastation, for Louis XIV's removal of the monarchy to Versailles and for Louis XV's ineptitude. By the end Marie Antoinette looked like an old woman, but she remained dignified and refuted all of the ridiculous charges – of lesbianism, of drunken orgies and of sexual abuse. She was condemned to death by guillotine. She travelled to her execution dressed in white in an open cart, her head shorn and her hands bound. She was executed on 16 October, 1793.

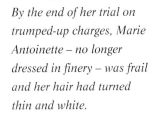

*By the end of her trial on trumped-up charges, Marie Antoinette – no longer dressed in finery – was frail and her hair had turned thin and white.*

### 'LET THEM EAT CAKE ...'

Marie Antoinette's biographer, Antonia Fraser, argues that it is extremely unlikely that she ever uttered this notorious phrase. She was frivolous and a spendthrift, but Marie Antoinette was not cruel. Her philanthropy shows how deeply she cared for the plight of the poor. By the end of the 19th century, the phrase had been attributed to various French queens and princesses for over 100 years, firstly to Louis XIV's queen, the Spanish Marie-Thérèse (1638–83), and then to two of Mesdames Tantes (Louis XVI's aunts), Victoire (1733–99) and Sophie (1734–82). In his memoirs, Marie Antoinette's brother-in-law, the comte de Provence – the future Louis XVIII (r. 1814–24) – attributed the phrase to his ancestress Marie-Thérèse.

# VICTORIA

## *1819—1901*
## Queen of the United Kingdom and Empress of India

*Victoria is Britain's longest-serving monarch to date. She was just 18 when she ascended the throne, and during her 64-year reign she presided over momentous changes in British society. The Victorian age witnessed rapid expansion of the country's industrial, economic and imperial might. At her death, Britain held sway over huge expanses of the world. But for all this, Victoria was a mere figurehead: her reign laid the foundations of the modern constitutional monarchy, a system in which the sovereign is consulted and advised by his or her ministers but is devoid of any real power.*

Prince Edward, duke of Kent (1767–1820) always believed his baby daughter Victoria would inherit the throne. '*Look at her well*', he told his friends, '*for she will be queen of England*'. Alexandrina ('Drina') Victoria was born at Kensington Palace on 24 May, 1819, the only child of Edward, the fourth son of George III (r. 1760–1820) and Victoire of Saxe-Coburg-Saalfeld (1786–1861), the widowed dowager princess of Leiningen. Her birth was the result of a race to the throne after Princess Charlotte (1796–1817), the daughter of the prince of Wales (later George IV; r. 1820–30) died in childbirth in 1817. George III had no other legitimate grandchildren, and so the dukes of Kent, Clarence and Cumberland all abandoned their mistresses to marry German princesses in their attempts to produce an heir.

### AN ISOLATED CHILDHOOD

When Victoria was eight months old, her 51-year-old father died of pneumonia – both her father and husband were to die as a result of poor nursing. She was left third in line to the throne and in the care of her possessive mother, who kept Victoria isolated from the royal family, fearing any influence beyond her own. Physically, Victoria resembled her grandfather George III: she was tiny, prone to plumpness, and had prominent blue eyes. She grew up at Kensington Palace, where she was solidly, but not well, educated by her governess Louise (later Baroness) Lehzen (1784–1870) and her tutor, Reverend George Davys. Her

*The young Queen Victoria, painted by the German artist Franz Xaver Winterhalter in 1842, when she had been on the throne for just five years. In the course of her reign, Britain became the greatest colonial power of the age. She was said to have commanded an empire 'on which the sun never set'.*

only companions were her half-sister Feodore (1807–72) by her mother's first marriage and her King Charles spaniel, 'Dash'. Her mentor was Leopold, later king of the Belgians (r. 1831–65), Victoire's brother and the widower of Princess Charlotte.

When Victoria was 11 George IV died. Her uncle William (the artless 'Sailor William') became William IV (r. 1830–7) and she became heiress presumptive to the throne. (William had ten illegitimate children by the actress Dorothy Jordan, but no legitimate heir.) A story tells of Victoria only learning of her closeness to the throne by reading a book, but this may be apocryphal; in response she allegedly told Lehzen: *I will try to be good*. The king was enraged by the duchess of Kent's rudeness to his wife Queen Adelaide (1792–1849), and he resented her possessiveness of Victoria. When Victoria was 17 he publicly humiliated her mother at his birthday dinner in August 1836, saying:

> *'I trust God that my life may be spared for nine months longer … I should then have the satisfaction of leaving the royal authority to the personal exercise of that young lady [Victoria] … and not in the hands of a person now near me.'*

His wish was granted. On 20 June, 1837, less than a month after Victoria's 18th birthday, William died and she ascended the throne. (The duchess had tried to put off her daughter's majority until her 21st birthday but was thwarted.) Victoria moved from Kensington to Buckingham Palace and sent her mother to far-off apartments, although Lezhen lived in the next room until Victoria was married.

She adored her Whig prime minister Lord Melbourne (1779–1848) – fatherless Victoria always looked to strong men to mentor her. This led to unwise partisanship in party politics in the early years of her reign during the 'Bedchamber Crisis', when she refused to admit Conservative ladies to the inner court. She loved her new-found independence and power, but had not learned yet to wield it: as her first cousin, Prince Albert (1819–61), whom she later married, wrote:

> *'Victoria … is said to be incredibly stubborn and her extreme obstinacy to be constantly at war with her good nature; she delights in court ceremonies, etiquette and trivial formalities … she is said not to take the slightest pleasure in nature and to enjoy sitting up at night and sleeping late into the day.'*

## A LIFELONG LOVE AFFAIR

In February 1840, aged 20, she wed the studious Prince Albert of Saxe-Coburg-Gotha, at the urging of her beloved Uncle Leopold (who was also Albert's uncle). As a reigning

*Prince Albert, Victoria's adored husband and consort. Their marriage lasted 21 years before he died of typhoid fever. Victoria was shattered at the prince consort's untimely death.*

monarch, Victoria had to propose; she confided to her diary, '*Albert ... is ... so extremely handsome ... a beautiful figure, broad in the shoulders and a fine waist; my heart is quite going*'. She tried to make him king consort, but was rebuffed by Melbourne, who told her, '*if you get the British people into the way of making kings, you will get them into the way of unmaking them*'. Nevertheless, Albert was the dominant partner in their marriage and Victoria happily submitted to him; he even chose her clothes. She wrote, '*I am every day convinced that we women, if we are to be good women ... are not fitted to reign*'. Albert pensioned off Lehzen and encouraged Melbourne to retreat; but he convinced Victoria to forgive the duchess of Kent, and mother and daughter were reconciled.

Albert undertook most of the work, going through Victoria's government boxes, drafting memos and advising ministers on her behalf; he also organized the Great Exhibition of 1851, which showcased Britain's growing empire. In 1845 Charles Greville (1794–1865), the clerk to the Privy Council, reported, '*the prince is become so identified with the queen, that they are one person ... it is obvious that while she has the title, he is really discharging the functions of the sovereign. He is the king to all intents and purposes*'.

She was passionate about him: '*... he does look beautiful in his shirt only*', she wrote. She did not like child-bearing, however, calling it the '*shadow-side of marriage*', and shocked her physician by asking him if there was any way to have sex without procreating. Even so, Victoria and Albert would have five daughters and four sons. Her children – who

*A postcard commemorating the Great Exhibition of 1851, organized by Prince Albert. The Crystal Palace, designed by the architect Joseph Paxton (1803–65) was built specifically for the event.*

all survived infancy, a rare feat for the age – were married into the royal families of Europe. In the later years of her reign it was said that most of European royalty addressed the queen of England as 'Grandmama'. But Victoria neither liked babies nor having them. She wrote to her eldest daughter Vicky (1840–1901) in 1858:

> 'What you say of the pride of giving life to an immortal soul is very fine, dear, but I own I cannot enter into that; I think much more of our being like a cow or a dog at such moments.'

In December 1861, 21 years into their marriage, Prince Albert contracted typhoid fever. It was misdiagnosed and the prince consort died on 14 December. Victoria was devastated and never fully recovered. *'Those paroxysms of despair and yearning and longing and of daily, nightly longing to die ... for the first three years never left me'*, she said. She never forgave her eldest son Edward, 'Bertie', prince of Wales (1841–1910), believing he contributed to his father's final illness. (Albert had travelled to Cambridge to rebuke Bertie for his affair with an actress and they had afterwards walked in the cold.) *'It quite irritates me to see him in the room'*, she said of her son.

## THE 'WIDOW OF WINDSOR'

Victoria spent the next decade in seclusion at the houses Albert had built for her at Osborne on the Isle of Wight and at Balmoral in Scotland, and dressed in mourning for the rest of her life. She built monuments to Albert at Buckingham Palace and on the site of the Royal Exhibition in Kensington. She would rule for 40 years without him, but in all her decisions she tried to imagine what the 'dear one' would have approved. Nevertheless, the retreat from public life (Victoria became known as 'the Widow of Windsor') damaged her popularity and boosted the early republican movement.

In the 1870s she returned to public life, at the urging of two men: her beloved servant John Brown (1826–83) and her favourite prime minister, the Conservative Benjamin Disraeli (1804–81). Disraeli flattered her and flirted with her; he was the only prime minister invited to sit down in her presence and he was able to persuade her to fulfil the

### 'MRS BROWN'

After Albert's death, Victoria became close to her outdoor servant, the Scotsman John Brown (1826–83). He had been a favourite of Albert, and Victoria, fond as she was of strong men, responded to his brusque candour. Her family, on the other hand, were shocked by the way he spoke to her. She described him in letters as *'my dearest best friend ... the most devoted, faithful, intelligent and confidential servant ...'*. Their intimacy was the subject of much unkind gossip in the 1860s. *Punch* wrote a spoof court circular: *'Mr John Brown ... partook of a haggis ... Mr John Brown was pleased to listen to the bagpipe'*, while the queen was nicknamed 'Mrs Brown'. When he died, she was so distraught she temporarily lost the use of her legs, as she had when Albert died.

*John Brown was Victoria's valued personal servant for many years, serving her and providing companionship in his informal manner, which was appreciated by the queen and resented by her family.*

*Victoria surrounded by her children and grandchildren from across Europe, including the German Kaiser, Wilhelm II (seated to the left of the queen). This photogrpah was taken in 1894.*

monarchical duties she had neglected whilst in mourning for Albert. She approved of the grandiose imperialist policy that Disraeli pursued. When Britain was moving towards war with Russia she wrote to him, '*Oh, if the queen were a man, she would like to go and give those horrid Russians ... such a beating*'. He secured her nearly half the Suez Canal and in 1876 he delivered the ultimate prize by passing the Royal Titles Act that made Victoria empress of India. As he lay dying, he was asked if he would like to see her. '*Better not*', he replied, '*she will only ask me to take a message to Albert*'.

Victoria died at Osborne on the evening of 22 January, 1901, with her family, including Bertie (soon to be Edward VII; r. 1901–10) and her grandson Kaiser Wilhelm of Germany (r. 1888–1918), by her side. She was buried in the Frogmore Mausoleum she had built for Albert in Windsor Great Park, with her widow's cap and her wedding veil. She had reigned for almost 64 years.

'*I have always felt that when I knew what the queen thought, you knew pretty certainly what views her subjects would take, and especially the middle classes ...*'

BRITISH PRIME MINISTER LORD SALISBURY

# LAKSHMI BAI
## c.1830–58
## Rani (Queen) of Jhansi

*Nearly 200 years after the death of the Mughal empress Nur Jahan, a new breed of woman arose in India. Unlike her predecessor, Lakshmi Bai, rani of Jhansi, did not use guile to stay in power. She fought her adversary, the British, on the battlefield. This rani battled for the hereditary rights of her son in the horrific bloodbath of 1857 – the Indian War of Independence, known to contemporaries as the Indian Mutiny.*

Lakshmi was born into a high-caste Brahmin family around 1830 and given the name Manukarnika. She grew up in the royal palace at Benares (Varanasi), where her father was political advisor to the brother of the last *peshwa* of Bithur. When she was 12 years old, she married Gangadhar Rao (r. 1838–53), maharajah of Jhansi. The maharajah was much older than her, reputedly liked to dress in women's clothes, was rumoured to be homosexual and sponsored theatre productions where he took the starring – and often female – role. Manukarnika adopted the name Lakshmi – the name of the goddess of luck, light and wisdom – and became the country's rani.

Jhansi, a small principality in northern India, owed its peace and prosperity to its friendly relations with the ruling British. Lakshmi was the maharajah's second wife and she and her husband presided over an uneventful court for 11 years. Then, in 1853, Gangadhar Rao became ill. Desperate to continue his line, he adopted his young cousin, Damodar Rao (r. 1853–60), and wrote his will, leaving his kingdom to the five-year-old boy and entrusting his rani with the regency. (Lakshmi was childless, although she may have given birth to a son who died young.) Gangadhar's will read:

> *'Should I not survive, I trust that in consideration of the fidelity I have evinced towards the British government, favour may be shown to this child and that my widow during her lifetime may be considered the Regent of the State and mother of this child, and that she may not be molested in any way.'*

The local political agent looked favourably on the maharajah's request. But when he died in November the governor general rejected the will. He refused to recognize the maharajah's adopted heir or Lakshmi's right to be regent, and annexed the principality.

### HUMILIATION AT THE HANDS OF THE BRITISH
Lakshmi desperately appealed against the decision but was rebuffed. Furious, she cried: *'I shall never surrender my Jhansi.'* After a self-imposed hunger strike she rallied, and

*Lakshmi Bai went into battle against the British wearing a magnificent pearl necklace and wielding a sword. This portrait, by an unknown artist of the Calcutta School, was painted in around 1890.*

petitioned London. The humiliating response was the confiscation of the state jewels, a pension of 5000 rupees a month (out of which she had to pay her late husband's debts), and permission to remain in the palace. There was nothing more she could do. She and her son languished in the palace for the next three years. The once-thriving Jhansi was abandoned as the British soldiers were ordered away and its merchants left.

But the rani, pragmatically, remained on friendly terms with the British. In the summer of 1857, news of a rebel insurgence at Meerut reached her. Fearful that it would threaten her own position, she begged the British to provide her with a bodyguard. On 4 June the revolution reached Jhansi, when some of her own garrison mutinied. After murdering the British soldiers, they went after the civilian British and Eurasian population.

There were only between 40 and 60 non-Indians in Jhansi, many of them women and children. They barricaded themselves in the inferior City Fort, together with a few of the British military who had survived, while the heavily armed mutineers occupied the Star

*Sepoys (Indian soldiers in the British Indian army) slaughter British residents of the garrison town of Cawnpore in June 1857 during the Indian Mutiny.*

Fort. The British, now finally acknowledging Lakshmi's leadership of her own kingdom, asked her for her help until they could send reinforcements. But with no troops and anti-British feeling at its height, there was little she could do.

## MASSACRE AND ITS AFTERMATH

On 8 June the mutineers attacked the City Fort. The local political agent's representative recorded the horror that followed:

*'Early upon the morning … the mutineers surrounded the fort … when Captain Gordon [Deputy Superintendent of Jhansi], after making a most gallant resistance, finding the place was no longer defensible and preferring death to surrender, shot himself through the head … The mutineers then made prisoner all the European officers with their wives and children … took them … outside the city walls … and there brutally murdered every soul of them … The next day the mutineers left Jhansi, taking along with them the treasure and magazine [ammunition].'*

The rani, who played no part in the appalling massacre, tried to prove her innocence; while it suited the British, they believed her. For now, as they slowly put down the rebel uprisings, they needed her to keep order. She was allowed to form a government and was at last recognized as the queen of a magnificent court. For a few months she could relax – she rode daily, went shooting (she was an excellent shot), read, and re-opened the theatre. By now in her late twenties or early thirties, Lakshmi was very attractive, with a magnificent figure and clothes designed to show it off. A British visitor reported that, *'The eyes were particularly fine and the nose very delicately shaped. She was not very fair, though she was far from black [and had] a remarkably fine figure … '.*

By the end of the year, however, it was clear to Lakshmi that the British would not let her retain control of Jhansi. Dubbing her 'the Jezebel of India,' they now blamed her for the massacre and ordered her to step down. This drove her into the arms of the growing rebel movement whose aim was the expulsion of the British from India. Lakshmi mustered an army of 14,000 troops, including

## REBEL TURNED NOMAD

Nana Sahib, the rani's fellow rebel, is celebrated throughout India. He was the adopted son of the last peshwa of Bithur and was driven to rebellion after his father's death by the British refusal to grant him his pension. The British accused him of perpetrating the massacre at Cawnpore (Kanpur), which was similar to the massacre at Jhansi, in June 1857. After the rebel defeat, Nana Sahib was driven to a nomadic existence – it is not known when or where he died. His reputation spread to Europe, when he was immortalized by Jules Verne (1828–1905) – Nana's championing of oppressed peoples inspired one of Verne's most famous characters, Captain Nemo in *Twenty Thousand Leagues Under the Sea.*

women, to confront a British force under the leadership of Major-General Sir Hugh Rose, which arrived at Jhansi on 21 March, 1858 . The general had allowed rebels to escape at Rahatgarh and Garhakota, and was determined not to repeat his mistake. For ten days, British cannon fire turned the night sky red as the rani's standard stood defiant above the fort. Tatya Tope, a fellow rebel leader, attempted to relieve her with 20,000 men, but the British fended him off and continued their assault. On 3 April Jhansi fell. The British looted, and murdered everyone over the age of 16. An Indian eyewitness recorded that *'In the squares of the city ... hundreds of corpses* [were collected] *in large heaps and covered with wood, floorboards and anything that came handy and set on fire. Now every square blazed with burning bodies and the city looked like one vast burning ground ...'*. Five thousand Indians were slaughtered in retribution for the 60 or so Europeans who had been killed.

Nevertheless, the British troops admired the warrior Rani. They marvelled at her ability to ride like a man, calling her *'a perfect Amazon in bravery ... just the sort of daredevil woman soldiers admire'* and *'... a wonderful woman, very brave and determined. It is fortunate for us that men are not all like her'*. When she fled the city to join Tatya Tope in Kalpi, they set off in determined pursuit.

## REBELS GAIN GROUND

The British caught up with Lakshmi on 6 May at Kunch. Cleverly, Tatya Tope had led the exhausted British troops on as far as possible before engaging them in battle. Although the rebel army was defeated, the British, dying of heatstroke, were unable to press home their advantage. On 22 May the British rallied and defeated the mutineers again at Kulpi, one of India's most impregnable forts. Then, however, came an unexpected victory for the rebels over the 2000-strong force of the maharajah of Sindhia (who, convinced the rebels could never win, had adopted a pragmatically pro-British stance).

Sir Hugh Rose was sick from the heat and desperate to rest. But again the pursuit went on, this time to Kotah-ki-Serai, where the two armies met on 16 June. The rani was in command of the rebel army's eastern flank. She wore her armour and the maharajah of Sindia's glorious (and plundered) pearl necklace around her throat. But on the second day of fighting the rani was shot in the back. She returned fire, but her adversary, probably a soldier of the 8th Hussars, ran her through with his sword, and killed her.

The rebel army lost the battle; its leaders scattered or were captured and hanged as the British stamped out the 'mutiny'. Yet Sir Hugh Rose paid tribute to his enemy: *'The rani was remarkable for her bravery, cleverness and perseverance; her generosity to her subordinates was unbounded. These qualities, combined with her rank, rendered her the most dangerous of all the rebel leaders.'* In its regimental history the 8th Hussars added their own praise: *'... in her death the rebels lost their bravest and best military leader.'* The rani had fought for the hereditary rights of her adopted son, Damodar Rao, but he surrendered in 1860 in return for a pension. The British remained in India for another 100 years.

## TIMELINE

**1842** Lakshmi marries the maharajah of Jhansi, Gangadhar Rao

**1853** Gangadhar names his adopted son Damodar as heir; when he dies, the British authorities refuse to accept his wishes and annex Jhansi; Lakshmi's appeal falls on deaf ears and she is forced to live on a meagre pension

**1857** Rebels attack Meerut; Lakshmi asks the British for help in defending Jhansi; mutineers massacre European women and children barricaded in the City Fort; the British entrust Lakshmi to form a temporary government; later that year she is outlawed

**1858** Lakshmi leads an army against the British at Jhansi, but the Indian troops are overwhelmed and butchered; further defeats occur at Kunch, Kulpi and Kotah-ki-Serai; Lakshmi is shot and killed in battle

**1860** Damodar surrenders to the British

# CIXI

## 1835–1908
## Empress of China

*Like her predecessor, the notorious Empress Wu, Cixi, a low-grade concubine, used any means – even the murder of members of her own family – to achieve power, yet in the end she destroyed a 200-year dynasty. The historian Barbara Tuchman describes her vividly:* 'a painted, brocaded despot amid her eunuchs, she presided over the final sinking years of the Manchu dynasty, lapped by approaching ruin.'

Cixi was born in the Anhui province of southern China, the daughter of a Manchu officer. She was extremely beautiful – petite, with a glorious face and figure. When she was 16, and happily betrothed to her handsome cousin, her name was put forward as a candidate for concubine to the new emperor Xianfeng (r. 1850–61). Cixi was forced to leave her family and enter the Forbidden City as a concubine, third grade.

She could never leave the febrile and pernicious harem. One of 3000 concubines who existed to provide pleasure to the 'Son of Heaven,' she was the emperor's property. If she was lucky she might bear a son and, if she outlived the emperor, she might eventually exercise power as a dowager empress.

While she languished in the harem, this clever and frustrated concubine paid court to Xianfeng's mother, the dowager empress. She also cultivated the eunuchs, those de-sexed guardians of the harem and surreptitious wielders of enormous political power.

*A Chinese erotic figurine made of ivory, depicting an imperial concubine. In this role, Cixi spent five years in the harem before Xianfeng chose to spend the night with her.*

### THE EMPEROR'S FAVOURITE
When Cixi was 21, the emperor finally chose her to be his companion for the night. On the appointed evening she was carried to his chamber on the back of a eunuch, naked beneath her scarlet silk sheet. On reaching the emperor's apartments the sheet was taken from her and she was placed at the foot of his bed, expected to crawl up towards His Celestial Majesty. Cixi must have spent the long five years learning how to please the jaded emperor. After their first night together, she was promoted to concubine of the second grade and swiftly became his favourite.

She became pregnant almost immediately and on 27 April, 1856 she gave birth to a boy. The child, Xianfeng's only son, was fated to become the next ruler of China. Now she was promoted again with the title Empress Cixi, and Xianfeng took her into his confidence. He allowed her to move beyond the claustrophobic world of the harem and to act as his informal advisor. When Cixi suggested he appoint General Zeng Guofan (1811–72) to quash the Taiping Rebellion (1850–64) in southern China, she basked in the acclaim the warrior's success brought her.

Cixi played for political power at a critical moment in China's history. The Qing, or Manchu dynasty, had ridden from the north and usurped the Ming dynasty in 1644. Now, after over 200 years in power, the dynasty – which had begun as a vibrant force – had become as corrupt and archaic as its predecessor.

The Manchu believed themselves superior to all other races; the 'Middle Kingdom' was the centre of the world and everyone outside its borders was a barbarian. European aggression in the form of the Opium Wars of 1839–42 and 1856–60, followed by a humiliating defeat, forced an unwilling China to open its doors to trade. The country was faced with a choice: modernize and trade with the West, as their despised neighbour Japan had agreed to do, or face ruin.

*Portrait of Cixi as a young woman. She ruled China as empress and then as dowager empress from 1861 until her death in 1908.*

## CIXI UNDER THREAT

In 1860 Xianfeng died. It should have been a glorious moment for Cixi; as regent for her young son, the Tongzhi emperor (r. 1861–75), she could begin to wield real power. But she had fallen from favour during the emperor's final years and he maliciously nominated her enemy, Minister Su Shun, as head of the regency council, denying Cixi power. In the emperor's last days Su Shun had whispered spiteful tales of the empress's adultery with Jung Lu (1836–1903), commander of the Bannerman bodyguard. Xianfeng, delirious with opium, ordered their son to be taken from Cixi's care. But Cixi's cultivation of the eunuchs and of Xianfeng's brother, Prince Gong (1833–98), now bore fruit.

Su Shun appointed a regency council of eight officials and made both Cixi and the late emperor's former favourite, Ci'an (1837–81), dowager empresses. Then he ordered their assassination. But a eunuch loyal to Cixi had stolen the emperor's seal as he lay dying; no proclamations could be made without it. Jung Lu's men saved their women's lives and Cixi, aided by the prince, usurped the council of regents. She mitigated the excruciating sentence of 'slicing' – death by thousands of cuts – to the honourable option of suicide for Su Shun's co-regents. But Su Shun was decapitated; his head was not re-attached to his body as custom dictated, and he would not go into the next world intact. Instead it was put on public display. Although Cixi and Ci'an nominally held the regency together, power lay with the cleverer and more ambitious Cixi.

Cixi feared her power would be curtailed when Tongzhi reached his majority at the age of 14, in 1873. Her regency would end and Tongzhi, encouraged by his uncle, Prince Gong, was already a reformer. Under his minority China began to modernize: schools were established and an attempt was made to understand and learn from the Western 'barbarians'. But Cixi had no intention of stepping down in favour of her son. To avoid this, it is possible she murdered him.

## A RIVAL AT COURT

When he was 16, the young emperor chose a wife, Alute (1854–75). Like Cixi, she was a Manchu. But the dowager empress hated her: she feared that if her daughter-in-law became pregnant she would usurp her; after marrying, Tongzhi began to make decisions alone – without his mother. In 1874 the emperor contracted smallpox – believed to be a good omen in China – and temporarily withdrew from government to recover, leaving his affairs to Cixi.

When his mother visited his sick room she overheard her now pregnant daughter-in-law criticize her. Enraged, she attacked Alute. Cixi's rages were typical, and a courtier described the scene as the dowager empress attacked: '*her cheekbones were sharp and the veins on her forehead projected; she showed her teeth as if she were suffering from lockjaw.*' Some contemporary sources suggest that when Cixi visited her son he was beginning to improve but, disturbed by Alute's critical remarks, she arranged for Tongzhi to be re-infected with smallpox; he never recovered and died on 13 January, 1875.

Cixi determined that her unborn grandchild, if male, would never rule – if that happened, Alute would have too much power. She bullied the council into accepting her three-year-old nephew Guangxu (r. 1875–1908) as emperor and probably murdered Alute. She continued her regency with Ci'an but the latter held no power. Cixi's biographer Keith Laidler suggests that Cixi may have murdered her, too. After Ci'an's death in 1881 she finally ruled alone.

## CIXI ALL-POWERFUL

Cixi's court was corrupt and she made only desultory attempts to modernize a country that had not changed in thousands of years. China suffered a humiliating defeat in its war with the inferior 'eastern dwarf men' of Japan in the mid-1890s as the dowager empress failed to provide the glorious new ships of the 'modernized' navy with any artillery. Modernization challenged the rule of Cixi and her élite, and she swiftly reversed any attempts at reform. Meanwhile foreign powers encroached on the Middle Kingdom and China, reactionary and weak, was unable to resist.

But Guangxu, like his predecessor puppet emperor, realized that if China was to remain a viable power, change was vital. At the end of the century he introduced sweeping reforms. But his experiment lasted a mere 100 days before Cixi and her reactionary forces triumphed. Guangxu was confined to an isolated palace in the middle of a lake in the Forbidden City, while the dowager empress continued her reign.

But the empire was dying. Cixi's support of the Boxer Rebellion of 1900 – a revolt of ultra-nationalists who sought an end to Western influence in China – caused 19,000 European troops to march on Beijing, forcing a punitive treaty on China. Cixi fled with the emperor and only returned after two years, to live in splendid isolation in the Forbidden City.

On 14 November, 1908 Guangxu died; he had not participated in government for nearly ten years and, again, it is possible that Cixi murdered him. She immediately nominated her three-year-old nephew Pu-yi (r. 1908–24) as emperor; he would be the last emperor of China. The following day, she died at the age of 73. Her final words were '*Never again allow a woman to hold the supreme power in the state*'.

> ## 'FOREIGN DEVILS'
>
> To the Chinese China was the centre of the world, the civilized 'Middle Kingdom'. All non-Chinese were 'barbarians' and 'foreign devils'. Before the disastrous Opium Wars foreigners were not allowed a permanent presence in China and there was no word for 'ambassador' in the Chinese language – only 'tribute bearer'. All foreigners – 'hairy' and 'long-nosed' – were to be avoided lest Chinese purity be affected. Before 1898 there was no ministry for foreign affairs – only the Hall for Governance of Barbarians.

*Illustration from the French magazine* Le Petit Journal *showing a European being murdered by members of the nationalist Society of Right and Harmonious Fists, or 'Boxers', who staged an anti-foreign rebellion in China in 1900.*

# LILIUOKALANI
## *1838—1917*
## Queen of Hawaii

*Liliuokalani was the first and last queen of Hawaii. A staunch monarchist, she fought a bitter battle against the annexation of the islands by the United States at the end of the 19th century, always believing that she and her people had been sold out to the vested interests of the provisional government. Her struggle continued until her death.*

Liliuokalani was born in Honolulu on 2 September, 1838, a Hawaiian princess and member of the royal family. Her father, Kapaahea, was a high chief and her mother, Keohokalole, was an important political figure, one of 15 advisors to King Kamehameha III (r. 1824–54). Liliuokalani was the third of ten children; at her birth she was named Lydia Kamakaeha Kaolamali.

Hawaii was first inhabited by Polynesian settlers as early as the fifth century. When Europeans arrived at the wondrously fertile group of islands in 1778 in an exploration led by Captain James Cook (1728–79), the country was fragmented into several tribal leaderships. However, by 1810 Kamehameha I (r. 1795–1819) – known as 'the Great' – had united most of the islands under his rule; Liliuokalani was to be the last of his dynasty. By the 19th century Hawaii had become a desirable land – appealing both to Christian missionaries, who flocked to convert the 'heathen', and to merchants, drawn by the irresistible lure of sugar, which they called 'white gold'. Many of the indigenous population abandoned their faith, and an ever-increasing American and European presence led to the Westernization of the country as European dress, transport, accommodation and education systems were adopted.

*Kalakaua, the last reigning king of Hawaii. He had no surviving children, and so his sister Liliuokalani was appointed as his successor*

So when Lydia was four she began a thoroughly Western – missionary – education at the Royal School, where she learned to speak fluent English. Surviving photographs of the queen show a stately woman, rigidly correct in sombre Victorian dress and large crinoline skirts. In September 1862, aged 24, she married a non-Hawaiian, a government official named John Owen Dominis (1832–91). The marriage was unhappy and they had no children.

### APPRENTICE QUEEN
In 1874 Lydia's brother, David Kalakaua (r. 1874–91), became king and three years later, after the death of their brother Leleiohoku, Lydia became heiress apparent. She adopted her royal name, Liliuokalani, for the first time and acted as the king's regent during

*Liliuokalani was the first and last reigning queen of Hawaii. Her memory endures today, as composer of Hawaii's national anthem, 'Hawaii Oe'.*

his absences. She was conscientious; she established schools and acted as Hawaii's representative on a world tour in 1887. During her trip to Europe she met Queen Victoria (r. 1837–1901), whom she thought of as '*one of the best of women and greatest of monarchs*'. In her autobiography she vividly describes their meeting:

> ' *… the queen of England again kissed me on the forehead; then she took my hand, as though she had just thought of something which she had been in danger of forgetting, and said, "I want to introduce to you my children"; and one by one they came forward and were introduced.* '

Under Western and missionary influence, Hawaii was turning into a constitutional monarchy. Liliuokalani decried the enormous loss to royal power her brother, among others, was sanctioning. In 1887, while his sister was on her world tour, pressured by a

## MUSICAL TALENT

Liliuokalani, a talented musician, composed numerous Hawaiian songs. Her best remembered is the wonderful 'Aloha Oe' (Farewell to Thee), which she wrote in 1898. Tradition tells us that this beautiful song, full of sorrowful sentiment, was composed as Liliuokalani watched two lovers saying goodbye in the moonlight, and that it symbolizes the pain she felt when her country was taken away from the Hawaiian people.

cabal of American financiers and sugar-plantation owners, the king agreed to a punitive new constitution that would drastically curtail the power of the monarchy. He granted the United States unprecedented trading rights and even ceded them the port of Pearl Harbor. Four years later he died, and Liliuokalani became queen.

Liliuokalani was 52 years old and the first female in Hawaiian history to rule in her own right. A journalist wrote that her face was 'strong and resolute … Her voice was musical and well modulated … and she spoke remarkably pure and graceful English. Her manner was dignified, and she had the ease and the authoritative air of one accustomed to rule'. The local press acclaimed her: *The Friend* praised 'her gentle and gracious demeanor, her good sense, and her fine culture … '. But, its editor presciently continued, ' … it can hardly be doubted by anyone that this kingdom is advancing through a period of transition from monarchy to government by the people'. This was certainly not the stance of the royalist Liliuokalani.

### CALLS FOR ANNEXATION

*Honolulu harbour in the mid-19th century. Honolulu means 'Fair Haven.' This was the name given to the place by the captain of the first European vessel to enter the harbour.*

She was mistrusted by the powerful *haole* – the community of foreign businessmen and traders – and the punitive McKinley Tariff Bill of 1890 created enormous economic hardship for Hawaii. The American Congress set a high tariff on sugar imported into the United States, a move intended to favour American sugar producers. Sugar was the backbone of the Hawaiian economy and, as a result, the country endured a slump with high unemployment and rising property prices. Now, a powerful pro-American lobby began to moot the idea of Hawaiian annexation by the United States.

Liliuokalani was determined to overthrow her brother's constitution and institute a new one that would restore power to the monarchy. At the beginning of 1893, she went to the government building resplendent in a diamond-studded coronet and a feather cloak to proclaim her new constitution. However, she was frustrated when two cabinet ministers who had previously agreed to back her changed their minds at the last minute. An angry crowd gathered outside the government building screaming their support for their queen. The delay that this event forced upon her proved fatal to her plans.

The reform movement, on the other hand, was superbly organized. It represented American interests and its leader, Sanford Dole (1844–1926), the son of American missionaries, was a veteran of Hawaiian politics. Dole was convinced he had American support for an armed democratic coup. He later wrote, '*We knew that the United States minister was in sympathy with us*'. American troops landed at Honolulu.

The queen was forced to abdicate, and Dole formed a provisional government as the country awaited annexation by the United States. Liliuokalani had no choice but to concede. But it was not to the provisional government she conceded, but to the United States itself:

> *That I [Liliuokalani] yield to the superior force of the United States of America whose minister plenipotentiary, His Excellency John L. Stevens, has caused United States troops to be landed at Honolulu and declared that he would support the said provisional government.*'

She put her faith in the justice of American government policy and in a letter to the new president, Grover Cleveland (1837–1908), she expressed:

> ' ... *the certainty which I feel that your government will right whatever wrongs may have been inflicted upon us* ... '

## EMOTIONAL OUTPOURINGS

When Grover Cleveland discovered the majority of native Hawaiians were against the coup he refused to condone annexation and demanded the queen's reinstatement. Dole and his provisional government ignored him; in 1894 they declared the independent Republic of Hawaii. Liliuokalani vainly protested to the United States and Britain but she too was ignored: the new republic was recognized by foreign powers. She may have been complicit in a failed uprising at the beginning of 1895, when she was placed under house arrest at the former royal palace and forced to recognize Dole as the chief authority in Hawaii. She also had to renounce her claim to the throne. Following annexation in 1898, Hawaii became a United States territory in 1900 and Dole was appointed its first territorial governor.

Liliuokalani spent the next 20 years of her life wandering the globe in a desperate bid for aid; but she would never again play a role in government and her cause had failed. She suffered a stroke and died on Hawaii in 1917.

## TIMELINE

**1778** European explorers first arrive on the Hawaiian islands

**1810** Most of the islands are united under Kamehameha I

**1862** Lydia marries John Dominis

**1874** Lydia's brother, David Kalakaua becomes king

**1877** Liliuokalani becomes heiress apparent and acts as regent in the king's absence

**1887** Kalakaua introduces a new pro-American constitution, severely curtailing the powers of the monarchy

**1890** Economic hardship in Hawaii gives rise to calls for annexation

**1891** Kalakaua dies and Liliuokalani becomes queen

**1893** American troops land at Honolulu, and Liliuokalani is obliged to abdicate

**1894** The provisional government declares the independent Republic of Hawaii

**1895** Liliuokalani is implicated in a failed insurrection and placed under house arrest

**1898** Hawaii is annexed by the United States

**1900** Hawaii becomes a United States territory

**1917** Liliuokalani dies of a stroke

# GOLDA MEIR

## 1898–1978
## Prime Minister of Israel

*Golda Meir was a founder member of the state of Israel and one of the first female prime ministers of the 20th century. A highly controversial figure, she governed a nascent Israel, working tirelessly to create a country for the Jewish people. A decade before Margaret Thatcher was dubbed 'the iron lady of politics', Golda was already earning a reputation as a tough stateswoman, refusing to shy away from hardline policies in the defence of her newly created homeland.*

Golda Meir was born in 1898 in Kiev, now the capital of Ukraine but then part of the Pale of Settlement, a large tract of land in western Russia to which the Jews were restricted by Tsarist law. Her parents, Moshe and Bluma Mabovitch, had eight children but only Golda and her two sisters survived infancy; all of her brothers died.

The vicious pogroms of her childhood had a huge impact on the young Golda Mabovich; later, she recounted how during one attack on the Jewish community, she and her elder sister hid in a graveyard. When she was six, the Jews of Kiev experienced the worst pogrom in living memory. Crippled by the physical attacks and economic sanctions against the Jews, Moshe took action. A skilled carpenter, he sailed alone to America to earn enough money to pay for his family's passage away from the dangers of anti-Semitic Russia.

In 1906 Golda and her family sailed for the United States, where they settled in Milwaukee. But life in America was hard for new immigrants. Moshe failed to support his family financially so his wife Bluma opened a grocery store. Golda worked in the store every morning before school, where she was a brilliant student. By the time she reached high school she had decided to become a teacher.

Golda was a rebel. She refused to accede to her parents' demands for an arranged marriage and saved enough money teaching English to run away from home, to her married sister Sheyna in Denver, Colorado. Denver was a huge centre of Russian Jewry and it was here that Golda became politically conscious.

Sheyna's home was a meeting place for anarchists, socialists, Marxists and Zionists, all fiercely debating the destiny of the Jewish people. But Golda and Sheyna argued, and

when Golda was 17 she returned to her parents in Milwaukee. They promised not to interfere in the life of their stubbornly independent daughter; she completed high school in just two years, then she pursued her dream of training to be a teacher.

## BOUND FOR PALESTINE

Meanwhile Golda rapidly acquired a reputation as a gifted orator. In 1915, still just 17 years old, she joined Po'alei Zion, a socialist Zionist movement, and she spoke eloquently in both English and Yiddish. She gradually rejected diaspora Zionism and embraced the idea of an independent Jewish state. As a committed socialist, she eagerly subscribed to

*Golda Meir was a natural leader all her life, from her schoolgirl campaign for textbooks through to helping found the State of Israel. This photograph was taken in 1971, during an official visit to the United States.*

the nascent kibbutz movement. She left for Palestine in 1921, accompanied by her new husband, a mild-mannered sign-writer called Morris Myerson.

Palestine was under a British mandate following the disintegration of the Ottoman empire at the end of the First World War. The country encompassed modern-day Israel, the West Bank, Gaza and Jordan.

Golda and Morris went to Kibbutz Merhavia in the north. Golda loved it; she picked almonds, raised chickens, planted trees, ran the kitchen and in her spare time studied Hebrew and Arabic. But Morris was miserable. Kibbutz conditions were harsh and although the swamps had been drained, malaria and dysentery were rife. When Morris became ill Golda reluctantly moved with him to Tel Aviv. It would be the backdrop of her transition from housewife to politician.

## POLITICS COSTS GOLDA HER MARRIAGE
In Tel Aviv Golda was offered a job with the Jewish Agency – the Sochnut. But as her career soared, her marriage disintegrated. Although she and Morris had two children, Menachem, born in 1924, and Sarah, born in 1926, the marriage failed. Golda had abandoned politics to care for her children but, frustrated with being a full-time mother, she returned to her first love. In 1928 she became secretary of the Women's Labour Council. Her daughter's illness (she suffered from a kidney complaint) forced her to return to America in 1932 for two years but still she used the time productively, raising funds for a national homeland for the Jews in Palestine. When she returned in 1934 she joined the executive of the Histadrut, the Jewish trade union movement. By 1940 she was head of its political department.

In 1938, as Hitler massed his forces and Europe moved towards war, Golda attended the Evian Conference as one of the Palestinian representatives. Here, 32 nations of the world discussed the plight of German Jewry – and decided to do nothing. Golda, mindful of the likely fate of European Jewry, acted with political allies such as David Ben-Gurion (1886–1973) to smuggle Jews illegally into Palestine.

During the war years and its immediate aftermath Golda and her political allies fought to expel the British from Palestine. On 29 November, 1947 the British handed the situation over to the United Nations; they decided to slice Palestine into two separate parts – an Arab state and a Jewish state.

## A SENSE OF BETRAYAL
Golda was furious. As far as she was concerned an Arab state – Jordan – had been carved for the Palestinians out of four-fifths of the mandate in 1922. But there were more pressing concerns. Golda Meir knew that when Israel declared statehood, it would immediately be invaded by its Arab neighbours. And so she went to the United States and led the biggest fund-raising drive in the history of American Jewry. She told her audiences: *'Six million Jews died and you stood aside. There are half a million Jews in Palestine and*

*we will fight and we will die unless you save us.'* When David Ben-Gurion met her at the airport on her return, he told her: '*Madam, you have saved the Jewish state.'*

In May 1948 the state of Israel was founded; Golda was one of the 38 signatories to the declaration of independence. During the inevitable Arab–Israeli war of 1948–9, she returned to the United States to raise funds and was, once again, extremely successful. Her first post after the armistice was that of ambassador to Moscow, where the socialist Israeli state received tacit backing from Stalin. The Russian Revolution of 1917 had abolished the practice of all religions. But when Golda visited Moscow, 40,000 Jews came to greet her and Stalin realized, belatedly, that he had a Jewish problem.

On her return to Israel Golda became a member of the Knesset in David Ben-Gurion's socialist Mapai Party. He appointed her minister of labour and development, with responsibility for the vast influx of Holocaust survivors and Arab Jewry, the latter fleeing persecution from Israel's neighbours. It was at this point, in recognition of her formidable political skill, that David Ben-Gurion called her '*the best man I ever had*'.

Ben-Gurion, the idealist, envisaged a perfect democracy. He believed proportional representation was the best way to achieve this, but the results were chaotic. By 1955, a country of just 3 million people had 33 political parties. When US president Lyndon Johnson (1908–73) complained to her how difficult it was being the president of a country of over 250 million people, an exasperated Golda Meir replied: '*Mr President, you have no idea how difficult it is to be the leader of a country of over 3 million prime ministers.'*

*David Ben-Gurion wishes farewell to the final contingent of British troops to leave Israel, in 1948.*

*Golda Meir speaking at the United Nations in 1953. She was an exceptional orator.*

## THE SUEZ AFFAIR

In 1956 Golda, now Minister for Foreign Affairs, changed her name from Myerson to the more Hebraized Meir. This year was dominated by the Suez crisis. Gamal Abdel Nasser (1918–70), the Egyptian president, nationalized the Suez Canal, against British and French interests (the British owned the canal). In a secret deal, it was agreed that the Israelis would attack and seize the canal, and the British and French would step in to separate the combatants. But the international community, particularly the United States, exposed the plan as a put-up job, embarrassing the conspirators. The débâcle had two far-reaching consequences: Nasser's standing was assured among the Arab nations, and the whole world became aware of the exceptional fighting prowess of the Israeli Defence Forces. As foreign minister, Golda was obliged to explain Israel's actions to the United Nations.

1960 found Golda at the centre of an international incident again when she faced the United Nations to justify Israel's kidnapping of the notorious Nazi leader, Adolf Eichmann (1906–62).

## THE EICHMANN TRIAL

The Eichmann trial was one of the most sensational events of the latter half of the 20th century. Together with Heinrich Himmler (1900–45) and Reinhard Heydrich (1904–42), Eichmann had been chiefly responsible for the implementation of the Final Solution – Hitler's plan to annihilate European Jewry. In 1960 he was the only one of these leading Nazis left alive – Hitler (1889–1945) and Himmler had committed suicide, while Heydrich was assassinated by Czech partisans in 1943. After the war Eichmann fled to Argentina but Mossad – Israel's military intelligence agency – was finally alerted to his presence.

Israel wanted to place Eichmann on trial but they had no extradition treaty with Argentina. So the government kidnapped him; they sent a trade delegation to Argentina, including a Mossad agent who bore a striking resemblance to Eichmann. When they reached Argentina, the agent was admitted to hospital, allegedly suffering from injuries sustained in a fake accident; as he recovered, the authorities provided a letter stating he was fit to be repatriated. Eichmann was kidnapped and drugged, his details were substituted on the hospital letter and he was flown to Israel. Meanwhile Israel introduced the death penalty for crimes against humanity. Eichmann was found guilty and executed in 1961.

Golda later said of her speech to the United Nations: *'Of all the public addresses I have made, that was the one that drained me most, because I felt I was speaking for the millions that could no longer speak for themselves.'*

## THE MUNICH MASSACRE

By 1967 Yasser Arafat (1929–2004) had radicalized the PLO (Palestine Liberation Organization) and was using terror tactics to bring the Palestinian cause to the centre of world attention. During the Olympic Games in the German city of Munich in 1972 a group of Arab terrorists calling themselves 'Black September' murdered 11 members of the Israeli Olympic team. Golda gave Mossad the order to act, and every terrorist but one who had taken part in the plot was later assassinated.

## GOLDA AS PRIME MINISTER

Golda retired in 1968 at the age of 70. But when the prime minister, Levy Eshkol (1895 – 1969), died, she was asked to take over as interim prime minister. She received a resounding vote of confidence at the subsequent general election.

Golda Meir's premiership was defined by her efforts for peace; she travelled throughout Europe in pursuit of a diplomatic solution to the Middle East crisis. But the Yom Kippur War of 1973 brought about her downfall. After its extraordinary victory in the 'Six-Day War' of 1967, Israel had grown complacent. There was a failure of intelligence, and when Egypt, Syria, Jordan and Iraq attacked on the holiest day in the Jewish calendar, the country was caught unawares. If America had not stepped in to provide the state with weapons, Israel would have lost. Golda was blamed for the near-calamity. Her popularity declined and she was unable to form a new coalition government on two occasions.

She resigned in 1974. Although she remained active in the Labour Party she became bitter when her political enemy, Menachem Begin (1913–1992), took power in 1977. However, when Begin made peace with Egypt's president Anwar Sadat, it was Golda who presented him with a gift, 'from a grandmother to a grandfather'.

Golda Meir died on 8 December, 1978 after a long battle with cancer. The obituary in the *New York Times* paid her fitting tribute: '*The miracle of Golda Meir was how one person could embody the spirit of so many.*'

*Golda Meir with her Labour party colleagues Shimon Peres and Yitzhak Rabin, plus other dignitaries, including former German chancellor Willy Brandt, at a international socialist conference in 1977.*

# SIRIMAVO BANDARANAIKE

## *1916 – 2000*

## Prime Minister of Sri Lanka

*Sirimavo Bandaranaike spent her married life as a housewife and helpmeet to her husband Solomon, the prime minister of Ceylon. When he was assassinated she succeeded him as the world's first female prime minister and went on to serve three terms in office. As a politician she was woefully underestimated. As Sirimavo assumed power, Solomon Bandaranaike's cousin, Paul Pieris Deriyanagala, commented,* 'What does she know of politics? In Solla's time, Sirima presided over nothing fiercer than the kitchen fire …' *He added, maliciously,* 'She'll end by spoiling her personal reputation and ruining the family name'.

*Solomon Bandaranaike founded the Sri Lankan Freedom Party, promoting Sinhalese culture and language and championing the Buddhist religion.*

Sirimavo (the 'vo' at the end of her name denotes respect) Bandaranaike was born into a country still very much a part of the British empire – Ceylon. The nation did not achieve independence until 1948 with the fragmentation of the British empire. Her parents were wealthy landowners who belonged to the highest *goyigama* caste, and were members of an Anglicized, although staunchly Buddhist, aristocracy. Their daughter was given the best education available at a Roman Catholic convent in Colombo, the country's capital. When she left school she used her privileged position to informally aid the plight of the poor and to promote the rights of women. In 1940, when she was in her early twenties, she married the ambitious, Oxford-educated Solomon Bandaranaike (1899–1959).

Sirimavo spent the next years bearing children – she had three, two girls and a boy, between 1943 and 1949 – and taking the subordinate role in her marriage. She played no part in Solomon's increasing political involvement. His biographer, James Manor, tells a story to illustrate the nature of the marriage: when serving tea to a group of her husband's

political friends, Sirimavo forgot to bring a spoon, to Solomon's irritation. He berated her in front of their guests: '*Sirima! These gentlemen drink tea with sugar. For the sugar to get into the cup, there must be some instrument. You have not put a spoon in the sugar bowl.*' She did not protest.

## FORMATION OF THE SLFP

Solomon, however, evidently admired her intellect and her loyalty. She encouraged his role within the ruling United National Party (UNP) but it was Sirimavo who eventually persuaded him to resign and to form his own political party, the democratic socialist Sri Lankan Freedom Party (SLFP) in 1951. She campaigned on his behalf and, although he received the largest vote for any single candidate, his nascent party won only nine seats. In 1956, however, he achieved a landslide victory. Three years later a Buddhist monk shot him in his home. He died the following day.

Sirimavo stepped into the political spotlight. Her views – Sinhalese revival, and the promotion of the majority Buddhist Sinhalese culture and language over English to the detriment of the Hindu Tamil minority (which would have far-reaching and dire consequences) – were in concert with those of her murdered husband. Accordingly,

*Sirimavo Bandaranaike, pictured on taking office in 1960. She was her husband's natural successor as leader of the SLFP after his assassination in 1959.*

members of his party pleaded with her to take his place as party leader. If they hoped she would be a malleable president they were mistaken. In 1960 she was swept into power on a sympathy vote and became the world's first female prime minister.

## DOMESTIC REFORM AND INTERNATIONAL NEUTRALITY

Her first term in office saw a whirlwind of reform. She promoted industrialization, pursued international neutrality, nationalized foreign oil companies, reformed the education system and took the country into the Non-Aligned Movement (NAM) of nations. She played a significant role on the international stage and in 1962 she successfully arbitrated peace between India and China. When she was ousted from office in the elections in 1965, she spent the next five years as the leader of the opposition.

In 1970 she was returned to power with a leftist coalition government. Two years later she changed the country's name from Ceylon to Sri Lanka, and instituted a republic; an elected president replaced the British queen as head of state. But the 1970s were cataclysmic years for Sirimavo. She faced the violence of Tamil separatist insurrections as her government continued to favour the Buddhist Sinhalese majority and made Buddhism the state religion. Her policies were economically flawed, and one-fifth of the population was unemployed, leading to riots which were brutally suppressed. To curb the violent insurrections, Sirimavo was forced to seek help from abroad. Her suppression of the Tamils, combined with her programme of nationalizing industry and poor economic judgment, caused disaster at the 1977 polls. Sirimavo was accused of autocratic tendencies and nepotism – a remarkable number of her relatives and friends filled government-funded posts – and she was ousted as prime minister.

The end of the 1970s and the beginning of the 1980s were years of political failure and familial discord for Sirimavo. Political humiliation was mirrored in her family life as her son, Anura (b.1949), joined a breakaway movement of her own Freedom Party. Her political enemy Junius Jayawardene (1906–96) instituted a witch-hunt against her; she was found guilty of corruption in office and was barred for seven years from participating in the most important thing in her life – politics. It was a terrible blow.

## FAMILY RIVALRY AND PARTY SPLITS

She spent the next years desperately trying to keep her fractured party together. In 1985 she received a pardon from President Jayawardene and campaigned for the presidency of the SLFP; she failed by only a narrow margin. Meanwhile, her children fought bitterly for political power as her son Anura and her daughter Chandrika (b.1945)

*'She donned her [leadership] like a cloak that had been lying in her wardrobe for years, unworn, but which had been pressed and kept ready for wearing at any given moment.'*

SIRIMAVO BANDARANAIKE'S BIOGRAPHER, MAUREEN SENEVIRATNE

both contested the party leadership. Chandrika had married a film star and together they left the SLFP to form their own left-wing party, one that sought accommodation with the Tamils. But when her husband was murdered in 1988, Chandrika returned to the SLFP fold. She was as startling a political operator as her mother, and when Sirimava resigned office in 1994, Chandrika secured the party leadership. Anura, enraged, crossed the house and joined the opposing United National Party, to Sirimavo's immense disappointment. Chandrika – the new political force in the family, and the country's first female president from 1994 to 2005 – granted her mother the now largely ceremonial post of prime minister.

## THE FIRST – AND THE LONGEST SERVING

Sirimavo Bandaranaike was not only the world's first female prime minister, she was also the longest serving. She held office for a total of 18 years over three administrations: 1960–5; 1970–7; 1994–2000. In India, Indira Gandhi (1917–84) held power for 15 years (1966–77; 1980–4), while in the United Kingdom Margaret Thatcher (b. 1925) served for 11 years as prime minister, between 1979 and 1990.

Sirimavo Bandaranaike was an extraordinary political trailblazer. She was a major force in navigating a nascent Sri Lanka from government by empire to an independent state. Her greatest fault was her failure to deal with minority Tamil needs because, as an ardent nationalist, she refused to appreciate the extent to which their marginalization and victimization threatened Sri Lanka – until it was too late. In 1983, when she was out of office, the country indulged in an orgy of violence against the Tamils; they responded with a wave of armed resistance. The problem is unresolved today.

Dogged by ill health, frail and unable to walk, Sirimavo died of a heart attack on election day, 10 October, 2000, exactly 60 years after her marriage to Solomon; she was buried beside him. She was 84 years old. The Sri Lanka Freedom Party acclaimed her as ' … *a heroic mother of the nation*' and the country went into two days of national mourning.

*Chandrika Bandaranaike Kumaratunga (b.1945) followed in her mother's pioneering footsteps by becoming Sri Lanka's first woman president in 1994. She is seen here with Indian prime minister Manmohan Singh in 2004.*

# Indira Gandhi
## 1917–84
## Prime Minister of India

*Voted the most popular woman of the millennium in a 1999 poll, Indira Gandhi – India's only female prime minister – won overwhelming support from the poor and dispossessed of the Subcontinent. But ambition, the lack of an effective opposition and her own increasing feelings of insecurity led her to behave like a despot, ultimately bringing shame and violence to her nation.*

Indira Gandhi was born into India's first political family, in Allahabad on 19 November, 1917, the only child of Jawaharlal 'Pandit' Nehru (1889–1964) and Kamala Kaul (1899–1936). Nehru was a brilliant, Western-educated politician who devoted his life to securing independence for India from the British; he was India's first prime minister from independence in 1947 until his death. He recorded proudly how his daughter was born in the very month of the Bolshevik revolution in Russia. It was a typically political reflection.

Indira's early life was steeped in politics and she was formally politically active from the age of 12. Her parents' house was the meeting place for Congress Party members in the hot, fervent years leading up to the end of imperial rule, and she witnessed the frequent arrest and imprisonment of family members and friends. Later, she would proclaim, *'politics is the centre of everything'*.

*Indira Nehru photographed in 1937 with her father Jawaharlal Nehru, president of the Indian Congress, before she left Bombay for England to study at Oxford University.*

She was educated in India and then at Somerville College, Oxford; on her return in 1942 she married a Parsi, Feroze Gandhy (1912–60), a fellow member of the Congress Party. (Nehru later persuaded him to change the spelling of his surname to Gandhi to disguise his Parsi origins. Once in office, Indira would exploit the resonance that the name Gandhi had for millions of Indians, though she was unrelated to Mohandas 'Mahatma' Gandhi.)

Indira and her husband had two children: Rajiv, born in 1944, and Sanjay in 1946. Feroze worked sporadically as a journalist for *The National Herald*, the newspaper founded by Nehru, although his father-in-law was dismissive of his archaic style of writing. The year Sanjay was born, Indira left Feroze. He was adulterous and they had very little money. She took the boys to her father's house in New Delhi.

## KINDLING OF POLITICAL AMBITION

In 1947 Nehru became the first prime minister of a newly independent India and Indira, living with him at his grand official residence, was again thrust into the political spotlight. Her mother was dead and she now acted as her father's hostess, frequently travelling abroad with him. Although many of her father's associates approached her to stand for parliament, Nehru never entertained the possibility that she might succeed him. Her detractors claim he did not think she had a sufficiently astute political mind, and that she was merely his aid. But after a visit to the Soviet Union in 1953 – the year in which Joseph Stalin died – Indira became enchanted by the idea of power.

Nehru died in 1964, to be succeeded by the gentle and courteous Lal Bahadur Shastri (1904–66), who offered Indira the post of minister of information and broadcasting. Shastri did not appoint her for her political abilities; it was merely an act of courtesy. She accepted because she needed the money. Feroze had died in 1960 and left her nothing.

Prime Minister Shastri died two years later, bequeathing a Congress Party riven by faction. Party elders approached Indira to lead; they were attracted not by her political skills, which were untested, nor by her passion, which was negligible. They chose her because they mistook her for a *goongi gudiya* – a 'dumb doll' – whom they believed they could easily manipulate.

*In March 1971, on the eve of elections, premier Indira Gandhi addresses a public meeting gathered at the Red Fort in Delhi.*

## A TROJAN HORSE

Too late, the Congress elders came to realize that she was anything but their puppet. Now almost 50 years old, she had been steeped in politics all her life, and on entering the political fray discovered her natural métier. She would bide her time until the general elections of 1967, when the Congress Party was returned – but with a greatly reduced majority. In her district, however, Indira won by a landslide. It was a mandate to impose radical change on the archaic Congress Party structure as she took the party further towards the left and swept away the old guard. Indira, charismatic and in touch with the electorate, soon fostered a cult of personality. She was immensely popular and her simple campaigning slogan 'Remove Poverty' won her the mass vote among the poor.

Thanks to her championship of the poor, the underdog and women, Indira triumphed again in the 1971 general elections. In December that year, war with Pakistan over Bengali nationalism thrust her once again into the international arena; when Pakistan invaded, Indira's victory was seen as a dazzling success. Many Indians still revere Mrs Gandhi for her stunning leadership during this conflict.

However in the 1971 war, one worrying new development was the US backing for Pakistan. When Indira first came to office she had made strenuous efforts to charm the superpower. President Lyndon Johnson (1908–73) was beguiled, and pledged $9 million of aid to India, keen to ensure that *'no harm comes to this girl'*. Now Indira's triumph over Pakistan earned her the enmity of President Richard Nixon (1913–94), who called her an *'old witch'*. Although India belonged to the Non-aligned Movement of nations, Nixon, paranoid in the prevailing Cold War climate, believed that under Gandhi's rule the country was moving too close to the USSR. But at home and on the wider international stage she was fêted, and many Indians compared her to the goddess of power, Shakti.

> *'She started as Joan of Arc, and ended as King Lear.'*
>
> A.J. AKBAR, EDITOR-IN-CHIEF OF *THE ASIAN AGE*

## AUTOCRATIC BEHAVIOUR AND EMERGENCY POWERS

Indira pursued an assertive foreign policy, hammering out a settlement with Pakistan over disputed Kashmir, and, in 1974, announcing that India had gone nuclear. But her rule at home became ever more autocratic. Her restructuring of her party meant in practice that she enjoyed far more power as prime minister than her predecessors. She abused her large electoral majority to govern an India that she increasingly viewed as her personal fiefdom.

During the mid-1970s, India's poor economic performance sparked a wave of unrest. Indira was accused of electoral fraud and threatened with being disbarred from parliament for six years. In June 1975, wrongly believing there was a plot to depose her, she imposed a state of emergency and awarded herself draconian powers.

The crisis lasted for nearly two years. The opposition press was silenced, political rivals were incarcerated and mass sterilizations occurred – the women who 'volunteered' were frequently from the poorest classes. Slums were destroyed and their inhabitants cleared away, as Indira rode roughshod over the democratic principle. Her actions left a stain on her name. When she called a general election in 1977. she was defeated at the polls.

Amazingly, however, by 1980 she had recovered enough political ground to be elected for a fourth term. She cultivated an image of herself as 'mother India', synonymous with the history of the subcontinent. She achieved a resounding victory, but this last term was disastrous. Her vain, arrogant son Sanjay was killed in a plane crash during the summer, depriving her of a successor. She faced uprisings as regionalist movements throughout the country sought a greater degree of independence. In the Punjab the Sikh community, appalled at the suspension of powers in the previous decade and under the charismatic leadership of the religious preacher, Jarnail Singh Bhindranwale (1947–84), agitated for a homeland – Khalistan.

*Indira Gandhi greeting Congress Party supporters in 1977, the year in which she lost the general election.*

## SLAUGHTER AT AMRITSAR

The result was a catastrophe. In June 1984 Bhindranwale and his followers barricaded themselves in the Sikhs' most sacred shrine, the Golden Temple at Amritsar. Acting under orders from Indira, the Indian army launched a devastating attack. Over 450 people were slaughtered in the ensuing violence.

On 30 October, 1984 Indira addressed a political rally. She told the crowd: *'I don't mind if my life goes in the service of the nation. If I die today, every drop of my blood will invigorate the nation.'* The following day, in revenge for the storming of the holy shrine, she was killed by two of her own Sikh bodyguards.

The dynasty endures, however. Mrs Gandhi's son Rajiv (1944–91) became prime minister after her death in 1984 but, forever associated with his mother's politics and predilections, he, too, fell prey to an assassin. Today Mrs Gandhi's daughter-in-law Sonia (b.1946) is a hugely influential figure, while her grandson, Rahul (b.1970), is a member of parliament.

## THE POPULARITY POLL

Indira Gandhi remains an extremely controversial figure. In a BBC poll in 1999, she was voted the greatest woman of the past millennium, ahead of Elizabeth I of England (r. 1558–1603), Margaret Thatcher (b.1925), Marie Curie (1867–1934), Eleanor Roosevelt (1884–1962), Joan of Arc (c.1412–31), Mother Teresa (1910–97) and the Burmese opposition leader Aung San Suu Kyi (b.1945).

# EVA PERÓN

## 1919–52
## Wife of President Juan Perón of Argentina

*A British Foreign Office internal memo of 1950 described Eva Perón as* 'a dangerous but very remarkable woman', *but to her supporters she was* la dama de la esperanza – *the lady of hope. She was both adored as a saint and abhorred as a fascist and a Nazi sympathizer. With the looks of a starlet, Eva escaped rural poverty and made for the bright lights of Buenos Aires to become an actress; later, as the wife of a rising politician, she abandoned the theatre for a wider stage. A champion of the poor, she attracted world renown as she ruled Argentina with her husband, President Juan Perón. Her death at the age of 33 only enhanced her iconic image. But Evita – 'little Eva' – was complicated. Vain, single-minded in her pursuit of power and absolutely dedicated to the cult of the Peróns, she is no less divisive a figure today.*

María Eva Duarte was born in the spring of 1919 in Los Toldos, one of the countless isolated and barren villages that dot the vast plain of the Argentinian *pampas*. She was the youngest of five illegitimate children (although she attempted to conceal her illegitimacy all her life). She was slim, blonde and striking, and at the age of 15 – ambitious and desperate to escape the harsh conditions of life in rural Argentina – she fled to the capital, Buenos Aires. There she enjoyed moderate success as a film and radio actress. She was not particularly talented but was extremely persistent, and by the time she met the labour secretary Colonel Juan Perón (1895–1974) at a fund-raising gala in 1944, she was one of the highest paid women in the media. He was 49, she was 24.

Perón was a career soldier and politician. A European tour in 1939 had convinced him of the merits of fascism. He was extremely ambitious and may have recognized Eva's potential to aid his cause. Later, he claimed that his first impression of her was electrifying: *'Eva was pale but when she spoke her face seemed to catch fire.'*

*'My biggest fear in life is to be forgotten.'*

EVA PERÓN

*With her filmstar looks and presence, Evita captivated the hearts and minds of the Argentine people, inspiring their devotion with her work for women and the poor.*

## CHAMPION OF THE POOR

Evita (the diminutive form of Eva, by which she preferred to be known) may not have been well educated but she did have uncanny political acumen. Now, as Perón's girlfriend, she too became ambitious. She began to fashion herself as the champion of the unions and of *los decamisados* – 'the shirtless', or poor. She swiftly gained enormous popularity among Argentina's working classes. She was one of them, but simultaneously a blonde goddess who stood above them; she beguiled them. The landed and the middle classes, however, distrusted and despised her as a showgirl and an upstart.

Juan Perón and Evita married in 1945. She was his second wife. The following year he was elected president, his campaign aided enormously by Evita's laudatory radio broadcasts. Although not elected to office, Evita became the unofficial minister of labour and social welfare. She cannily established the María Eva Duarte Social Help Foundation, which further personalized her work as it funded the building of thousands of schools, hospitals and orphanages for the poorest classes throughout Argentina.

*Eva Perón's popularity was such that the public called for her to stand as vice-president. Although she eventually chose not to do so, her husband appointed her as 'Spiritual Leader of the Nation'.*

## A MIXED RECEPTION IN EUROPE

In 1947 Evita embarked on a European tour – the so-called Rainbow Tour. She was fêted in Spain, where she was welcomed by the dictator General Francisco Franco (1892–1975), and was also granted an audience with Pope Pius XII (r. 1939–58) in Rome. Although Evita hoped to receive an honour for her charitable work, the pope only presented her with a rosary. She travelled on to Paris but cancelled her planned visit to England. The official reason was exhaustion, but the truth was that Evita, having been denied permission to stay at Buckingham Palace, refused to go.

Back in Argentina, Evita fiercely promoted the rights of women and in 1947 a female suffrage bill was passed. She established the Perónista Female Party in 1949, a mass organization with half a million members and thousands of local headquarters. She painted her husband as a Christ-like figure and would tolerate no criticism of him. She also facilitated her own veneration throughout the country – Evita's picture could be seen in streets and plazas everywhere. A city (Ciudad Evita) was even named after her.

She became one of the most photographed women in the world. Beautiful, always fashionably dressed and seemingly tireless in her work on behalf of Argentina's poor, she became an icon as she governed Argentina – although unofficially – by Perón's side. She was his greatest political asset and exercised absolute control over his image – and her own. Any publication critical of the Peróns was banned and she wrote an immensely popular weekly column, 'Eva Perón Says', which further broadened her influence and accessibility. But in public she took the subordinate, feminine role. It was from behind the scenes that she exercised her power.

## FASCIST OR SAINT?

To her supporters Evita was a saint, despite the pope's refusal to canonize her. Her detractors, however, saw her as a fascist and possibly a Nazi sympathizer who worked with her husband to offer Nazis a safe haven at the end of the Second World War. Juan Perón certainly facilitated the escape via the Argentine embassy in Barcelona of the notorious Nazi war criminals Dr Josef Mengele (1911–79, the concentration-camp doctor who conducted hideous

### DON'T CRY FOR ME, ARGENTINA

During the 1982 Falklands War between Britain and Argentina, the hugely popular song 'Don't Cry for Me, Argentina' from Andrew Lloyd Webber's musical *Evita* was not banned outright. However, disc-jockeys on the BBC were politely asked to consider the suitability of playing it – a very British ban.

experiments on inmates), Adolf Eichmann (1906–62, one of the chief executors of Hitler's 'Final Solution') and Klaus Barbie (1913–91, a murderous Gestapo chief in occupied France), among countless others. Although there is no evidence that she actively aided the escape of any Nazis to Argentina, she must have been aware of her husband's actions. On the other hand, even her most outspoken critics believe Evita was too unsophisticated to fully embrace an ideology such as fascism.

In 1951 she decided to court official political support and mooted the idea of running alongside her husband in the forthcoming presidential campaign as vice president. But the military hated the idea; they feared that should Perón die, Evita would become president.

Her popularity culminated at a mass rally in Buenos Aires in August 1951 where a hysterical crowd of over a million people begged her to stand for the vice presidency. She told them, '*I shall always do what the people wish, but I tell you, just as I said five years ago, that I would rather be Evita than the wife of the president, if this Evita could do anything for the pain of my country …* '. With an actress' perfect sense of timing, she left it several days before acceding to their request.

## RELINQUISHING POWER

However, at the end of the month, under pressure from a nervous Perón and lacking the support of the military and the upper classes, she withdrew. Her decision was also swayed by the fact that she had developed cervical cancer, which a hysterectomy failed to stem. She announced her change of mind in a radio broadcast and begged to be judged by history as '*a woman alongside General Perón who took to him the hopes and needs of the people to satisfy them, and her name was Evita*'. She claimed she would always defer to the president.

When Perón was re-elected in June 1952, Evita, as always, was by his side at the victory parade. But she was desperately thin and unable to walk. Concerned for her public image, she masked her frailty by wearing an enormous fur coat, beneath which she was supported by a frame.

Evita, the 'Spiritual Leader of the Nation' since her husband's re-election, died the following month. She was 33 years old. She had achieved the status of a living saint, and a radio broadcast announcing her death proclaimed that she had 'entered immortality'. Shrines were erected in every village, on every street, as the country submitted to a torrent of mass mourning and came to a standstill.

In 1955 Juan Perón was overthrown in a military coup. It became illegal to speak the names of the former president and his late wife. Evita's remains mysteriously disappeared and only resurfaced 16 years later – they had been secreted beneath a crypt in Milan by her enemies, desperate to prevent her shrine becoming a focus of resistance. In 1971 Juan Perón reclaimed Evita's corpse and kept it with him in exile in Spain. Following his death in 1974 his third wife, Isabel, brought her body back to Buenos Aires.

## TIMELINE

**1935** Eva arrives in Buenos Aires and finds work as an actress

**1944** Eva meets Juan Perón at a fund-raising event

**1945** Eva becomes Perón's second wife

**1946** Juan Perón is elected president of Argentina; Evita becomes unofficial minister of labour and social welfare

**1947** During her 'Rainbow Tour' of Europe, Eva visits Spain, Italy and France; back in Argentina, she is instrumental in passing the female suffrage bill

**1948** Inaguration of the María Eva Duarte Social Help Foundation

**1949** The Perónista Female Party is founded

**1950s** Juan facilitates the escape of leading German Nazis to Argentina

**1951** Eva announces her decision to run as vice president in the forthcoming elections but later declines the nomination

**1952** Juan is re-elected; Evita dies

**1955** A military coup ousts Juan Perón, who seeks exile in Madrid

**1971** Evita's remains are returned by her enemies to Juan Perón in Madrid

**1974** Isabel Perón returns Evita's body to Buenos Aires

# Margaret Thatcher

## born 1925
## British Prime Minister

*Margaret Thatcher rose to become the first woman to lead a political party in the UK, and served three consecutive terms as prime minister from 1979 to 1990 – the longest continuous period in office since Lord Liverpool in the early 19th century. Tireless in pursuit of the causes in which she believed, the 'Iron Lady' came to epitomize both the entrepreneurial zeal and the philistine greed of the 1980s. Almost two decades after leaving office, her legacy still makes itself felt in contemporary politics and society like that of no other post-war British leader.*

Margaret Hilda Roberts was born in 1925 in Grantham, Lincolnshire. Life in the Roberts household was austere. Her father, a local grocer and alderman, inculcated in her the corner-shop values of thrift, hard work and self-reliance. She worked her way to Oxford University through a scholarship, where she studied chemistry at Somerville College. While Oxford was no social paradise for Margaret, it gave her a first taste of office: president of the Oxford University Conservative Association; only the third woman to hold that post. Even at the tender age of 21, her ambition was obvious. She told a friend that part of her reason for joining the Conservatives was that there was more chance to be noticed.

Graduating in 1947, she needed a job. She became a junior research chemist at BX Plastics, where her employer remembers her as hard-working and conscientious. She did not hide her obsession with politics from her colleagues. They enjoyed teasing her: *'There goes the future prime minister.'*

During the 1950 election Margaret was adopted as the Conservative Party's candidate for Dartford, a Labour stronghold. She lost, but the campaign she fought brought her to the attention of the party's headquarters. Eight years later, she was selected for the north London seat of Finchley, which she won in the election of 1959. At the age of 34, she had succeeded in her ambition of becoming a member of Parliament.

As the first female prime minister of a Western nation,
Margaret Thatcher's place in history is assured. She loomed
large over the British political landscape, and her name still
evokes admiration and antipathy in equal measure.

'The eyes of Caligula, the voice of Marilyn Monroe.'

FRENCH PRESIDENT FRANÇOIS MITTERRAND

## FAMILY LIFE

She was also a wife and mother. She married Dennis Thatcher (1915–2003) – divorcé, businessman and traditional Conservative – in 1951. Dennis was 'old school'; when the twins Carol and Mark were delivered on 15 August, 1953, he was watching cricket at The Oval. But he was her rock. Dennis was supportive throughout her career and always told her the truth, when few others dared.

In the years that followed, her rise was rapid. She won a place as the 'statutory woman' in the Shadow Cabinet in 1967; initially she was given the brief for Power, before being moved to Transport and finally to Education.

The Conservative Party under Edward Heath (1902–69) unexpectedly won the 1970 general election, and Margaret Thatcher was made Education Secretary. Most Britons remember this appointment only for her decision to cut free milk from primary schools, earning her the soubriquet 'Thatcher, Thatcher – Milk Snatcher'. In fact, it had seemed a sensible policy at the time: much of the available milk was not drunk, and the government had discovered it was spending more on milk than on books.

## LEADERSHIP VICTORY

Margaret Thatcher's moment came in 1975. A year after Heath lost the election, she stood for the Tory leadership after the candidate from the party's right wing stepped down from the contest. When she went into Heath's office to break the news, he not did even bother to look up. *'You'll lose'*, he said. *'Good day'*.

Thatcher surprised everyone by her triumph; it was a tribute to her willingness to take advice. Airey Neave (1916–79), an anti-Heath MP and former member of the security services, masterminded a brilliant campaign. He launched Thatcher on a charm offensive to meet, flatter and coax the Conservative backbenches that Heath had ignored, simultaneously planting disinformation to lull the leader's camp into complacency.

If the Labour prime minister Jim Callaghan (1912–2005) had called the election in 1978, she would almost certainly have lost. The economy was improving, inflation was falling and the polls had Callaghan a clear ten points ahead. But he delayed, and she won the 1979 election to become the first ever female prime minister of a Western nation.

The country she inherited was floundering. Britain had been in slow decline for 30 years and was now at best a third-rate power. The economy had limped through the 1970s, earning Britain the unenviable title of the 'sick man of Europe'. Trade union power was crippling the economy, and the last years of the decade were marred by strikes and high unemployment, culminating in a bitter confrontation between unions and government at the end of 1978, dubbed the 'winter of discontent'. With a 44-seat majority in the House of Commons, Margaret Thatcher now had a mandate to roll back the state.

## Monetarism and conviction politics

As Opposition leader she surrounded herself with right-wing thinkers who rejected the postwar economic consensus. She was introduced to the doctrine of monetarism, an approach to economic management that focuses on the supply of and demand for money, and which was entirely untested on a mature Western economy. She began pushing up interest rates and raising indirect taxes in order to lower inflation. The early results were grim: for a government that had won an election with an advertising campaign that proclaimed 'Labour isn't working', her policies doubled the level of unemployment.

But Margaret Thatcher's hallmark was conviction politics and, defying her critics, she was dogged in pursuit of her controversial policies. To roars of approval at the 1980 Conservative Party conference, Thatcher was defiant towards those who urged a U-turn: *'I have only one thing to say: you turn if you want to; the Lady's not for turning.'*

These were the years of austerity budgets, recession and an unprecedented 4 million Britons without work. The early optimism had vanished and her government's popularity fell to an all-time low. Then, in April 1982, the Argentinian military junta invaded the Falkland Islands. Invoking the spirit of her beloved Winston Churchill (1874–1965), Thatcher ignored those who advised her to pursue diplomatic channels and despatched a task force to retake the islands. A thousand men died in the ten-week campaign, but the Falklands were returned to British hands. Thatcher's handling of the conflict provoked a huge swell of patriotic fervour and provided a much-needed boost to her popularity.

## War with the unions

Assisted by the 'Falklands factor', economic recovery and a ramshackle Labour Party campaign, she trounced the opposition in the 1983 election, winning a 144-seat majority. Now the real work of Thatcherism began. She set herself the task of curbing the trade

## TIMELINE

**1950** Margaret contests the Dartford seat for the Conservative Party, but loses

**1951** Marriage to Dennis Thatcher

**1953** Twins Carol and Mark are born

**1954** Margaret is called to the Bar

**1959** Margaret wins the seat of Finchley to become an MP

**1967** Margaret joins the Shadow Cabinet

**1970** Conservatives win the general election; Margaret becomes Education Secretary

**1974** Conservatives face defeat at the polls

**1975** Margaret wins the party leadership contest

**1978** Winter of discontent

**1979** Margaret becomes Britain's first female prime minister

**1980** 'U-turn' speech at Conservative Party conference

**1982** Falklands War

**1983** The Conservative government is re-elected

**1984–5** Miners' strike

**1987** The Thatcher government wins a third term

**1990** Margaret resigns and is succeeded by John Major; Margaret is awarded the Order of Merit

**1992** Margaret is elevated to the House of Lords

unions and introduced a series of laws to strip the movement of its power. She banned secondary pickets, demanded a compulsory membership ballot before strike action and an end to the closed shop. Her war against union power came to a head with the miners' strike in 1984. This dispute lasted a year and was a bruising experience. Thatcher's determination to win was evidenced by her support for brutal police tactics, although the country was equally shocked by television images of miners beating 'scabs' who wished to return to work. The defeat of the miners led to a widespread programme of pit closures, which had a devastating effect on mining communities. But – combined with the raft of anti-union legislation – it left the trade union movement shorn of its power. Never again would anyone ask, as they so often had in the 1970s, 'Who governs Britain?'

*Thatcher found a close political ally in Ronald Reagan, who was US president from 1981 to 1989.*

These were the years of radical reform – and nothing was more radical than the privatization of Britain's nationalized industries and utilities. Thatcher tore through state-owned shibboleths one by one – British Airways, British Steel, Rolls-Royce – and sold them off to the private sector. She realized that privatization was not only good economics, but it could be a vote-winner too. The sale of British Telecom in 1984 had provoked a mad dash for shares among the public; when British Gas was sold two years later, the share issue was supported by a publicly financed advertising campaign called 'Tell Sid'. She brought the fleshpots of capitalism to ordinary people and gave birth to a powerful new electoral force: the share-owning democracy. By the end of the decade, one in four of the population owned shares while some 40 former nationalized businesses were in private hands.

## STRENGTHENING FOREIGN RELATIONS

In Opposition, she had fashioned a reputation as a Cold War warrior, attacking the Soviet Union at every opportunity. Moscow denounced her as the 'Iron Lady', a description she relished. Once in office, she found a political soul mate in US president Ronald Reagan (1911–2004), based on their shared enthusiasm for free-market economics and their visceral hatred of communism.

Nevertheless, she was the first Western leader to talent-spot the future architect of *glasnost*, Mikhail Gorbachev (b.1931), describing him as '*a man we can do business with*' in 1984, shortly before he became leader. Together with Reagan, she encouraged Gorbachev to pursue his reformist instincts to their limits and, in doing so, helped bring about the eventual unravelling of Soviet communism.

## AN UNCEREMONIOUS END

At the 1987 election, Thatcher won her third consecutive victory. It was an extraordinary achievement, but she would not see out the full parliamentary term. Against advice, she introduced the 'poll tax' to replace the local government rating system. It was a mistake: despised by everyone, it was the single most unpopular reform of her time in office. Her popularity was further eroded as the effect of recession began to bite. Dark mutterings were exchanged among her own MPs that perhaps it was time for her to go.

The unlikely catalyst was her implacable opposition to any closer integration with Europe. It divided her party and provided a focus for the malcontents. Geoffrey Howe (b.1926), one of her oldest and most faithful colleagues, resigned as deputy prime minister in November 1990, citing differences over Europe. His resignation speech was a scorching indictment of her style, judgement and direction, and was timed to coincide with a formal challenge to her leadership. She scraped through the first round of voting, but it was not enough. She was persuaded to resign, to be succeeded as prime minister by John Major (b.1943).

## SINGLE-MINDED OR NARROW-MINDED?

Margaret Thatcher was loved and loathed. Her supporters adored her for her tenacity, her single-mindedness and her courage; to her detractors, she was a cruel, narrow-minded ideologue. In *Spitting Image*, the 1980s TV satirical puppet show, she was shown in a double-breasted suit, smoking a Churchillian cigar and ordering steak from a waiter. He asks: '*And the vegetables?*' As the camera pans out to reveal her entire Cabinet, she replies: '*They'll have the same*'.

Today, Margaret Thatcher continues to cast a long shadow over British politics. She affected a seismic shift in what passes for political consensus in the UK. New Labour, under both Tony Blair (b.1953) and Gordon Brown (b.1951), has embraced privatization, the enterprise culture, the primacy of the financial services industry and the reduced role of trade unions – all fundamental tenets of Thatcherism.

*The hugely unpopular community charge, or 'poll tax,' hastened Thatcher's downfall. Her obduracy in championing this heavy-handed and unfair policy convinced her political allies that she had lost touch with the popular mood of the country.*

# ELIZABETH II

## born *1926*

## Queen of the United Kingdom of Great Britain and Northern Ireland

*Elizabeth II is England's sixth queen regnant and its second-longest serving monarch after Queen Victoria. Elizabeth's reign has endured the greatest erosion to the power and mystique of monarchy since William I conquered England in 1066. Her reign has seen the loss of empire and the break-up of the Commonwealth, as well as much personal disappointment. Elizabeth stands at the centre of the tempest, consciously modelling herself on her most successful antecedents as she remains semper eadem – always the same.*

*Elizabeth with her parents, George VI and Elizabeth, sister Margaret, and husband Philip in the late 1940s.*

Elizabeth, like every other English queen regnant, was not expected to rule. She was born in London on 21 April 1926, to Albert, duke of York (1895–1952), the shy second son of George V (r. 1910–36), and the commoner Elizabeth Bowes-Lyon (1900–2002). Her childhood was idyllic; her father had a distant relationship with the tyrannical George V and was determined that his daughters Elizabeth and Margaret Rose (1930–2002) would have a loving home. Winston Churchill (1874–1965) met her when she was very young and remarked, '[*she has*] *an air of authority and reflectiveness astonishing in an infant*'.

When the princess was seven, everything changed. Her uncle David, the charming, irresponsible prince of Wales met and fell in love with Wallis Simpson (1895/6–1986), a married American society hostess. When George V died at the beginning of 1936, David came to the throne as Edward VIII (r. 1936) but, advised by the Conservative prime minister Stanley Baldwin (1867–1947) that he could not marry a divorcée and retain the throne, he abdicated. Elizabeth's father reluctantly became George VI (r. 1936–52) and the ten-year-old princess became his heir. The young princess – polite, dutiful, attractive and solemn – was immensely popular.

*Queen Elizabeth II at her coronation. In later life, she recalled, 'When I was 21, I pledged my life to the service of our people and I asked for God's help to make good that vow. Although that vow was made in my salad days, when I was green in judgement, I do not regret nor retract one word of it.'*

## MARRIAGE TO PHILIP

When she was 21, Elizabeth became engaged to her distant cousin Prince Philip of Greece and Denmark (b.1921) – both are descendants of Queen Victoria (r. 1837–1901). She first met him when she was 13 years old, and despite her mother's efforts to introduce her to other young men, Elizabeth had set her heart on him.

After a long courtship, they married on 20 November, 1947 and for a time she lived the life of an aristocratic naval wife; she gave birth to a son, Charles, the following year and to a daughter, Anne, in 1950. (Prince Andrew would follow in 1960 and Prince Edward in 1964.) Two years later, on 6 February, 1952, George VI died of lung cancer. Elizabeth was informed by Philip while on tour in Kenya. The couple were staying at the Treetops Hotel, and it was remarked that she '*went up a princess and came down a queen*'.

Elizabeth was now 25 – the same age as the Tudor monarch Elizabeth I (r. 1558–1601) on her accession – and queen of England, Australia, Canada, Ceylon, New Zealand, South Africa and Pakistan, as well as head of a vast Commonwealth. In total, she ruled 539 million subjects.

Philip, duke of Edinburgh would play no role in government. At Elizabeth's coronation ceremony in June 1953 he was not crowned alongside her – there was no precedent for a male consort to be crowned and Elizabeth, never innovative and bowing always to tradition, did not break that precedent. It was the first coronation to be televised, exposing the theatre of monarchy to the British public as no event had done before. Under the guidance of her prime minister Winston Churchill and her mother, she agreed that their children would bear her surname – Windsor – and not Philip's – Mountbatten. In 1960, however, she announced that descendants without the title prince, princess or royal highness would carry the surname Mountbatten-Windsor.

Winston Churchill thought Elizabeth an ideal queen: '*All the film people in the world, if they had scoured the globe, would not have found anyone so suited to the part*', he gushed, and the queen's polite attention to duty, hard work and courtesy won her subjects' affection. But Elizabeth's empire was slowly disintegrating as modernity required a changing monarchy, and later, with the fractures in her family, many would publicly discuss its abolition. Elizabeth was the first queen regnant to rule a country ambivalent about its desire for a monarchy.

## GROWTH OF REPUBLICANISM

The turning point was 1977, the year of the queen's Silver Jubilee, when the nation was divided between those who marked her reign with street parties and a younger generation who questioned the purpose of monarchy. The biggest-selling single that year was British punk-rock band the Sex Pistols' irreverent 'God Save the Queen'. Lyrics such as '*God save the Queen, The fascist regime, They made you a moron, Potential H-bomb*' reflected the discontent of an emerging generation. Born after the war and coming of age at the end of the 1960s, they had none of their parents' inherent respect for authority. The following years saw race riots at home and calls for independence by many Commonwealth countries. As Britain became increasingly multicultural, many questioned the validity of a Protestant defender of so many faiths. The behaviour of some members of the queen's own family exacerbated the schism between republicans and monarchists and exposed the problems of an Edwardian-style royal family adapting to a modern, media age.

In 1981 the prince of Wales married Lady Diana Spencer, the 19-year-old daughter of Earl Spencer (1924–92) in a fairytale-like wedding at St Paul's Cathedral in London. Diana, beautiful and with a shrewd sense of how to manipulate the media, was immediately popular, and outshone her husband. But Charles' continuing affair with his married mistress, Camilla Parker Bowles (b.1947), and Diana's confessed eating disorder and her consequent mental frailty, eventually undermined the marriage. The saga was played out daily on the pages of the national press.

Anne's marriage to Captain Mark Phillips (b.1948) also failed, as did Prince Andrew's to Sarah Ferguson (b.1959). Incidents such as the still-married Sarah, duchess of York photographed with her lover irrevocably damaged the queen's careful maintenance of the mystique of monarchy.

## RELUCTANCE TO MODERNIZE

Compromises were made: limitations were imposed on the civil list and in 1993 Elizabeth was obliged to pay income tax for the first time. When Charles and Diana divorced in 1996 the media, so important to the perception of the modern monarchy, remained firmly on Diana's side. And when, in August 1997, Diana died in a car crash in Paris, the queen's initial reluctance to mourn publicly was greeted with national incomprehension, which quickly turned to rage.

The queen failed to read the popular mood correctly, as thousands of mourners gathered outside Kensington Palace to lay flowers in tribute to Diana. The royal family remained in seclusion at Balmoral in Scotland, whilst the tabloid press fanned the flames of hysteria. For a brief moment the monarchy teetered. But, following the advice of her prime minister Tony Blair (b.1953), who well understood the power of the media, to return to London to address the nation 'as a grandmother', Elizabeth survived.

At the beginning of the 21st century, the crisis has passed. Charles's marriage to Camilla Parker Bowles in 2005 has generally been accepted (the queen vetoed a sumptuous wedding and the couple wed in a Register Office in Windsor). But the monarchy seems far less important to modern life than it did at Elizabeth's accession. To most 'baby boomers' (those born after the Second World War) and their children and grandchildren, it is a charming anachronism – little more than a lucrative draw for tourists.

Elizabeth II has never courted popularity. She has not been England's most thrilling queen but she has had none of her predecessors' opportunities. She reigns in an age in which parliament, not monarchy, exercises power and her role is largely ceremonial, her scope limited.

*In 1981, the prince of Wales married Lady Diana Spencer, who became immensely popular with the public. Although the marriage did not last, it produced two grandsons for Elizabeth, William (b.1982) and Henry ('Harry'; b.1984).*

## TWO STRONG WOMEN

Elizabeth's most intriguing relationship with a prime minister was with the Conservative Margaret Thatcher (b.1925), who became increasingly regal throughout her time in office between 1979 and 1990. On occasion she scandalously sat down, exhausted, in the Queen's presence. Elizabeth II's response was, apparently, *'Oh look! She's keeled over again.'* But it was not all antipathy. When Margaret left office Elizabeth, allegedly shocked by the brutal disposal of a British prime minister by her own parliamentary party, acknowledged her achievements by presenting her with the Order of Merit.

# BENAZIR BHUTTO

## *1953–2007*
## Prime Minister of Pakistan

*On 10 April, 1986, Benazir Bhutto returned to Pakistan in triumph. She had been imprisoned and exiled after her father's execution by the military dictator General Zia in 1979; now she returned to lead his party and to fight Zia at the polls. Millions turned out to adore her; she was their great hope of secular democracy for a Pakistan free of corruption. Both Pakistan and the world expected great things from Zulfikar Ali Bhutto's daughter, when she swept to victory as the first female prime minister of a Muslim country.*

*Benazir Bhutto at her wedding to Asif Zardari in 1987. The following year, as the first female prime minister in Pakistan's history, and also the youngest, she offered the prospect of change for the country.*

Like Indira Gandhi in neighbouring India, Benazir Bhutto was born into one of her country's foremost political families. Her grandfather, Sir Shah Nawaz Khan Bhutto, was a key figure in the fight for independence from the British, which was finally achieved in 1947. Her father, the veteran politician Zulfikar Ali Bhutto (1928–79), was the founder of the Pakistan People's Party (PPP), president from 1971 to 1973, and from 1973 until 1977, the country's first prime minister. He was a member of the wealthy landowning classes, educated at Berkeley and Oxford, and had spent his political career striving for a nascent Pakistan's independence from the West. His was one of the few premierships not dominated by the military.

### ASSUMING THE MANTLE OF LEADERSHIP

Benazir was born in Karachi in June 1953. Like her father, she was educated in the West – at Harvard, and then at Oxford, where she studied Politics, Philosophy and Economics, and was a much-praised President of the Oxford Union. She returned to Pakistan in 1977, days before General Zia (1924–88) overthrew her father in a military coup. He was hanged in 1979; his daughter spoke of Ali Bhutto as a saint and resolved to take on his mantle. Benazir spent the next five years in prison, often in solitary confinement. She described the horrific conditions in her autobiography:

*'The summer heat turned my cell into an oven. My skin split and peeled, coming off my hands in sheets. Boils erupted on my face. My hair, which had always been thick, began to come out by the handful. Insects crept into the cell like invading armies. I tried pulling the sheet over my head at night to hide from their bites, pushing it back when it got too hot to breathe.'*

In 1984, under pressure from the West, she was finally released. She fled to London, where she became the focus of widespread resistance to Zia's regime. When martial law was lifted in 1986, Benazir – bright, beautiful and the symbol of hope for a better Pakistan – returned to be Zia's most potent adversary. She recalled that *'one million people'* greeted her at the airport and claimed that the figure swelled to *'three million… hundreds of coloured balloons soared into the sky as the airport gates opened. Rose petals, not tear gas, filled the air …The black, green and red colours of the PPP seemed the only colours in Lahore that day.'* She heard the crowd cry: *'Live, Live, Bhutto Live!'*

The following year, when she was thirty-four, she married Asif Ali Zardari (b. 1956), a polo player and property developer and also a wealthy member of the landowning classes. It was a small, private ceremony in Karachi in December 1987; she avoided the ostentatious wedding that few of her supporters could afford. She recollected that *'the sweet shops in the cities were sold out for three days as the public celebrated the event. For ten years we've been mourning'*, she reported her supporters crying: *'Finally we can rejoice.'*

She determined that marriage would not interfere with her political commitments, and Zardari agreed. Benazir was now established on a path as her father's successor; she would, she promised, lead Pakistan to a brilliant future. In 1988 Benazir, now pregnant, prepared to fight General Zia at the polls. Later she accused him of scheduling the elections to coincide with her pregnancy, hoping that she would be incapacitated.

Before the country could go to the polls, Zia died in a plane crash. In the election, Benazir and the PPP won a convincing victory on

*During her election campaign in 1986–8, Bhutto roused Pakistan with plans to end discrimination against women and pledges of more aid for the poor. But she failed to deliver on her promises.*

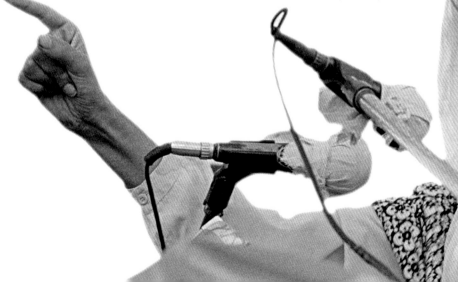

a platform of aid and better services for the poor, and rights for women. She was sworn in on 2 December, the youngest female prime minister in history. She was lauded everywhere; *People* magazine named her one of 'The Fifty Most Beautiful People' in the world.

However, this sense of euphoria was short-lived. Benazir Bhutto was in power for just 20 months, during which time she accomplished little. Charged with corruption, she was sacked by the president, Ghulam Ishaq Khan (1915–2006). Her husband Asif, nicknamed 'Mr Ten Percent' for alleged financial abuse of his wife's power, was arrested and imprisoned for two years.

## A SECOND CHANCE

In 1993 Benazir swept to power again. She released her husband and gave him a post in the cabinet – as investment minister. Although she remained leader of her party, she was dismissed as prime minister once more in 1996, again charged with corruption. She claimed she was the victim of a smear campaign. Her husband, meanwhile, was said to have channelled millions of dollars out of Pakistan, depositing them in secret bank accounts in Switzerland. He was also accused of taking bribes and, rather fantastically, of attaching a remote-control bomb to the leg of a business rival, of being complicit in the murder of Benazir's estranged brother Mir Murtaza Bhutto, and of assassinating other rivals of his wife. To date, he has served eight years in prison, although none of the charges against him have been proved in court. He was released in 2004; Benazir and Zardari furiously denied the charges, claiming the documentary evidence had been 'fabricated' by her opponents.

Catastrophe dogged Benazir and her family. Her brother, Shahnawaz, died in France in mysterious circumstances in 1985, and her other brother, Murtaza, was murdered, perhaps by Pakistan's military government, in 1996. But her years in office were also tainted. She faced numerous corruption charges, while Amnesty International claims Pakistan had an appalling human rights record during her time in office.

In 1999, Benazir and her three children left Pakistan for Dubai. Zardari joined them on his release in 2004. Meanwhile her party remained enormously popular in Pakistan – in 2002, despite its leader being *in absentia*, the PPP received the largest proportion of the vote. She was made welcome by many Western leaders, including the United States – she made an annual visit to the White House – which believed she may be useful in their 'war on terror', notwithstanding the assistance she gave to the Taliban in its early years. She was popular on the European lecture circuit and appeared frequently on current affairs programmes.

Western opinion is divided. In May 2007, *The Economist* published a review of Benazir's autobiography:

> *'It is hard to like her refusal to admit any serious misjudgment. Undemocratic transfers of power are deplorable; but the incompetence and corruption of her regimes contributed to their own downfall, a sad truth she ignores.'*

*Benazir Bhutto waves to her supporters in Karachi on her return from seven years of self-imposed exile in Dubai. Less than three months later, she was assassinated by a suicide bomber at a PPP campaign rally in Rawalpindi.*

By contrast, a former government minister in the UK, Roy Hattersley, wrote that '*whatever the truth of the allegations that her enemies have made against her – [she] represents Pakistan's best hope of taking its place among the democratic nations of the free world*'.

In 2007 the beleaguered President Musharraf (b. 1943), who had threatened her with arrest if she returned to Pakistan, mooted the possibility of making a deal with her; he would drop the charges in return for her political support.

She returned in October to run for prime minister. Despite her two uninspiring periods in office, thousands of PPP supporters joyfully welcomed her home. But on 27 December she was assassinated while addressing a mass rally at Rawalpindi. Her will dictated that her 19-year-old son, Bilawal Bhutto Zardari, assume leadership of the PPP. Her husband is to serve as caretaker until Bilawal completes his law studies at Oxford. Appearing on news bulletins throughout the world the day after his mother's death, he declared, '*My mother always said democracy is the best revenge*'. The paradox remains, however, that Benazir Bhutto's final act smacks of familial dynastic ambitions, and not of the hope of a democratic future for Pakistan.

## RULING IN THE SHADOW OF DEATH

It is extraordinary that almost all of Asia's female leaders in the 20th century were the widows or daughters of assassinated or executed politicians – not only Benazir Bhutto (father killed by Zia), but also Cory Aquino of the Philippines (husband Benigno, an opposition senator, executed), Sirimavo Bandaranaike of Sri Lanka (husband Solomon, assassinated), Sheikh Hasina of Bangladesh (father Sheikh Mujibur Rahman was the country's first leader, murdered in an army coup along with 17 close relatives), and Aung San Suu Kyi (daughter of the hero of Burmese independence, General Aung San, assassinated by opponents).

Indira Gandhi is the exception. Although she inherited the mantle of leadership from her father Panditji Nehru, he died of natural causes. It was she and her son Rajiv who were assassinated.

# INDEX

# FURTHER READING

Arranged in the sequence of chapters

Tyldesley, Joyce, *Hatshepsut: the Female Pharoah* (Viking, 1996)

Fletcher, Joann, *The Search for Nefertiti: the True Story of a Remarkable Discovery* (Hodder & Stoughton, 2004)

Macqueen, J. G., *The Hittites and their Contemporaries in Asia Minor* (Thames & Hudson, 1986)

Bryce, Trevor, *The Kingdom of the Hittites* (Oxford University Press, 2005)

*Encyclopaedia Judaica* (Jerusalem: Encyclopaedia Judaica, c.1971–1972)

Newsom, Carol A. & Ringe, Sharon H. (eds), *Women's Bible Commentary* (John Knox Press, 1998)

Finkelstein, Israel, *The Bible Unearthed: Archaeology's New Vision of Ancient Israel and the Origin of its Sacred Texts* (Free Press, 2001)

Herodotus, *The Histories* (Penguin, 1972)

Briant, Pierre, *From Cyrus to Alexander: a History of the Persian Empire* (Eisenbrauns, 2002)

Cary, M. & Scullard, H. H., *A History of Rome* (Macmillan, 1991)

Graves, Robert, *I Claudius* (Methuen, 1977)

Hughes-Hallett, Lucy, *Cleopatra: Histories, Dreams and Distortions* (Bloomsbury Publishing, 1990)

Chaveau, Michel, *Cleopatra: Beyond the Myth (*Cornell University Press, 2002)

Barrett, Anthony A., *Livia: First Lady of Imperial Rome* (Yale University Press, 2002)

Fraser, Antonia, *Boadicea's Chariot* (Weidenfeld & Nicholson, 1988)

Marsden, Peter, *Roman London* (Thames & Hudson, 1980)

Stoneman, Richard, *Palmyra and its Empire: Zenobia's Revolt against Rome* (University of Michigan Press, 1992)

Watson, Alaric, *Aurelian and the Third Century* (Routledge, 1999)

Browning, Robert, *Justinian and Theodora* (Weidenfeld & Nicholson, 1971)

Fitzgerald, C. P., *The Empress Wu* (Barrie & Jenkins, 1968)

Bradbury, Jim, *Stephen and Matilda: the Civil War of 1139 - 53* (Alan Sutton, 1996)

Weir, Alison, *Eleanor of Aquitaine: by the Wrath of God, Queen of England* (Jonathan Cape, 1999)

Pernoud, Régine, *Blanche of Castile* (Collins, 1975)

Tuchman, Barbara, *A Distant Mirror: the Calamitous Fourteenth Century* (Alfred A. Knopf, 1979)

Doherty, Paul, *Isabella and the Strange Death of Edward II* (Constable, 2003)

Weir, Alison, *Isabella: She-Wolf of France, Queen of England* (Jonathan Cape, 2005)

Etting, Vivian, *Queen Margrete I (1353–1412) and the Founding of the Nordic Union* (Brill, 2004)

Maurer, Helen, *Margaret of Anjou* (The Boydell Press, 2003)

Weir, Alison, *Lancaster and York: the Wars of the Roses* (Jonathan Cape, 1995)

Jansen, Sharon L., *The Monstrous Regiment of Women: Female Rulers in Early Modern Europe* (Palgrave Macmillan, 2002)

Fernández-Armesto, Felipe, *Ferdinand and Isabella* (Taplinger, 1975)

Aram, B., *Juana the Mad: Sovereignty and Dynasty in Renaissance Europe* (Johns Hopkins University Press, 2005)

Bradford, Sarah, *Lucrezia Borgia: Life, Love and Death in Renaissance Italy* (Penguin, 2004)

Barber, Noel, *The Lords of the Golden Horn: from Suleiman the Magnificent to Kamal Atarturk* (Macmillan, 1973)

Lamb, Harold, *Suleiman the Magnificent: Sultan of the East* (International Collectors Library, 1951)

Beem, Charles, *The Lioness Roared: the Problems of Female Rule in English History* (Palgrave Macmillan, 2006)

Waller, Maureen, *Sovereign Ladies: the Six Ruling Queens of England* (John Murray, 2006)

Frieda, Leonie, *Catherine de Medici* (Fourth Estate, 2005)

Starkey, David, *Elizabeth: Apprenticeship* (Chatto and Windus, 2000)

Plowden, Alison, *Lady Jane Grey: Nine Days Queen* (Sutton, 2003)

Fraser, Antonia, *Mary Queen of Scots* (Weidenfeld & Nicholson, 1969)

Weir, Alison, *Mary, Queen of Scots and the Murder of Lord Darnley* (Ballantine Books, 2003)

Findly, Ellison Banks, *Nur Jahan: Empress of Mughal India* (Oxford University Press, 1993)

Kleinman, Ruth, *Anne of Austria, Queen of France* (Ohio State University Press, 1985)

Buckley, Veronica, *Christina, Queen of Sweden* (Fourth Estate, 2004)

Trevelyan, George Macaulay, *England Under Queen Anne* (Longman, 1934)

Pick, Robert, *Empress Maria Theresa: the Earlier Years, 1717–1757* (Weidenfeld & Nicholson, 1966)

Wheatcroft, Andrew, *The Habsburgs: Embodying Empire* (Viking, 1995)

Pevitt, Christine, *Madame de Pompadour: Mistress of France* (Grove Press, 2002)

Rounding, Virginia, *Catherine the Great: Love, Sex and Power* (Hutchinson, 2006)

Sebag-Montefiore, Simon, *Prince of Princes: the Life of Potemkin* (Weidenfeld & Nicholson, 2000)

Fraser, Antonia, *Marie Antoinette: the Journey* (Weidenfeld & Nicholson, 2001)

Weintraub, Stanley, *Albert: Uncrowned King* (The Free Press, 1997)

Laidler, Keith, *The Last Empress* (Wyley, 2003)

Hibbert, Christopher, *The Great Mutiny, India 1857* (A. Lane, 1978)

Robinson, Jane, *Angels of Albion: Women of the Indian Mutiny* (Viking, 1996)

Tuchman, Barbara, *Stilwell and the American Experience in China 1911–1945* (Grove, 2001)

Coffman, Tom, *The Island Edge of America: a Political History of Hawai'i* (University of Hawaii Press, 2003)

Kuykendall, R. S. & Day, A. G., *Hawaii: a History: from Polynesian Kingdom to American State* (Prentice Hall, 1976)

Liliuokalani, *Hawaii's Story by Hawaii's Queen* (Boston, 1898)

Meir, Golda, *My Life* (G. P. Putnam, 1975)

Frank, Katherine, *Indira: the Life of Indira Nehru Gandhi* (Houghton Mifflin, 2001)

Fraser, Nicholas & Navarro, Marysa, *Eva Perón* (W. W. Norton, 1985)

Goñi, Uki, *The Real Odessa: How Perón Brought the Nazi War Criminals to Argentina* (Granta Books, 2003)

Campbell, John, *Margaret Thatcher: The Grocer's Daughter* (Jonathan Cape, 2000)

Campbell, John, *Margaret Thatcher: Iron Lady* (Jonathan Cape, 2003)

Bhutto, Benazir, *Daughter of the East* (Pocket Books, 2008)

# PICTURE CREDITS

# AUTHOR'S ACKNOWLEDGEMENTS

I should like to express my thanks to my agent Vivienne Schuster; to Richard Milbank and everyone at Quercus; to Dr Karen Radnor at University College London for her guidance on women in the ancient world; to Raymond Levine for his insights into goddess worship; to the ever-helpful staff at the London Library; to my mother, Trudy Gold, and my sister, Tanya Gold, for hours of joyful discussion on which women to include and which, regretfully, to omit; and to my husband Phil and our son Asher, who have made the past year the most wonderful imaginable.

First published in Great Britain in 2008 by

**Quercus**
**21 Bloomsbury Square**
**London**
**WC1A 2NS**

A CIP catalogue record for this book is available from the British Library

Cloth case edition: ISBN-978 1 84724 542 7

Printed case edition: ISBN-978 1 84724 191 7

Printed and bound in China

10 9 8 7 6 5 4 3 2 1

Designed and edited by BCS Publishing Limited, Oxford.